MYSTICISM, MYTH AND CELTIC IDENTITY

Mysticism, Myth and Celtic Identity explores how the mythical and mystical past informs national imaginations. Building on notions of invented tradition and myths of the nation, it looks at the power of narrative and fiction to shape identity, with particular reference to the British and Celtic contexts. The authors consider how aspects of the past are reinterpreted or reimagined in a variety of ways to give coherence to desired national groupings, or groups aspiring to nationhood and its 'defence'.

The coverage is unusually broad in its historical sweep, dealing with work from prehistory to the contemporary, with a particular emphasis on the period from the eighteenth century to the present. The subject matter includes notions of ancient deities, Druids, Celticity, the archaeological remains of pagan religions, traditional folk tales, racial and religious myths and ethnic politics, and the different types of returns and hauntings that can recycle these ideas in culture.

Innovative and interdisciplinary, the scholarship in *Mysticism, Myth and Celtic Identity* is mainly literary but also geographical and historical and draws on religious studies, politics and the social sciences. Thus the collection offers a stimulatingly broad number of new viewpoints on a matter of great topical relevance: national identity and the politicization of its myths.

Marion Gibson is Associate Professor of Renaissance and Magical Literatures at the University of Exeter, UK. Her publications include *Witchcraft Myths in American Culture* (2007), *Possession, Puritanism and Print: Darrell, Harsnett, Shakespeare and the Elizabethan Exorcism Controversy* (2006) and *Reading Witchcraft: Stories of Early English Witches* (1990).

Shelley Trower is a Lecturer at the Department of English at the University of Roehampton, UK. Her publications include *Senses of Vibration* (2012) and *Place, Writing, and Voice in Oral History* (2011).

Garry Tregidga is a Senior Lecturer and Assistant Director of the Institute of Cornish Studies at the University of Exeter, UK. His publications include *Memory, Place and Identity: The Cultural Landscapes of Cornwall* (2012) and *Mebyon Kernow and the History of Cornish Nationalism*, co-edited with Dick Cole and Bernard Deacon (2003).

MYSTICISM, MYTH AND CELTIC IDENTITY

Edited by Marion Gibson, Shelley Trower and Garry Tregidga

Routledge
Taylor & Francis Group

LONDON AND NEW YORK

First published 2013
by Routledge
2 Park Square, Milton Park, Abingdon, Oxon OX14 4RN

Simultaneously published in the USA and Canada
by Routledge
711 Third Avenue, New York, NY 10017

Routledge is an imprint of the Taylor & Francis Group, an informa business

British Library Cataloguing in Publication Data
A catalogue record for this book is available from the British Library

Library of Congress Cataloging in Publication Data
A catalog record for this book has been requested

ISBN: 978-0-415-62868-6 (hbk)
ISBN: 978-0-415-62869-3 (pbk)
ISBN: 978-0-203-08018-4 (ebk)

Typeset in Bembo
by HWA Text and Data Management, London

CONTENTS

CONTRIBUTORS

Maura Coughlin is Associate Professor of Visual Studies at Bryant University in Smithfield, Rhode Island. Her recent research is concerned with the visual culture of Brittany and the themes of death, mourning rituals and the interpretation of Brittany's prehistoric and medieval past in the nineteenth century.

Elizabeth Edwards is a Research Fellow at the University of Wales Centre for Advanced Welsh and Celtic Studies, Aberystwyth, where she works on the AHRC-funded project 'Wales and the French Revolution'. Liz has published articles on war poetry in 1790s Wales and the stonemason-poet Edward Williams ('Iolo Morganwg'), and her anthology, *English-Language Poetry from Wales 1789–1806*, is forthcoming from the University of Wales Press.

Jo Esra is nearing the end of her AHRC-funded PhD at the University of Exeter, Cornwall Campus. Her thesis explores the impact of early modern Barbary captivity on the maritime communities of Devon and Cornwall, contributing to narratives of place and identity. She is also working on *Shakespeare's Demonology* with Marion Gibson (Continuum, forthcoming).

Marion Gibson is Associate Professor of Renaissance and Magical Literatures at Exeter University and works on witches, magic and the supernatural in literature c.1500–present. Most recently, she is the author of *Imagining the Pagan Past* (Routledge, forthcoming).

David Hesse received a PhD from the University of Edinburgh's School of History, Classics and Archaeology. He works as a political correspondent for a Swiss daily newspaper in Washington, DC. He is a member of the Scottish Centre for Diaspora Studies.

Ronald Hutton is Professor of History at Bristol University, and the author of 14 books and 75 essays on different aspects of his subject, including *Blood and Mistletoe: The History of the Druids in Britain* (Yale University Press, 2009).

Chris Manias is a specialist in the history and wider cultural impact of the human and biological sciences in modern Britain, France and Germany. He completed his PhD at Birkbeck, University of London, with support from the AHRC in 2008, and is presently a Lecturer in Modern European History at the University of Manchester.

Peter Merchant is Principal Lecturer in English at Canterbury Christ Church University. He collaborated with Suzanne Bray and Adrienne E. Gavin on the essay collection *Re-Embroidering the Robe: Faith, Myth and Literary Creation after 1850*, which they co-edited for Cambridge Scholars Publishing in 2008.

Dafydd Moore is Professor of Eighteenth-Century Literature at Plymouth University. He has published widely on James Macpherson and the poems of Ossian, and related areas of national and cultural identity.

Carl Phillips is a Teacher of Geography at Tuxford Academy in Nottinghamshire. His doctoral thesis, 'Mystical Geographies of Cornwall', studied the cultural and historical geographies of religion and spirituality in Cornwall since the late nineteenth century (including the late nineteenth-century Anglican revival, mid-twentieth-century Arthurianism and post-1960s neo-Pagan witchcraft), and can be read or downloaded at http://etheses.nottingham.ac.uk. Previous work has also appeared in *Cornish Studies*.

Garry Tregidga is Director of the Cornish Audio Visual Archive and Assistant Director of the Institute of Cornish Studies, University of Exeter, at the Cornwall Campus in Penryn. His research interests include the political and religious identities of Celtic Britain since the late nineteenth century.

Shelley Trower is a Lecturer at the University of Roehampton, and was previously the researcher for the AHRC-funded 'Mysticism, Myth, and "Celtic" Nationalism project'. Publications include *Senses of Vibration* (Continuum, 2012) and *Place, Writing, and Voice in Oral History* (Palgrave, 2011), as well as essays in journals and edited collections including *Victorian Literature and Culture*.

Rebecca Welshman is completing a PhD in English at the University of Exeter. She is a representative on the Thomas Hardy Society management council and the Richard Jefferies Society executive council. She is an organiser of conferences on both authors.

Jason Whittaker is Professor of Blake Studies and Acting Head of the Department of Writing at University College Falmouth. He is the author of a number of books and articles on the reception of William Blake, including *Blake 2.0* (Palgrave 2012), *Blake, Modernity and Popular Culture* (Palgrave, 2008) and *Radical Blake: Influence and Afterlife from 1827* (Palgrave, 2002). He has also worked for many years as a journalist and writes on a wide variety of technology subjects.

Andrew Fergus Wilson is Senior Lecturer in Sociology at the University of Derby. His research and writing embraces prophecy in new media contexts, political extremism in new religious contexts and modern millenarianism.

MYSTICISM, MYTH AND CELTIC IDENTITY

Marion Gibson, Shelley Trower and Garry Tregidga

This book explores notions of 'Celtic' identity in a series of different contexts and time periods and through readings of a range of literary and dramatic forms, from epic poetry to historical re-enactment. It can be considered in the context of wider developments in the global field of Celtic Studies. The early development of the discipline in the nineteenth century, notably through the creation of centres like the Académie Celtique in France in 1804, resulted in an emphasis on archaeology, early medieval literature and historical linguistics that essentially endures to the present day. In recent decades, however, the study of the Celts has been a controversial subject with a growing number of scholars challenging both their historical origins and the assumption of a sense of continuity with the present (Chapman, James, Collis). Responses to these critiques of Celtic Studies have varied in approach. For example, Barry Cunliffe (1997) focused on evidence that contradicted Chapman's assertions. Yet for other scholars the debate provided an opportunity to reassess the aims and objectives of the discipline. It was accepted that meanings relating to the word 'Celtic' are multiple and sometimes contradictory. These can draw upon a variety of spheres of social construction such as art, dance, landscape, literature, religion and politics. Paradoxically, this ambiguity led to a number of useful studies that have moved beyond debates on origins and traditional Celtic Studies to consider issues associated with contemporary notions of 'Celticity' (e.g. Hale and Payton; Harvey *et al.*). *Mysticism, Myth and Celtic Identity* seeks to build on these pioneering investigations.

Questions and answers

The collection of essays had its beginning in the papers given at the 'Mysticism, Myth, Nationalism' conference in July 2010 at the University of Exeter's

Cornwall Campus. The conference, in turn, was part of the Arts and Humanities Research Council-funded project 'Mysticism, Myth and "Celtic" Nationalism: A Case Study of Cornwall', whose principal investigator, co-investigator and associate research fellow were Marion Gibson, Garry Tregidga and Shelley Trower respectively. This volume brings together elements of that case study with the wider, related debates of the conference, with the aim of provoking further discussion of, and research, into its key terms.

Some of the questions that this volume asks and answers, in different ways in different chapters, are:

- What do we mean by 'mysticism', 'myth', 'Celtic identity' and 'nationalism'?
- How do these ideas work together to define and give political and cultural impetus to a series of groups of people from Brittany to Scotland?
- How does our broadly literary, text-based approach relate to the existing scholarly literature on nationalism?
- What is the role of oral tradition and cultural memory in the construction of contemporary Celtic identities?
- How far have traditional understandings of 'Celtic Studies' moved on in the twenty-first century from their origins in separate and often nationalistic groupings?
- How far can comparative studies of small and large polities, geographically-defined and online communities, contribute new insights to the field?
- What can be gained from the comparative analysis of written and visual texts and material culture and practices?

As was discussed earlier, our aim in bringing together the contributors to this volume was to move away from the traditional 'Celtic Studies' foci of medieval textual and language studies and archaeology to look at cultural productions from the early modern period onward. We chose further to limit the book's scope to a particular focus on literary and performative work from the Romantic period to the present, to explore the ways in which this period was a key one in developing modern notions of nationalism and identity. Although texts of this period often drew on earlier work, as some of our chapters show, the period also saw great changes in political and cultural understandings of the nation and its myths and the establishment of myths and trends that endure to the present day. Finally, much of the work relates to Cornwall, a 'Celtic' area not often discussed alongside Wales, Brittany, Scotland and other 'Celtic' nations, as it is here. The book thus builds on the project's case study to offer a different view of Celtic Studies that we hope will provoke new questions and new reflections on established matters of interest. In its interest in modernity, popular culture, representation and commodification this volume contributes to 'New Celtic Studies' as defined by Amy Hale and Philip Payton in their *New Directions in Celtic Studies* in 2000. But it also aims to situate the discussion of one label – 'Celtic' – in a wider context of reflections on mysticism, myth and nationalism and to highlight the fictive, contested and unreliable nature of all these terms, which are too often taken for granted. These are terms that shape real lives, lived in contemporary society by people who may seldom have cause to read scholarly literature about them.

Mysticism, myth, nation

The association between myth and nation is by now somewhat familiar to scholars and to the wider public, having been established especially through the work of Ernest Gellner and Eric Hobsbawm in the 1980s and 1990s. In the process of developing his argument concerning the invention of nations, Hobsbawm cites Gellner:

> Nations as a natural, God-given way of classifying men, as an inherent ... political destiny, are a myth; nationalism, which sometimes takes pre-existing cultures and turns them into nations, sometimes invents them, and often obliterates pre-existing cultures: *that* is a reality.
>
> (Hobsbawm 10)

For Gellner and Hobsbawm, among others, the idea of nations as natural is a myth that belongs to modernity (see also, for example, Colley; Brockliss and Eastwood; Anderson; Samuel, 4–5). Our focus is both more and less specific, engaging with the plurality of ways in which an often mystical past (or at least a past that is imagined as mystical) is used and re-used in conceptions of the 'Celtic' from the early modern period onward, registering how such conceptions feed into myths of 'Celtic' nations and identities. By 'mystical' we mean to refer to a wide range of ancient and modern spiritual ideas and practices and also to the imagined existence of supernatural entities – a wide definition that encompasses notions as diverse as druidry and ghosts. We are interested in how the mystical past is sometimes taken up in 'Celtic' nationalism, how it is used to support nationalist aims and identities, but also in how mystical characteristics are at times imposed upon 'Celts', contributing to certain stereotypes. While 'nationalists' and 'mysticists' are often distinct groups with very different aims, both have at times fed into a conception of places like Cornwall and Brittany as special, mystical and separate from the apparently more mundane, rational England or France.

What kinds of mysticism are most relevant here? Most obviously, we are dealing with the content and consequences of the 'Celtic Revival', a movement to revive or invent traditions in the interests of local self-assertion. The movement, which originated in eighteenth- and nineteenth-century antiquarianism (or even before that) and its reception by Romantic and nationalist writers, was particularly influential in Ireland, Scotland, Wales, Cornwall and Brittany as well as smaller polities such as the Isle of Man. It continues today in contemporary forms both there and in additional regions such as Galicia, after a second wave of revival around the period 1890–1930. In more recent decades there has even been a renewed interest in the Celts amongst the various diaspora communities located in countries like the USA, Canada and Australia (e.g. Payton 1999; Ray, McCarthy; Hague). The revival was a symptom of, and led to more of, an enhanced interest in the origin of 'Celts', their languages and ancient literatures, the prehistoric and medieval beliefs and practices of 'Celts' and survivals of these which could be observed by folklorists in contemporary customs. In Cornwall, for example, the folklorists Robert Hunt, William Bottrell and Margaret Courtney and, in the late nineteenth and early twentieth century, linguistic and historical scholars like Henry Jenner popularised notions of 'Celtic' survivals in Cornish culture. They identified the Celts as an immigrant people whose culture – arguably – flourished during the late Neolithic and/or Iron Age periods, and at least some of whose language and customs had successfully resisted Anglo-Saxon influence into the present day. By the mid-twentieth century such survivals were popularly believed to include seasonal customs like the Helston *hal-an-tow* performance and Furry Dance, or Midsummer bonfires (British Pathé; Vince) and these were (and still are) promoted and revived by, among others, a network of Old Cornwall Societies (http://www.oldcornwall.org/). The events were often linked by participants and observers to a reconstructed calendar of 'Celtic' festivals such as Beltane and Samhain (the calendar and its history is discussed by Hutton, 1996). The Cornish landscape was spiritualised by reconstructions of ancient rites.

Two main factors gave new impetus to the sense of Celtic regions and nations as distinctly mystical in the second half of the twentieth century: an upsurge in Celtic nationalism in Scotland, Wales and Cornwall, and the emergence of the New Age movement. In the 1960s the Welsh political party Plaid Cymru and the Scottish Nationalist Party won parliamentary seats (in by-elections at Carmarthen 1966 and Hamilton 1967), marking a period of growth in the strength of the nationalist parties which continued through to the next decade (Morgan; Nairn; Wilson; and contextually Newman; Watson; Reece). In this context the Cornish pressure group Mebyon Kernow attempted to transform itself into a political party, gaining increased membership and seeking electoral impact in both local elections and general elections. Several candidates won seats in the local elections, and although the new party did not succeed in the general election (no candidates were voted into parliament), this move encouraged some interest in Cornwall as a potential Celtic nation (see Deacon, Cole and Tregidga). At the same time, the sixties, of course, saw the flowering of new kinds of 'alternative' lifestyles and forms of spirituality. The 'Celtic nations' were considered in this context as an alternative space from the conventionalities of England, where distinctive kinds of spirituality, artistic freedom and experimentation with 'mind-expanding' drugs could flourish (Chapman 219*ff*). By the 1970s, participants in various forms of alternative – often 'Celtic' – spiritual practices became newly aware of themselves, according to Wouter Hanegraff, as belonging to a unified though highly disparate 'New Age' movement (17). This is a vague term which incorporates many different kinds of spiritual activities including channelling, astrology, geomancy and dowsing, and also various activities imagined more specifically as Celtic, such as Goddess worship. Although some nationalists have tried to distinguish themselves from mystical movements, both of these trends – a rising interest in Celtic spiritualities and an upsurge in Celtic nationalism – have tended to work together in what we could describe as a form of mystical 'Celtic nationalism'. Such representations often reinforce earlier trends as explored in this book (for example, Celts were described by Julius Caesar as a spiritual, superstitious people as early as the first century BC).

The construction of Cornwall as a mythical, mystical and haunted landscape is still in operation today, for tourists as much as for nationalists (although in different ways and for different purposes). Popular texts on the region tend to focus on its 'mystical' identity as an ancient land of legend and superstition. In an early tourist guide, *The Cornish Riviera* (1928), S.P.B. Mais promised visitors 'an atmosphere of warlocks and pixies, miracle-working saints and woe-working witches' (Mais 1). This formula is still attractive: 'King Arthur's' Tintagel Castle received 182,000 visitors in 2006–7 (English Heritage, personal communication). The notion of the supernatural plays a prominent part in this discourse and is, paradoxically, even deployed in landscapes defined by modern industrial waste: important attractions of Cornwall's mining World Heritage sites are ghost tours (e.g. Poldark Mine). It can be argued that the way in which the past impacts on the present is as a form of 'haunting', especially when this haunting is embodied in supernatural tales with a politicised element emphasising locality. Cornwall is an excellent example of this process and its cultural, political and economic impact. Although mining meant that Cornwall played a prominent role during Britain's Industrial Revolution, its subsequent dependence on tourism, and the emergence of an essentially antiquarian Celtic Revivalist movement, meant that memory and remembrance took on great significance in cultural constructions of place (Bhabha). Significantly, the 'spirit' of legendary and historical figures, such as the prehistoric 'Celts', King Arthur and Myghal Josef An Gof (who led the 1497 Cornish rebellion) has been resurrected to serve the changing needs of the present. This is bound up with perceptions of Cornwall as un-English, 'Celtic' and 'different' (see for example Deacon, Cole and Tregidga). Here, then, are some examples of mystical and myth-making activities directly linked to the preservation and building of a 'Celtic' identity.

Nation, race, writing back

The notion of 'Celtic nationalism' as a label is a problematic one. What exactly does it mean? At its most precise, 'Celtic' refers to a carefully defined linguistic grouping and it can be deployed in that sense without quotation marks. More often it has an ethnic aspect, involving questions of whether Celts were or were not Palaeolithic, Neolithic or Iron Age immigrants, and were or were not a British, Germanic, Aryan or Gallic-Hispanic people – or even Greek,

Phoenician (Borlase; Stukeley) or black Ethiopian Cushite (Higgins). What one means by ethnic 'Celts' definitely requires quotation marks to indicate its use as a matter of highly individual choice. Whilst Colin Renfrew suggests that Celtic languages and thus 'Celts' date back as far as 4500BC, and Barry Cunliffe and Anne Ross have both delineated features of 'Celtic' artistic and ritual culture in an Atlantic arc stretching from the Pyrenees to Scotland with roots in middle Europe, others, like Simon James and Malcolm Chapman, do not believe that the term means anything except 'other' (Payton 1996, 26–7, 46–61; Hale; Pittock). Recently, these questions have extended into the sphere of genetic science, with claims that inhabitants of parts of the British Isles often considered 'Celtic' may have a set of identifiable genetic characteristics. They may look different from other Britons, for instance, with paler skin or redder hair (Sykes; McKie). If so, then they could be seen as part of a distinct biological grouping, perhaps with a history of migration west and north under threat from Anglo-Saxon and Danish settlers in the east. If proven, this would add scientific weight to traditional histories of the displacement of Britons by new arrivals, offering choices of historical narrative from peaceful intermarriage to massacre and rape. What might be the consequences of this set of ideas, which split certain established groups (inhabitants of the United Kingdom) whilst lumping others together (Scottish, Cornish and Welsh)?

The notion of 'lumping together' also opens up a further problem: can the term 'nationalism' be used in this context to describe the motivation of Cornish, Scottish, Irish, Breton and Welsh peoples (to name only the usual core 'Celtic' group) not only without a nation, but also without the aspiration to a shared one? This question has haunted writers on nationalism, especially in recent years (Smith; Özkirimli). 'Nationalism' appears to be a neat, defined term until it is subjected to scrutiny in the context of particular groupings and their narratives of their aims or wishes. At one level Celtic organisations have campaigned to create a common future. There have been regular calls for some form of Celtic federation or confederation dating back at least to the 1867 Pan-Celtic Congress held at St Brieuc in Brittany. Established groups like the Celtic Congress and Celtic League continue to promote the cultural and political interests respectively of their members. In recent years the growth of social networking sites has been providing further opportunities to bring activists together in defence of the Celtic world. A good example is Celtic Solidarity, which is a Facebook site that has been created to counter racist statements in the media about the Celts in contemporary society (celticsolidarity@groups.facebook.com). At the same time nationalist movements operate in vastly contrasting cultural, economic and political environments. Although parties like Mebyon Kernow, Plaid Cymru and the Scottish National Party might seek to work together, they have been shaped by different historical processes and naturally have to focus on articulating the concerns of their specific territories.

When we look specifically at mystic aspects of culture, too, we are also treading the line drawn between Hutchinson's notion of nationalism, in which to become a modern polity nationalists reject the 'other-worldliness' of their folk culture, and Gellner's belief that nationalisms expressed initially through romantic 'fancies' will become politicised regardless of their self-deceptions (Hutchinson, 12–13; Gellner, 49). In other words, how much does a mystical narrative help or hinder nationalist aims? How far might it be termed 'culturally healthy'? Mysticism could be seen to make a polity backward-looking or damage its claims to a 'real' history of difference, yet a nation without a soulful or spiritual dimension is hard to imagine. At each step, the exact meaning of 'nationalism' – here, specifically Celtic nationalism – becomes less clear, though its insistent cultural power remains, since the contested 'Celts' have been endowed with a surprisingly rigid set of characteristics for a people so elusive in every other way.

In 1862, for instance, in *The Races of Man* Robert Knox was able to sum up what he saw to be the truth about 'Celts' as a distinct race: they possessed 'furious fanaticism; a love of war and disorder, a hatred for order and patient industry' and were 'restless, treacherous, uncertain: look at Ireland' (as cited in Stout, 57). Knox's irritation is plain: Ireland was seen to be an example of a Celtic polity left too much to itself, with the results being famine, insurrection and terrorism. Even fellow Victorians sympathetic to counter-claims of Celtic cultural genius – such as Matthew Arnold – reiterated elements of this stereotype even whilst deploring its overall logic and tone. In Arnold's famous 1867 essay, 'On the Study of Celtic Literature' the 'Celts' were idealised as being magical, imaginative and egalitarian, but were also accepted to be superstitious, excitable and subversive, as a concession to current racial theories. 'Celts', for Arnold, were western Britons troubled by a 'perpetual straining after mere emotion', and prevented from reasoned progress by an inability in 'the skilful and resolute appliance of means to ends'. Thus they could not govern themselves, could never form their own polities, and should in fact not be allowed to do so. Their very defining languages were dead or dying and this might be no bad thing (Arnold, 344–5; Dodd, 96).

Celts were thus often represented even by their partisans as a typical Victorian subject people: childlike, effeminised by unreasoning spirituality and doomed to nostalgic impotence. Fear lurked beneath such a dismissal. Words like 'chafing' and 'straining' suggested a violent resentment of authority that might one day erupt and the Fenian movement coloured the common view of a 'Celtic' threat in the mainstream of Victorian racial, nationalist and cultural politics. Other contemporary victims of this process of racialised 'othering' were colonised peoples in Asia and Africa, as documented by Said (1978, 1993) and Spivak. Figures like John Beddoe in his *The Races of Britain* (1885) frequently made comparisons of 'the Celt' and the 'African Negro', both imagined to be lower on the evolutionary scale. Cornwall, along with Scotland and west Ireland, contained the highest proportion of 'nigrescence', claimed Beddoes (cited in Vernon, 156–7). Amongst a range of negative stereotyping in Victorian thought, then, 'Celts' were portrayed as imaginative but unreasonable, too feminine in their sensitivities but too masculine in their violence, free but anarchic, weak but dangerous. Against this stereotyping, Celtic nationalism developed a literature of 'writing back' which laid claim to positive characteristics within the stereotype and attempted to rework negatively-portrayed attributes – such as a mystical temperament – as good.[1]

The writing back took diverse forms. It encompassed everything from literary forgery to the finest fiction. Sometimes the literary endeavour had a very high ambition: a nationalist epic or a series of antiquarian-inspired poems. Often, though, the writing or performance was in the form of approachable and educative work for the general reader or participant (Borlase; Bottrell; Graves; and on recent fiction Bell; Richards; Westland). Nationalist enterprises are usually strongly didactic: whilst an epic poem may reach educated readers already engaged in scholarly pursuits, an accessible collection of folklore tales or the opportunity to attend a re-enacted folkloric or historical event is likely to gain wider attention. Often fantasy was a key element: an invitation to the imagination was effective where a scholarly article or dictionary of Celtic words was not. Yet sometimes writing back could occur in unexpected places: a geological textbook, the obituary of a political figure, or a guide to local prehistoric sites. Generically, it could cross boundaries: whilst many of the chapters in this book deal with traditional 'Gothic' forms, there is also an attention to related and unrelated genres where similar concerns about identity and its spiritual or magical elements are explored. In many cases, then, mysticism was a key element of the texts and practices considered, but in all of them myth – the other central term of our title – was vital. In political life, in particular, a mythic narrative in which historical fact was unsure but the lines of a good narrative were, in contrast, clear and enticing was indispensable. Politicians, cultural critics and propagandists of all kinds thus lifted myth from fiction and in their turn inspired fictional responses. They still do so today. This collection examines all these arenas of cultural production and debate, asking how the interrelated themes of mysticism, myth, nationalism and identity operate in each one.

The book and its chapters

Here, then, are the contexts in which the collection exists and in which it intervenes: a strong tradition of scholarly and popular engagement with the notion of Celticity in mystical and mythic discourses; a regular use of the term 'Celtic' in mainstream and extreme political and cultural contexts; but multiple difficulties of definition. We have also found in some quarters a reluctance to historicise the cultural politics of Celticity or to accept that it has a 'cultural politics', or to explore new representations and their contexts. This is perhaps explained by the fact, noted above, that in the past the 'Celt' was so often associated with negative stereotypes. Perhaps also it is feared that interrogation will inevitably be a hostile act, and may mean the disintegration of the concept – at least to the satisfaction of those originally hostile to it. The passions that can be generated in such discussion are exemplified by the work of Michael Hechter and its reception (Hechter 1971, 1999; Birch; Michie; Sloan; Hunter; Hanham; Jackson) and by discussions in Dietler, Hale, Howlett, James, McDonald *et al.*, Nairn, Williams and Shumway. Our feeling is that the discussion of cultural politics only makes the notion of Celticity more interesting: its strength is demonstrated by the fact that it can withstand such discussion, and the range and complexity of its representations add richness and depth to what might otherwise seem a flat assertion of difference on questionable historical and literary grounds. It is important not to let such assertions stand without question, as our chapters on extremist politics demonstrate in the wider context of English and European discussions of the Celtic, mystic past. Once questioned, however, most of the representations that are discussed here tell us a great deal about the shared, multicultural history of 'Celts' and 'non-Celts' (and those who may claim to be something of both) in Britain and beyond.

Ideas of what it means to be Celtic may be based on problematic and sometimes extremist assumptions about race, but in another context Celticity can contribute to a sense of Britishness as multicultural. Vron Ware's study of British national identity from the perspective of people who have settled in the UK and have family origins in Bangladesh, India and other countries that were once part of Britain's empire indicates how a British, as opposed to an English, identity can seem more inclusive. Pratap, who grew up in London and whose family is Indian in origin, finds Englishness more exclusive: 'I think British is easier – it's clearly a bit more plural as it includes the Celtic fringe: Northern Ireland, Wales, Scotland. It seems to accommodate regional difference' (Ware 32). The interrogation of Celticity helps to explain how and why differences and divergent narratives exist, and allows us to look clearly at their pleasures and pitfalls: how most productively to live with and simply to *live* them.

The collection is thus designed to offer a series of interlinked discussions on diverse and provocatively combined texts, bringing together literary, historical, geographical and political scholars with widely divergent areas of interest. Some chapters provide background to others, whilst some are in juxtaposition or dialogue, and others stand alone. The collection is a mosaic, whose patterns may be designed in advance but whose multiple significances will be contributed by each reader looking at the finished product. Good scholarship in this area seems to us duty-bound to raise more questions than it answers, since the consequences of any identity politics built on glib conclusions and prejudiced verdicts can be serious to the point, literally, of warfare and genocide. The volume begins and ends with chapters by two of the conference's keynote speakers, Ronald Hutton and Jason Whittaker.

Part I is edited by Marion Gibson, and focuses on prehistory and paganism, examined by engagement with the myths and fictions that result from science and pseudo-science.

Ronald Hutton's chapter builds on his work (2007, 2009) on representations of druids in history and literature from the earliest accounts to the present, offering a closer look at British fiction since 1950. As he points out, the druid priesthood described by writers and archaeologists up to 1950 was 'both vivid and insubstantial', offering contemporary fiction writers a rich but confusing diversity of images from which to choose. The breadth of the choices on offer means that fictions about Celtic paganism reveal a surprising amount about the societies and eras that produce them. Unlike some of their earlier representations, druids in British fiction post-1950 are almost uniformly unpleasant figures. Hutton argues that this reflects anxieties springing from the end of the British empire, with the resentments and regrets of decolonisation still fresh in the public mind. Whilst there are changes over time in representation in the work of individual authors such as Rosemary Sutcliff, then, in English and Scottish work druids are almost always the repositories of fantasies of violence, sex and religious fanaticism. In Welsh, Australian and North American writing and in European portrayals such as the *Asterix* cartoons, however, things are different. In the last section of the chapter Hutton focuses on several positive fictions about druids to suggest how the specific political and cultural politics of each nation and era have shaped them. English and Scottish writers are often trapped in the paradigms of Victorian imperial fantasy whilst writers from what might be described as more assertively Celtic post-colonial backgrounds can create more positive mythic representations.

Marion Gibson's chapter focuses on deities rather than priests, as imagined in a selection of British fictions and histories from the medieval period to the present. She suggests that such depictions are often associated with – and indeed facilitate – subversive thought. The first attempt to recreate imaginatively British pagan modes of thought was that of Geoffrey of Monmouth in the 1130s and since then a range of surprisingly inclusive and positive images of pagan deities and their worshippers have been produced. In particular, classical goddesses such as Diana have been imagined as the focus of beautiful and legitimate mystery rites, although, of course, they have also been imagined as demonic too. Nevertheless, the 'demonic' tag sometimes has the appearance of second thought or necessary gesture toward convention, and what remains with the reader are the exciting possibilities of imagining alternative forms of religious thought. Gibson traces these through some representative medieval and early modern examples – Laȝamon, Ranulph Higden and Robert Fabyan – suggesting that these writers laid the groundwork for Renaissance and later writers to 'think like pagans'. The second part of the chapter moves on to examine this ability in a selection of twentieth-century British writers, such as T.C. Lethbridge, Margaret Murray and Harold Bayley – who in discussing pagan deities also opened their minds to the subversive possibilities of alternative archaeologies and new paganisms. The chapter concludes by looking at the fiction of Mark Chadbourn, which brings together notions of fantasy Celtic paganism and revolution in his influential *Age of Misrule* series.

Chris Manias' chapter expands on the notion that the names of particular ethnic groups were used in imprecise and often contradictory ways as nineteenth-century writers strove to make them carry unrealistically heavy cultural burdens.

He points out that two conflicting narrative models grew out of historians' and archaeologists' attempts to theorise their past. One was a narrative of successive waves of invading peoples, whilst the other was a stadial model of indigenous development from savagery to civilisation. Individual accounts of prehistoric British practices, monuments and artefacts had to be fitted into 'comprehensible systems', a task that often perplexed scholars, particularly because it was inflected by hotly contested contemporary notions of race and progress. Manias surveys a number of such debates, from the craniology of John Barnard Davies and John Thurman, through the ethnology of Robert Latham to the archaeology of William Boyd-Dawkins and the folklore of George Lawrence Gomme. From these debates emerged constructions of Aryan, Celtic and Germanic tribes who were thought to be identifiable through language group, artefactual or biological remains in a bewildering variety of ways. Manias shows how contemporary mythologies of identity are influenced by contradictory but still-authoritative Victorian scientific narratives.

Rebecca Welshman's chapter moves on from the divine and human element in prehistoric paganism to consider its material remains. Her chapter considers the place of archaeology in the cultural world of late Victorian authors such as the novelists Thomas Hardy and Richard Jefferies. She argues that the contemplation of prehistory through the medium of archaeology was one way in which nineteenth-century writers could come to terms with the gigantic questions of origin and purpose that perplexed them: 'for late Victorian authors the new dimension to human history afforded by archaeology was potentially less alienating than considering human life in the context of geological or astronomical time' (Welshman, this volume). Perhaps the description of archaeological sites and the use of them as settings for some of their works' most central scenes offered writers a way to engage with the implications of the work of such troublesome figures as Lyell and Darwin obliquely, lending *gravitas* to fictional works but also evading the problems posed by harder physical sciences. Welshman suggests, too, that prehistoric landscape features helped to reconnect industrial, modern humanity with the natural world. Barrows and the like are thus 'an embodiment of past human cares and desires carried through time to impact upon the modern mind in new and unpredictable ways'. The word 'Celtic' was often shorthand for this kind of cultural work, an insight that will recur throughout the volume.

Finally in Part I, Carl Phillips picks up on themes explored in the first four chapters to offer a case study of Cornish alternative archaeologies. As a geographer, his focus is on material remains in the Cornish landscape and their representation in gazetteers, fictions and mystical works by such writers as Craig Weatherill, Cheryl Straffon and Paul Devereux. The construction of landscapes of ley lines and energy centres in these texts springs directly from the writers' reading on archaeology, race, prehistoric paganism, etymology, folklore and Celtic difference, allowing these topics to be synthesised and mapped out on the landscape. There, they can also be played out in political battles over the conservation and custody of particular sites and finds and their cultural 'ownership'. Thus, Phillips suggests, that which appears to be spectral, mystical and mythic is actually manifested very solidly in the environment. Phillips' chapter ends Part I, then, by demonstrating how notions of mysticism, myth and nationalism can come together to produce tangible and topical results that continue to be measured in the sciences as well as the arts.

Part II is edited by Shelley Trower and concentrates on the notion of Celticity in Wales, Scotland, Brittany, Devon and Cornwall, focusing in particular on Romantic and Gothic narratives, but also taking in a range of other textual forms including travel narratives and visual images. Thus it cuts across some of the usual boundaries in both Celtic Studies and Romantic and Gothic Studies, offering new work in each field, and considering how a range of texts recycle the past to help consolidate distinct and contested national visions.

Elizabeth Edwards' chapter on Anglophone Welsh poetry and drama in the Gothic mode makes a point that is transferable to many of the other chapters: 'the most important aspect of national Gothic is its tendency to foreground *contested* histories' (emphasis added). Nothing can be taken for granted as labelled and closed. Edwards shows once again how ancient history is readily conflated with contemporary events in the service of a myth of identity. In this case, in the eighteenth and early nineteenth centuries, the French Revolution and the subsequent war combined with understandings of the medieval conquest of Wales by the English to produce a rhetoric of national victimhood which was perfectly suited to Gothic notions of terror and misery. Yet, contrasting with this image of Wales as subject to the depredations of English power was another: Wales as both a tourist destination to revive the flagging urban soul and a haven of liberty beyond the reach of tyranny. Was Wales a prison or a paradise? Gothic literature portrayed it as both in the context of late eighteenth-century political events. Edwards argues that the creative friction between past and present needs a subtle analysis that takes into account locality, chronology and genre as its starting points and can rewrite traditional Celtic studies accordingly.

Dafydd Moore also chooses a non-traditional focus for his chapter on the creation of Celtic history: the English county of Devon and its neighbour, Cornwall. As he explains, adding to Edwards' insights, the field of Romantic studies is now a focus of particularly intense efforts to revise the canon and incorporate regional literatures. One major beneficiary has been the Scottish poet James Macpherson, and Moore looks at a south-western English group of writers who drew inspiration from his Ossianic work and its contextual discourse of the heroic epic. The south-west was being refigured as a site of new cultural value. Much as Scotland had negotiated the difficult period after union by celebrating warrior romance within a polite modern literary culture, so Devon and Cornwall asserted both a claim to politeness and to a warrior past, presenting their literary culture as nationally central but also distinct and worthy in its own right. Moore examines how Celtic this culture was, finding Saxons and Danes active in the literature as well as more obviously 'local' Druids, and problematises the notion of a divide along the line of the river Tamar. He argues that Macpherson's legacy is one of malleability: it was available for translation and conversion into all kinds of local and national myth, so that once again we are reading contested histories.

Shelley Trower returns to Cornwall with a chapter that works in dialogue with Carl Phillips' Cornish case study to show how the nineteenth-century folklorist Robert Hunt reimagined the Cornish landscape, which he knew primarily as a geologist, as a 'primitive' landscape, in ways that laid some of the groundwork for modern earth mysteries. As a collector of information for the Geological Survey, Hunt could have seen the landscape simply as a source of granite, kaolin and tin, but instead – influenced by earlier writers like William Buckland – he read Cornwall as a 'nation' of abundance, sublimity and Gothic potential linked to the enduring qualities of the 'ancient race' thought to dwell there. Cornwall's 'primitive' and 'Celtic' nature was thus entwined with the imaginative power invested in its rocks, which influenced the character of its inhabitants, and Trower revisits Manias' themes of racial 'science' to conclude that discourses that appear at first sight to be contradictory and unrelated (such as geology and poetry, in this case) can in fact be synthesised to produce potent myth.

The forced synergy of disparate fields of enquiry is a recurrent theme of the collection. In a similar spirit of revisionism to that of Edwards, Coughlin surveys the Breton Celtic Revival of the eighteenth and nineteenth centuries, examining the wide range of practices and representations that were labelled 'Celtic' with abandon, from prehistoric stone monuments of uncertain age and equally debatable pagan significance (see also Welshman's chapter) to Catholic architectural features and mortuary rites. As in Edwards' chapter, Coughlin emphasises the importance of historicising depictions of national or local difference, of examining history as well as myth. Coughlin draws on visual representations as well as textual ones, and contextualises them within theories of place – for example, the art historian Nina Lübbren's notion of 'place myth' – widening the focus of this collection beyond text.

Finally in this section, Peter Merchant's chapter explores the reactions of Samuel Johnson and James Boswell to the Scottish culture that they found on their journey to the Western Isles, the outcomes of which were published in the 1770s and 1780s. As they encountered a network of cultural practices seen to be either in decline or already faded into history, both men reflected upon processes of change: Johnson on changes in the community, Boswell on changes in Johnson. Merchant notes that Boswell is both the cause and the observer of these latter changes, bringing Johnson 'exotic' foods to 'Scottify' his palate and by extension experiment with and alter other aspects of his persona, from his clothing to his English name. Johnson's interest in the stadial theory of social development (see also Manias' chapter) meanwhile provided a framework for him to discuss notions of the 'primitive' and the contemporary 'commercial', leading him ultimately to ask 'whether the Savage or the London Shopkeeper had the best existence'. Johnson's working out of this issue foregrounds myths of Celt and Caledonian, Jacobite and moderniser, and Merchant explores the unresolved tensions stirred up thereby. The chapter concludes by examining the echoes of this vacillating attitude in fictions by Walter Scott, George Meredith and Dinah Craik as well as key theorists of British identity Robert Knox and Matthew Arnold.

Thus Part II offers a range of eighteenth- and nineteenth-century perspectives on ideas of Celticity raised in Part I, showing how each perspective is both highly localised and nationally and internationally resonant, and how the perspectives are often in sharp conflict with one another. This part examines how a range of narratives and images contribute to the imagination of 'Celtic' regions and nations in this period, to the romanticisation of 'Celts' as heroic and spiritual but also to their dispossessed victimhood, or even their denigration as threatening savages. Wales is potentially prison or paradise (Edwards); the South West is a place of heroism or of primitive savagery (Moore and Trower); Brittany is home to a spiritual but 'backward' Celtic peasantry (Coughlin); while the question of whether Scotland's 'Savage' may or may not live a better life than the 'London Shopkeeper' remains unresolved.

Part III is edited by Garry Tregidga and broadens the scope of the collection further by examining ways of remembering and acting out these contested identity myths. The memorialisation of the past can draw on a variety of sources including written texts, oral traditions and visual representations. In these circumstances myth and mysticism can play a powerful role in the construction of communal and national identities.

Jo Esra's chapter returns to Cornwall to consider a neglected narrative of the county's multicultural past through the relationship between folk tales, apparent news-reporting and theatrical fiction about encounters with Islam. She focuses on the complex relationships between Barbary pirates, Cornish seafarers taken captive by them, crusaders and Cornish family members left behind. If captives or crusaders returned from Africa or the Levant, there was often concern about their 'true nature': their ability to resume an identity which was thought to have maybe been wholly altered by conversion to Islam and, even more subtly, by climatic changes in the body's humours. Three folk tales provide examples of this haunting anxiety. Esra argues that such tales dramatise tensions between a diverse and outward-looking Cornwall and an inward-looking, homogenous Cornwall. These tensions are only heightened by textual instabilities and the conflation of fictional and historical accounts, exemplified by a series of retellings of the same tale supposedly from a lost – and thus more mythically-charged – source. The notion of lost or questioned identity is here complicated by the 're'-telling of stories with no fixed point of original telling and no clear relationship to actual people and events.

Like Esra's chapter, David Hesse's is about the revisiting of totally fictive mythical pasts. He considers notions of the re-enactment of history, which has flourished beyond academia in the form of a hobby, particularly since 1960. As a 'discipline of global entertainment', it has helped to problematise notions of what exactly is being re-enacted or simply *enacted*. As Hesse notes, 'much of the history they re-enact never happened' and as anyone who has ever watched the re-enactment of a battle will know, re-enactors often have a sharply-defined polemical agenda in selecting their favourite contested moment of history: Roundheads versus Cavaliers, Union versus Confederacy or, surprisingly close to our own time, Nazis versus Soviet Russians. In this chapter, Hesse discusses the motivations of 're'-enactors of Scottish historical identities in Germany, France, the Netherlands, Belgium and the Czech Republic. He concludes that much of what is being enacted comes from literature (Macpherson's Ossian again, Walter Scott) and film (*Braveheart*) rather than from history books. Here again is identity as mythic commodity, a source of affective and even erotic pleasure where 'real' ethnic identity is not actually important and the notion of such reality is implicitly questioned.

Garry Tregidga's chapter also asks questions about the blurrings between identities sometimes considered to be quire separate: Cornish, Welsh and Breton. It examines the ways in which Cornish political developments were often intertwined with Welsh and Breton ones in the late nineteenth and early twentieth centuries. In particular, the focus is on the ways in which Cornish nationalistic aspirations were sometimes articulated by reference to particular Welsh or Breton figures or shared mythic narratives. For Cornish activists the choice of ally or role model was a difficult one. The Celtic Revival in Cornwall was very different to that in Wales, especially in its spiritual and class politics. Dominated as it was by high church Anglicans and Catholics like Henry Jenner and Louis Duncombe Jewell, whose politics tended towards conservatism, the Cornish Revival contrasted with the movement in Wales. In the principality, the Revival was more popular in its themes and participants and often it was linked to a Methodist and Liberal-centred politics of difference. Brittany was in many ways a more comfortable fit for Cornwall's Revivalists, since its social structures were more agrarian and conservative and it was also a Catholic polity. But this was unlikely to endear the Revival to the majority of Liberal-voting, chapel-going Cornish people who in reality lived in a mixed rural-industrial setting. Tregidga examines representation of Wales in Cornwall, and the ways in which the Cornish Revival might have been more quickly and widely successful had it taken the Welsh route.

The two final chapters move onto comparative approaches to Celtic mysticism, myth and nationalism, looking at these phenomena alongside white racist 'nationalism' linked with Nordic paganism, and British and English nationalism and its appropriation of the poet William Blake .

Andrew Fergus Wilson's chapter explores the strategy of entryism found in some white racist websites, to which, Wilson argues, naive readers and viewers can be attracted by a diverse mix of heavy metal music, 'glamour' photography, information about Nordic paganism and journalism on mainstream subjects. A particular focus is the racist writing of David Lane, which is sometimes then interspersed with these topics, giving it an apparent mainstream legitimacy.

Wilson finds that the term 'nationalism' is used anomalously in this *milieu*, since writers often explicitly reject the governance of their own national bodies, preferring to build an online community that – somewhat paradoxically given their politics of exclusion – transcends national and cultural boundaries. He also argues that on certain websites, ideas from the fields of both mysticism and myth, especially connected with the practice of Germanic-Celtic and Odinist paganism, are forced into an uneasy relationship with racist and sexist discourses that form no part of most of their adherents' interests. In summary, Wilson suggests that close attention should be paid to the kinds of semiotic slippage that appeared as benign 'malleability' in previous chapters. Here we are dealing with similar desires to appropriate the past – for example in the imagery of runes or the representation of Nordic gods – but in modernity these images can easily be co-opted by racist groups, often without less alert readers and viewers becoming aware of that process. It is our job to be alert and to alert other readers, as this book demonstrates.

Finally and relatedly in this part, Jason Whittaker's chapter examines the identity politics of the writings of William Blake, from Blake's use of the terms Albion, Britain and especially England, to his adoption by sections of the far right in contemporary Britain, notably the British National Party and English Defence League. Blake's ambivalence about 'England who is Brittannia' [*sic*] pervades his works, and Whittaker sees him as essentially a poet of anti-imperial views, even drawing for his criticism of jingoistic aggression on the long tradition of anti-British polemic stretching back to Gildas in c.540 AD. Thus the reading of him as a mystical prophet of English nationhood by either right or left wing politicians today is profoundly problematic and ironic. Whittaker documents the adoption of Blake by the BNP from 2000, facilitated by a shift from anti-Semitism to Islamophobia that made 'Jerusalem' (a hymn to the idea that Britons, especially Druids, could claim a personal religious connection with ancient Israel) a particularly apposite-seeming text. In response, he argues for Blake as a global and international prophet-poet, with his work commenting explicitly on the idea that nations are made by mythmakers, not the other way round. With this decisive separation of the mythic literature of identity from its possible political uses, Whittaker concludes the collection by reinforcing one of its main conclusions: that the cultural forms discussed here are capable of almost infinitely variable interpretations, and belong to no one group, nation or critical position.

Readers will notice from the discussions of the argument in each chapter some of the difficulties and slipperinesses of the language used to compare like with like, and occasionally like with unlike. The languages in which notions of identity are discussed, in this book as elsewhere, are deeply contestable. Words such as 'Celt', 'Welsh', 'Gothic', 'Nordic', 'English' and 'Cornish' are signifiers without clear signifieds, names without self-evident tribes, let alone nations. There are nations, there are identities stacked within them like Russian dolls: but exactly where are the borders, the gaps, the lines between them? The gap in each case between label and artefact must be a key focus of study in itself, lest we continue to mistake academic and poetic fictions for realities with the disastrous consequences seen across Europe in the twentieth century from – well, Sarajevo to Sarajevo. In this collection the term 'Celtic' has been the centre of attention, but the insights generated in the discussion by just fifteen contributors of one apparently fairly well-defined grouping are revealingly multiple and occasionally incommensurable.

Note

1   This writing back is the subject of the doctoral thesis arising from our project, Samantha Rayne's 'Henry Jenner and Old Cornwall: Haunting, Identity and 'Celtic' Nationalism'.

Bibliography

Anderson, Benedict. (1983, 2006). *Imagined Communities: Reflections on the Origin and Spread of Nationalism*. Revised edition. London: Verso.

Arnold, Matthew. (1962). 'On the Study of Celtic Literature' in R.H. Super (ed.), *Lectures and Essays in Criticism*. Ann Arbor: University of Michigan Press. 293–386.

Beddoe, John (1885) *The Races of Britain: A Contribution to the Anthropology of Western Europe*. Bristol: J.W. Arrowsmith.

Bell, Ian A. (ed.) (1995). *Peripheral Visions: Images of Nationhood in Contemporary British Fiction*. Cardiff: University of Wales Press.

Bhabha, Homi K. (1990). 'Introduction: Narrating the Nation' in Homi K. Bhabha (ed.), *Nation and Narration*. London and New York: Routledge. 1–7.

Birch, A.H. (1976).'The Celtic Fringe in Historical Perspective' [Review of the book *Internal Colonialism* by M. Hechter]. *Parliamentary Affairs* 39, 230–3.

Borlase, William. (1973). *Antiquities Historical and Monumental of the County of Cornwall*. Wakefield: E.P. Publishing.

Bottrell, William. (1870). *Traditions and Hearthside Stories of West Cornwall*. Vol. 1. Penzance: W. Cornish.

British Pathé. (1955). *Furry Dance* (also known as *Furry Dancer*). Retrieved from: http://www.britishpathe.com/record.php?id=22

Brockliss, Laurence and David Eastwood (eds). (1997). *A Union of Multiple Identities: The British Isles c.1750–c.1850*. Manchester: Manchester University Press.

Caesar, Julius. *De Bello Gallico*. Trans. H.J. Edwards. New York, 1917.

Chapman, Malcolm. (1992). *The Celts: The Construction of a Myth*. London: Macmillan.

Colley, Linda. (1992). *Britons: Forging the Nation 1707–1837*. New Haven: Yale.

Collis, John. (2003). *Celts: Origins and Re-inventions: Origin, Myths and Invention*. Stroud: Tempus Publishing.

Courtney, Margaret Ann. (1890). *Cornish Feasts and Folklore*. Penzance: Beare and Son.

Cunliffe, Barry. (1979). *The Celtic World*. London: Bodley Head.

——. (1997). *The Ancient Celts*. Oxford: Oxford University Press.

——. (2001). *Facing the Ocean: The Atlantic and its Peoples 8000BC–AD1500*. Oxford: Oxford University Press.

Deacon, Bernard, Dick Cole and Garry Tregidga. (2003). *Mebyon Kernow and Cornish Nationalism*. Cardiff: Welsh Academic Press.

Dietler, Michael. (2006). 'Celticism, Celtitude, and Celticity: the Consumption of the Past in the Age of Globalization' in Sabine Rieckhoff (ed.), *Celtes et Gaulois dans l'histoire, l'historiographie e l'ideologie moderne*. Glux-en-Glenne: Centre Archéologique Européen. 237–48.

Dodd, Philip. (1999). 'Englishness and the National Culture' in David Boswell and Jessica Evans (eds), *Representing the Nation: A Reader*. London and New York: Routledge. 87–108.

Gellner, Ernest. (1983). *Nations and Nationalism*. Oxford: Blackwell.

Graves, Robert. (1961). *The White Goddess*. Enlarged edition. London: Faber.

Hale, Amy. (1996). 'Foot in the Mouth or Foot in the Door? Evaluating Chapman's Celts'. *Cornish Studies* 4, 158–70.

Hale, Amy and Philip Payton (eds). (2000). *New Directions in Celtic Studies*. Exeter: University of Exeter Press.

Hanegraff, Wouter. (1998). *New Age Religion and Western Culture: Esotericism in the Mirror of Secular Thought*. New York: State University of New York Press.

Hanham, Harry. (1978). 'Review of *Internal Colonialism*'. *American Historical Review* 83:1, 173–4. http://0-www.jstor.org.lib.exeter.ac.uk/stable/1865963

Harvey, David, Rhys Jones, Neil McInroy and Christine Milligan (eds). (2002). *Celtic Geographies: Old Culture, New Times*. London: Routledge.

Hechter, Michael. (1971). 'Regional Inequality and National Integration: the Case of the British Isles'. *Journal of Social History* 5:1, 96–117.

——. (1999). *Internal Colonialism: The Celtic Fringe in British National Development*. 2nd edition. New Brunswick, NJ: Transaction.

Higgins, Godfrey. (1829). *The Celtic Druids*. London.

Hobsbawm, Eric. (1990). *Nations and Nationalism since 1780: Programme, Myth, Reality*. Cambridge: Cambridge University Press.

Howlett, Jonathan. (2004). 'Putting the Kitsch into Kernow', *Cornish Studies* second series 12, 30–60.

Hunt, Robert. (1865). *Popular Romances of the West of England: First Series*. London.

Hunter, James. (1977). 'Review of *Internal Colonialism*'. *The Scottish Historical Review* 56:161:1, 103–5.

Hutchinson, John. (1987). *The Dynamics of Cultural Nationalism*. London: Allen and Unwin.

Hutton, Ronald. (1996). *The Stations of the Sun: A History of the Ritual Year in Britain*. Oxford: Oxford University Press.

——. (2007) *The Druids*. London: London and Hambledon.

——. (2009) *Blood and Mistletoe*. London and New Haven, CT: Yale University Press.

Jackson, J.A. (1978). 'Review of *Internal Colonialism*'. *British Journal of Sociology* 29:4, 52–78. http://0-www.jstor.org.lib.exeter.ac.uk/stable/589680

James, Simon. (1999). *The Atlantic Celts: Ancient People or Modern Invention?* London: British Museum Press.

Jenner, Henry. (1904). *Handbook of the Cornish Language*. London: AMS Press.

Knox, Robert. (1862). *The Races of Men* (revised edn). London: H. Renshaw.

McCarthy, James and Euan Hague. (2004). 'Race, Nation and Nature: The Cultural Politics of "Celtic" Identification in the American West'. *Annals of the Association of American Geographers* 94:2, 387–408. http://0-www.jstor.org.lib.exeter.ac.uk/stable/3693994

McDonald, Maryon, Anthony P. Cohen, Ronald J. Frankenburg, R.D. Grillo, Teresa San Roman, Moshe Shokeid and Alex Weingrod. (1986). 'Celtic Ethnic Kinship and the Problem of Being English', *Current Anthropology* 27:4, 333–47. http://0-www.jstor.org.lib.exeter.ac.uk/stable/2743049

McKie, Robin. (2006). *Face of Britain*. London: Simon and Schuster.

Mais, Stuart Petre Brodie. (1928). *The Cornish Riviera*. London: Great Western Railway Company.

Michie, R.C. (1978). 'Review of *Internal Colonialism*'. *Journal of Economic History* 38:3, 779–80. http://0-www.jstor.org.lib.exeter.ac.uk/stable/2119510.

Morgan, Kenneth O. (1971). 'Welsh Nationalism: The Historical Background', *Journal of Contemporary History* 6:1, 153–72.

Nairn, Tom. (1977). *The Break-Up of Britain: Crisis and Neo-Nationalism*. London: NLB.

Newman, Gerald. (1987). *The Rise of English Nationalism: A Cultural History 1740–1830*. Basingstoke: Palgrave.

Özkirimli, Umut. (2000). *Theories of Nationalism: A Critical Introduction*. Basingstoke: Palgrave.

Payton, Philip. (1996). *Cornwall*. Fowey: Alexander Associates.

——. (1999). *The Cornish Overseas*. Fowey: Alexander Associates.

Pittock, Murray. (1999). *Celtic Identity and the British Image*. Manchester: Manchester University Press.

Ray, Celeste (ed.). (2005). *Transatlantic Celts*. Tuscaloosa: University of Alabama Press.

Reece, Jack. (1977). *The Bretons Against France: Ethnic Minority Nationalism in Twentieth-Century Brittany*. Chapel Hill: University of North Carolina Press.

Renfrew, Colin. (1987). *Archaeology and Language: The Puzzle of Indo-European Origins*. London: Jonathan Cape.

Richards, Jeffrey. (1997). *Films and British National Identity: From Dickens to Dad's Army*. Manchester and New York: Manchester University Press.

Ross, Anne. (1967). *Pagan Celtic Britain: Studies in Iconography and Tradition*. London: Routledge.

Said, Edward. (1978). *Orientalism*. London: Pantheon.

——. (1993). *Culture and Imperialism*. New York: Alfred Knopf.

Samuel, Raphael. (1999). *Island Stories: Unravelling Britain*. London: Verso.

Shumway, David. (1998). 'Nationalist Knowledges: The Humanities and Nationality'. *Poetics Today* 19:3, 357–73. http://0-www.jstor.org.lib.exeter.ac.uk/stable/1773424

Sloan, William B. (1979). 'Ethnicity or Imperialism: A Review Article'. *Comparative Studies in Society and History* 21:1, 113–25. http://0-www.jstor.org.lib.exeter.ac.uk/stable/178454

Smith, Anthony. (2000). 'Images of the Nation: Cinema, Art and National Identity' in Mette Hjort and Scott MacKenzie (eds), *Cinema and Nation*. London and New York: Routledge. 45–59.

——. (2004). *The Antiquity of Nations*. Cambridge and Malden, MA: Polity.

Spivak, Gayatri Chakravorty. (1988). 'Can the Subaltern Speak?' in Cary Nelson and Lawrence Grossberg (eds), *Marxism and the Interpretation of Culture*. Urbana: University of Illinois Press. 271–313.

Stout, A. (2008). *Creating Prehistory*. Oxford: Blackwell.

Stukeley, William. (1740). *Stonehenge: A Temple Restor'd to the British Druids*. London: W. Innys and R. Manby.

Sykes, Bryan. (2006). *Blood of the Isles: Exploring the Genetic Roots of our Tribal History*. London: Bantam.

Vernon, James. (1998) 'Cornwall and the English Imagi(nation)' in Geoffrey Cubit (ed.), *Imagining Nations*. Manchester and New York: Manchester University Press.

Vince, Ian. (2008). 'Strange Days: Fired by Ancient Zeal in Cornwall'. *The Telegraph*. 18 July. Retrieved from: http://www.telegraph.co.uk/earth/3347571/Strange-days-Fired-by-ancient-zeal-in-Cornwall.html

Ware, Vron. (2007). *Who Cares about Britishness? A Global View of the National Identity Debate*. London: Arcadia.

Watson, Cameron. (2008). *Basque Nationalism and Political Violence*. Reno: University of Nevada Press.

Westland, Ella. (1995). 'The Passionate Periphery: Cornwall and Romantic Fiction', in Ian A. Bell (ed.), *Peripheral Visions: Images of Nationhood in Contemporary British Fiction*. Cardiff: University of Wales Press, 153–72.

Williams, Colin H. (1979). 'Ethnic Resurgence in the Periphery', *Area* 11:4, 279–83.

Wilson, Gordon. (2009). *SNP: The Turbulent Years 1960–1990*. Stirling: Scots Independent.

PART I
Prehistory and paganism

1

DRUIDS IN MODERN BRITISH FICTION

The unacceptable face of Celticism

Ronald Hutton

One of the basic rules of Celticism is that Celts are cute: in most contexts of recent Western culture, things labelled 'Celtic' have a positive resonance, signifying mystery, magic, romance, and exciting and empowering encounters with a heavily spiritualised Otherworld. The great enduring exceptions to this rule have been the Celts to whom mainstream British culture has traditionally thought itself most familiar: the Druids, the most important spiritual figures in ancient Celtic culture. This anomaly is not by any means an inevitable result of the source material for them, consisting of Greek and Roman authors, almost all of whom were relying on data that was at least second-hand and generally out of date, and of Irish literature written centuries after the disappearance of the pagan world. The images that these texts provide are contrasting: some represent Druids as barbarous and ignorant priests, given to murderous rites, but others portray them as wise, learned, patriotic and pious. We have absolutely no means of telling which of these images, if any, are correct (Kendrick 1927, Chadwick 1966, Piggott 1968, Berresford Ellis 1994, Green 1997, Hutton 2007).

Figures which are at once so vivid and so insubstantial are excellent subjects for imaginative writing. The modern British have written poetry about Druids since the early sixteenth century, stage plays since the early seventeenth, and novels since the early nineteenth. These works have now been relatively well surveyed, at least in outline, as far as the early twentieth century (Owen 1962, Hutton 2009). By contrast, the role of Druids in British fiction published since 1950 has been almost completely neglected (Hutton 2007: 39–40, 120–24). This is a shame, because an examination of that role in novels, stage plays and screenplays promises to reveal many of the fears, hopes and divisions of recent British society, much as the analyses of it in earlier periods have done the same for the social and cultural movements of those times. Such an enterprise should be the more interesting in that during the past six decades Druids have featured as prominently in the British imagination as they did in the Georgian and Victorian eras, when they were major players in it, and much more than in the period of the World Wars and the years between them. It is also highly significant, as will be shown, that the portrayals concerned both buck the trend of associating Celticity with romantic and alluring images, and are sharply divided along national lines.

Druids appeared in the work of two of the most celebrated authors of British historical fiction to emerge in the 1950s, Rosemary Sutcliff and Henry Treece. Both wrote some of their most popular books about Roman Britain and its aftermath, and both approached the theme in a similar contemporary context: the dismantling of Britain's own colonial empire. This was accompanied by an increasing recognition by the British of their loss of status as a world power, and a fear of the necessary adjustments to be made as a result. Both authors identified strongly with the Romans, much as their Victorian predecessors had done, as a force for civilisation, rationalism and stability. Both also retained another characteristic of Victorian fiction, a deeply ambivalent attitude to the native British. On the one hand the latter are admired in these books for their pride, courage, flamboyance and passionate love of freedom; on the other, they are deplored for their savagery, unruliness and superstition. What firmly tips the balance of sympathy against the natives in the stories is their superstitious, oppressive and bloodthirsty Druidic religion. Sutcliff's Druids are malign and withdrawn figures, who dominate the spiritual life of their people while remaining detached from them, being instantly recognisable by their black robes: 'their influence lay heavy on the duns and villages, but nobody spoke of them, any more than they spoke of their gods and the prowling ghosts of their forefathers' (Sutcliff 1954: 158–9). To Treece, they are 'white-robed wolves who annually carried away the first-born or mutilated the cattle with golden knives to bring rain' (Treece 1952: 65 and 1958).

These images are based firmly on the more hostile writings of the Romans themselves, filtered through nineteenth-century fiction which adopted the Roman standpoint. The archaism of both authors is revealed again by the fact that both set Druid rituals inside megalithic monuments, in Treece's case including Stonehenge, following early Victorian precedent but ignoring almost a century of teaching from archaeologists that such structures had been erected long before Druids appeared. Treece incorporated into his portrait of Druidry accounts of human sacrifice reported by Victorian imperialists from India and Africa, to strengthen the identification of the modern British with the Roman Empire. The equivalent resonance in Sutcliff is to portray Druids as agitators working in secret within the Roman province of Britain, preaching holy war to foment rebellion among superstitious natives who are in actuality better off under the rule of Rome. The comparison with *mullahs* and *imams* who resisted the spread of British imperialism is clear, and would have renewed force in the 1950s as semi-religious resistance movements such as the Mau Mau appeared in British colonies. What marks these writers off from their nineteenth-century predecessors is a total lack of interest in Christianity as a redeeming and civilising force; its place in both is taken by a secular rationalism and tolerance, implied as present in Roman culture.

The two authors differed over their attitude to the consequences of the end of Roman rule. Both regarded this as regrettable, a triumph for barbarism, but in her work Sutcliff emphasises the manner in which descendants of the Romans kept aspects of civilisation alive through the ensuing darkness, so that it could flower again in better times. Furthermore, Druids are missing from her portrait of post-Roman times. Treece makes the collapse of empire far more complete, and claims that Druidry has continued to flourish in all its horror beyond the imperial frontier, and persisted as a secret cult inside the province. As Roman power disappears, Treece's Druids can try to regain their old power, led by Merlin, a figure straight out of hostile Georgian and Victorian stereotypes of evil Druidry, with clawed hands, burning eyes and foetid breath (Treece 1956a). Whereas nobody in Sutcliff's fiction wields supernatural power, in that of Treece Druids have the ability to alter their appearance at will, conjure up illusions, heal or blight humans with spells and communicate with animals and trees. He preaches the message that savage and uncanny forces lurk beneath the surface of civilised society and may break free as soon as the people in charge of that society lose the willpower to maintain it: a terrifying implied prophecy of the likely fate of Britain's colonies on independence, and perhaps even of Britain itself.

These themes, of the role of the Romans as a civilising force and the fragility of civilisation itself, survived the dissolution of empire, and manifested regularly in British culture in the late 1960s and 1970s, this time in screenplays and the heritage industry. In 1968 and 1973 they appeared in a pair of 'B' movies, the first now largely forgotten, and the second a cult classic. The former was *The Viking Queen*, which despite the title was a reworking of the story of Boudica's rebellion against Roman rule. It kept the traditional contrast between noble and glamorous but barbaric natives, and ruthless and aggressive but civilised Romans. Once again, the latter are made to seem the more familiar and sympathetic culture, and the balance of sympathy is again tipped by the natives' addiction to Druidic religion. The sacrifices practised by the latter include both the burning alive of captured Romans in cages, which has some basis in actual Roman texts, and the immolation of helpless young native women, which owes everything to the Victorian imagination. The second and much more famous film was *The Wicker Man*, which warns of the dreadful consequences of reviving paganism in the present day. Druids are never mentioned in it, but it draws heavily on the imagery associated with them, especially in the shocking final scene in which a Christian policeman is burned alive as a sacrifice to a sun god in a giant wicker effigy. This was taken directly and explicitly from an illustration in a work on Druids published in 1676, and based ultimately on an account by the Roman author Julius Caesar (Sammes 1676: 105; c.f. Caesar VI.13–18).

Between the dates of the two films there occurred the opening of the London Dungeon, Britain's main museum of waxwork horrors. One of its exhibits showed a Druid, equipped with the traditional white robe and sickle mentioned as Druidical garb by the Roman author Pliny, about to sacrifice a young woman stretched out naked on an altar.

Druids (and pagans in general) did no better on British television during the 1970s. In 1978 the time-traveller Doctor Who was made to arrive in modern Cornwall, in a story entitled 'The Stones of Blood'. There he uncovers and destroys a revived Druidic cult of human sacrifice, inspired by blood-hungry extra-terrestrial beings disguised as megaliths. In the same period, viewers could find 'The Goodies', the most popular British comedy team of the later 1970s, making a similarly perilous foray into a Celtic land. This time it is Wales, where they encounter another sect of revived Druids, and have to be rescued at the last minute from being sacrificed by them: the programme cleverly, if with no subtlety, parodied the opening ceremony of the leading modern Welsh cultural institution, the Gorsedd of Bards, which had been developed in the nineteenth century and blended Christian and Druidic elements. Meanwhile, Rosemary Sutcliff was continuing to publish, and to absorb changing cultural mores into her novels, such as feminism and an enhanced sympathy for the victims of colonialism. What she retained was a sense of essential savagery of Druidic religion. In 1977 she brought out a story set in Iron Age Britain which ends with the sacrifice of the hero as a prisoner of war by a neighbouring tribe. The rite is led by a Druid 'fat like an acorn-fed hog, in the way of the priests… who lived too richly on the offerings to the gods' (Sutcliff 1977: 110). The following year she published a novel about Boudica's rebellion, in which she largely reversed her earlier sympathies to portray the Romans as brutal and dishonourable invaders. None the less, the native religion is still atrocious, and when a Roman town is taken, the men and children are slaughtered and the women tortured to death as sacrifices. Their naked bodies are left as offerings 'like dreadful white fruit hanging from the branches of the dark and ancient trees' of a sacred grove which owes much to a famous description of one by the Roman poet Lucan (Sutcliff 1978: 116 and c.f. Lucan 3.5.399). For all their follies and crimes, her Romans still seem much more like 'us', the native British very much the 'other'. With their fey, romantic heroism, their intense, nature-based spirituality and their fatal lack of discipline, they embody the Victorian stereotype of the emotional, impractical, artistic Celt.

Indeed, what is striking about all these representations is how traditional they are in general. They fit perfectly into a luxuriant Victorian genre of fictional writing about Druids, in which a defence of Christianity and civilisation is mounted by portraying paganism and barbarism as inevitably associated with crimes against humanity. Just as under Victoria, the exercise licensed creative writers to provide erotic and violent images which could titillate an audience even while the activities concerned were being formally rejected and deplored (Hutton 2007: 107–20). This genre had almost disappeared during the early twentieth century, perhaps because two World Wars supplied a genuine experience of carnage and atrocity that removed much of the appetite for it in fiction. With the return of a society as prosperous and peaceful as that under Victoria, the taste for lubricious historical melodrama seems to have revived. Just as in the 1950s, the appropriation of nineteenth-century motifs included the association of megaliths with Drudical religion, found in all of the films and television programmes mentioned above. Sutcliff was now better attuned to scholarly opinion, and her Druids no longer frequented megalithic monuments. Instead, she projected onto them the cult of a single goddess, 'the Great Mother', which mid-twentieth-century archaeologists had imagined as characterising the Neolithic and which was being appropriated by some contemporary feminists (Hutton 1999: 278–82, 340–68). The sustained difference from the Victorian works was the absence of a commitment to Christianity as the religion of goodness and civilisation; instead, as in the 1950s, rationalism and science were deployed in its place. As Treece had done before, Sutcliff now credited the native British with innate magical abilities, based on their closeness to the natural world, which were ultimately unavailing when confronted with Roman mechanical skill and common sense.

What is missing in all this work is any sense of a countervailing tradition of sympathy for Druids, drawing on the more admiring ancient and medieval sources, of the kind that had been dominant in eighteenth-century Britain, and were still present in the nineteenth century (Hutton 2009: 86–145, 210–27). This was the more significant, in that the late twentieth century had seen the appearance all over Britain of a recreated paganism, which represented itself as a benign nature-venerating religion surviving from ancient times (Hutton 2009: 348–99; and 1999 *passim*). Thus far, its presence had mainly served to inspire warnings against the dangers that such a revival represented, delivered by *The Wicker Man*, *Dr Who* and *The Goodies*. In 1976 and 1977, however, Peter Timlott published two books which projected onto the ancient Druids almost all the motifs of the modern resurgence of sympathy for occultism and paganism. He portrayed them as a mystical order with the grades and costumes of the Welsh Gorsedd. From the British 'earth mysteries' movement, which had blossomed at the end of the 1960s, he took the idea that megalithic monuments had been erected at places where natural energies, embodied in the planet, were concentrated. He made the Druids the priests of these, and added the information, also taken from the same movement, that their wisdom had originally come from Atlantis. The British capital of these ideas in the 1970s was Glastonbury, which Timlott duly made that of his ancient Druidry, and he gave the latter the organisations and rituals of modern British occultists, with lodges, cubic altars, the tracing of elemental pentagrams, and contacts with higher beings on 'inner planes' of existence. As part of this package, Timlott reversed the sympathies of mainstream fiction, turning the Romans into forces of evil and condemning Christianity as a corrupted religion of intolerance and repression, lacking genuine spiritual contacts. His Druids, by contrast, are perfect counterparts of the modern 'permissive society', preaching carefree sexuality accompanied by an expert knowledge of contraception (Timlott 1976 and 1977).

As the 1980s ran their course it became clear that Timlott had been an aberration, and that the hostile view of Druidry was to remain dominant, even in contexts where a more favourable treatment might have been expected. One of these was in a new medium for the subject in Britain, the comic strip, collated and republished as the graphic novel. In this case the strip was that created by Pat Mills and starring an ancient Irish hero, Sláine, in the very popular magazine *2000 AD* (Mills, Mahon and Fabry 2000). Its sympathies are solidly with Sláine and his tribe, but they still adhere to human sacrifice. These gory ceremonies are led by a single male Druid, in the traditional white robe, accompanied by a circle of naked female witches: the latter may have been inspired by a passage in Pliny, where native British women paraded naked at festivals (Pliny XXII.2), but more probably by the modern pagan witch religion of Wicca, which is woman-centred and where members work nude. The sacrificial victims include prisoners of war, in conformity with ancient texts, but also the tribe's own sacred kings, immolated after a reign of seven years according to the vision of ancient religion propagated by the Victorian scholar Sir James Frazer, in his famous book *The Golden Bough*. In the realm of more conventional novels, the bloodshed continued apace. The biggest bestseller of the decade to feature Druids was probably Edward Rutherford's *Sarum*, an account of the fortunes of a group of families living in the area round what became Salisbury over six thousand years. One of the chapters included Druids, defined primarily as practitioners of human sacrifice who operate out of forest lairs like beasts (Rutherfurd 1987). Less celebrated, but still popular, was the series of novels by Guy N. Smith, starring an esoteric version of James Bond, called Mark Sabat, as a warrior against occult evil. The fourth book in the series was concerned with Druids, characterised as representatives of 'a religion most long thought vanished, its otherworldly horror deep buried and forgotten save in the nightmares of the deranged' (Smith 1983: dust cover).[1] The story has them return to modern England to punish the profanation of one of their ancient sacred sites by killing the perpetrators in horrible ways, usually by burning. Sabat does not vanquish so much as propitiate them, by beheading the surviving individuals who have offended them, at Stonehenge.

The Timlott view made only one appearance in the 1980s, and then only to be sent up, brilliantly, in one of the earliest of what became the long series of comic novels by Sir Terry Pratchett. Here too Druids are shown as masters of earth energies, flying around on rocks using a dowser's pendulum to steer them and a mistletoe bough (which Pliny, again, had made a familiar symbol of Druidry) to land them. Following the views of some earth mysteries enthusiasts, they work in megalithic monuments which function like giant computers, which means that they behave like real computers, crashing and needing huge efforts to repair them. Pratchett deftly combined the two traditional views of Druidry in one passage: 'they believed in the essential unity of all life, the healing power of plants, the natural rhythm of the seasons and the burning alive of anybody who didn't approach all this in the right frame of mind' (Pratchett 1986: 56). None the less, it is the bloodthirsty aspect that comes to dominate, though within the framework of slapstick comedy: in a perfect parody of Victorian melodrama, the heroes rescue a virgin from becoming a Druidical sacrifice, only to find her wildly indignant at being cheated of the immortality promised to her as a consequence of the rite. She is also furious at the waste of all those Saturday nights spent conserving her virginity for that moment. Furthermore, at the same time Pratchett does seem to take a swipe at the more benevolent portraits of Druids, declaring that 'all this stuff about golden sickles and cycles of nature and stuff just boils down to sex and violence, usually at the same time' (Pratchett 1986: 73).

Meanwhile, the sex and violence were still being delivered, without any leavening of humour. In 1987 the most famous living Scottish historical novelist turned his attention to Druids. This was Nigel Tranter, who published two books on the careers of early saints, in that year and 1993, as some of the last in a long list by him covering almost the whole of medieval and early modern Scottish history (Tranter 1987 and 1993). A consistent feature of them had been his enthusiastic adoption of a Protestant myth, created in the sixteenth century and still strong in the nineteenth, of a benevolent and admirable native 'Celtic Church', which had appeared on the arrival of Christianity in the British Isles and been subsequently obliterated by a power-hungry Roman Catholicism. This now gave him a perfect role for the Druids as the evil pagan priests overcome by this good new religion; and in doing so, he drew ultimately on a medieval Irish tradition, of the Druid as the natural foe of the early saint. This tradition was, however, filtered through Victorian melodrama, and Tranter, through writing almost a century after the end of that era, reflected Victorian ideas more fully than many earlier writers. He condemned the Druids relentlessly as slaves to superstition and enemies to good religion, science and progress alike. They are, of course, addicted to blood sacrifice, slaughtering animals of many different kinds and humans of all ages and both sexes. Just as in so many other works in this tradition, since the eighteenth century, horror is mingled with prurience: women are the favourite victims of the sacrificial rites, being stripped nude before dying, and one Druidical idol consists of a 'life-sized stone statue of a naked woman, painted all black...from between whose legs issued a serpent' (Tranter 1993:159). This is, of course, an artefact unknown to European archaeology. In classic Victorian fashion, the devotees of these rites respond to the blood-letting as if possessed by devils themselves, shouting and cavorting madly and engaging in promiscuous sex. Once again, the long-established opinions of archaeologists are ignored, to make Druids habitually worship in stone circles; and indeed in circles of the precise form imagined by John Toland in a work published in 1726 but influential until the early nineteenth century (Hutton 2009: 80–81). Unlike the preceding novelists to deal with Druids since 1950, Tranter made Christians his heroes, suggesting that their faith automatically turned converts into better human beings, with superior medicine and agricultural techniques as well as morals.

In just two respects does Tranter's portrait incorporate elements of more recent modernity. One is to give a sharper liberal edge to his condemnations by asserting that Druids especially selected as victims handicapped children and women who had defied their husbands or borne children out of wedlock. The other comes in a sudden, temporary and awkward change of heart in the second book, when Tranter seems to become briefly aware of the view, put about by the earth mysteries movement in the 1970s, that megalithic monuments reflected great scientific ability and natural wisdom. For a moment, his benighted heathen priests become remarkable scientists, their stone circles 'all sited accurately to link up with each other in relation to the sun's seasonal variations, an astronomical and geodetic wonder' (Tranter 1993: 154). They are also admitted to be quite good herbalists and acupuncturists, with pretty rites for children and some decent people among them who will make good Christians; but within a few pages we are back to witnessing scenes of horror and obscenity.

Tranter was approaching the end of his career, and creative abilities, when he wrote these works, but another prolific author tackled the subject a few years later at the height of his powers. This was Bernard Cornwell, who loaded Druids into his triple-decker retelling of the Arthurian legend published between 1995 and 1997 (Cornwell 1995, 1996 and 1997). He portrayed post-Roman Britain as one in which Druidry is still (somehow) in power in most areas and Christianity only just arriving. Once more, Druid religion is shown as a horrific one of human sacrifice, physical filth and superstition, with people cowering before apparently nonsensical symbols and actions: the chief Druid of the kingdom of Siluria is, typically,

> ...a tall old man...dressed in a dirty grey robe embroidered with hares and crescent moons. He had hung small bones on the end of his long, lank, white hair and the bones clattered together as he shuffled ahead of his king.
>
> (Cornwell 1995: 26–7)

Nonetheless, just as in the pages of Treece (who is Cornwell's closest predecessor) Druid magic somehow seems to work, especially in the hands of Merlin, who is shown as a personal devotee of the pagan god Cernunnos, not coincidentally the favourite god of modern pagan witchcraft. By contrast, Christianity seems to have no intrinsic power at all, and is characterised by sanctimony, hypocrisy and the repression of natural appetites and joys. It triumphs because it manipulates human self-interest and ambition: the preference of the author is clearly for an irreligious modernity free of the faults of either religion.

The 1990s went out with two other novels, which took an equally dim view of Druids, though from different perspectives. In 1997 came Julian Rathbone's recreation of the events leading up to the Battle of Hastings, which had the 'Old Religion' lingering in Wales and Ireland, but also in the wooded interior of Kent and Sussex, at that late date. These pagans emerge in stereotypical Druidic fashion 'at certain seasons… to celebrate their awful ceremonies and sacrifices' within a circle of oaks (Rathbone 1997: 54). A year later came *On the Edge of Darkness* by the Scot, Barbara Erskine, another story to portray ancient Druidry as a religion of fear and carnage, led by all-powerful priests who wield real occult powers. The latter are defeated by the invocation of a superior Christian magic, deployed by saints, though the author also suggests that there are equally benevolent forces inherent in the natural world, into which good people can tap (Erskine 1998). It is an answer to the question of what is correct in religion different from that of Tranter or Cornwell; but Druids are still an example of what is bad.

Given the strength of this tradition, the millennium represented no hurdle to it. A new historical novelist had arrived, Simon Scarrow, whose books were set during the Roman invasion of Britain. One dealt with Druids, who are portrayed in it as universally hostile to Rome but divided into sects, some more evil than others. Among the worst is the 'Dark Moon' cult, which combines features of modern occult societies, New Age Travellers and biker gangs, by wearing black robes, charms of twisted hair on their wrists and black tattoos of crescent moons. Their (never explained) aim is to destroy the world by empowering a terrible god to commit the act, burning women and children alive in wicker cages as offerings to him. In a note at the end, Scarrow identified some specific contemporary targets for his hostility. One was modern Druidry, described as 'that naïve and nostalgic reinvention of Druid culture that parades around Stonehenge at certain times of the year'. The other was religious fanaticism in general, which he held to be exemplified by the atrocity which had just been committed by Islamic terrorists on 11 September 2001 (Scarrow 2002: 432–33). On his heels, in 2003, came another female writer, Fay Sampson, who set a story like Scarrow's during the Roman conquest of Britain. Her tone is gentler than that of the other authors since 1980, and she makes a less stark division between heroes and villains. Both of the opposed societies are shown as having virtues and vices, and the true evil in the story is that of war itself, with its inevitably brutalising effect. The British Druids are shown as wise and (often) gentle, and, in a classic post-feminist manner, as including women on a basis of equality. None the less, when the Romans attack, the native British readily turn to human sacrifice to win divine support, as one of the corrosive effects of militarisation. The story ends with the promise of a peaceful union of Briton and Roman and the redemption of both by Christianity (Sampson 2003).

This review of popular fiction is of course not exhaustive, concentrating instead on the best-known works, purchased by public libraries or shown in cinemas. It reveals a clear pattern that since the Second World War, Druids have returned to being what they were in the poetry and novels of the nineteenth century: favourite figures of horror and disgust in the British imagination.

One reason for this has already been suggested: that they furnish a means of portraying and legitimising scenes of lurid violence, often seasoned with eroticism, to entertain a relatively stable, peaceful and prosperous society. This is one similarity between contemporary Britain and that of the Victorians, and there is another of relevance: that both societies are characterised by anxiety about religion. In the nineteenth-century case it was provoked by the decision to assimilate fully other forms of Christianity, and Judaism and atheism, into a nation formerly dominated by an established church. In the recent one it was induced by the growth of new forms of spirituality and religion, and the large-scale importation of foreign faiths such as Islam, Hinduism and Rastafarianism. In both periods, Druids are used to express hostility towards forms of religion of which an author disapproves (and so to commend others) or else to justify a dislike of religion in general.

In this connection, it is interesting to see what has happened to views of earlier British prehistory in recent fiction. It is plain that from the 1950s onward more and more authors have come to accept the decision of Victorian scholars that megalithic monuments were not built by Druids, but were the holy places of earlier religions and peoples in the Neolithic and Bronze Ages. During the twentieth century, professional archaeologists began increasingly to portray the Neolithic in particular as a relatively peaceful period of small social groups who engaged in joint works of monumental construction to honour ancestors and forces of the natural world (Hutton 2009: 414–15). This hardly seems to have affected novelists, to whom savagery remains a better stimulus. The portrait of the Neolithic presented in novels after 1960 – often by the same writers who dealt with Roman or post-Roman Britain – has been more or less that which most Victorian writers gave of Druids, with the Druids taken out: of a religion of callous and sadistic cruelty of which the main spiritual expression is human sacrifice. The main difference in them is one of gender, for in the earlier fantasies women were generally portrayed as sacrificial victims, while in a post-feminist age they are just as likely to be found wielding the lethal blade (Treece 1956b, Rutherfurd 1987, Burnett 1984, Cornwell 1999).

It is notable, however, that this attitude is not really a 'British' one: rather, it is Anglo-Scottish. During the nineteenth century the Welsh developed their own national myth of Druidry, by which a generally benevolent Druid religion turned into an exceptionally fine kind of Christianity, the two together nurturing an enduring Welsh disposition towards piety and love of the arts: it is this myth which is acted out in the Gorsedd ceremony at the National Eisteddfod (Hutton 2009: 146–82, 241–86, 313–17). As a result, Druids have become benign background figures in the Welsh mental landscape. When the playwright Emlyn Williams wrote a comedy about contemporary Welsh life in 1944, it was centred on a country pub called 'The Druid's Rest' (Williams 1944). Nine years later the most celebrated of all modern Welsh writers, Dylan Thomas, completed his 'play for voices', *Under Milk Wood*, set in a small Welsh coastal town in which the minister wears a 'Druid's seedy nightie' and a local child makes a Druidical stone circle (Thomas 1954: 20, 22). The exception to this pattern is one that certainly proves the rule: the series of detective novels set in a surreal version of Aberystwyth patterned on Raymond Chandler's Los Angeles, published since 2001 by Malcolm Pryce. The modern Druids of the Gorsedd are prominent in the first, where they control most organised crime in West Wales, especially gambling, prostitution and the supply of alcohol (Pryce 2001). As the basic joke of the series depends on giving a squalid and melodramatic twist to aspects of Welsh life that are actually humdrum and respectable, the implication is that 'real' Welsh Druids are similarly harmless: in the fiction they are succeeded in their role of crime bosses by the Meals on Wheels service. Modern Welsh culture has, however, generally been too defensive and inward-looking to make much impact on the rest of the British. Furthermore, there is every sign that if it did make a determined outreach in this respect, such a move would be resisted. That is, after all, the whole point of the joke against the Welsh in *The Goodies*, cited above. In the 1990s Sir Terry Pratchett went on to include in his imagined world a parody of Wales called Llamedos, populated by Druids who officiated in stone circles. To date, however, none of his stories have been set there, apparently because it is too damp, pious and musical (it features most prominently in Pratchett 1994). It seems likely, indeed, that English and Scottish hostility to Druids burgeoned in the nineteenth century partly because of the developing Welsh love affair with them (Hutton 2007: 19–40).

The unusual nature of the modern Anglo-Scottish dislike of Druids is highlighted still more effectively when it is compared with the attitudes of creative writers from nations outside Britain. The Druid most familiar to Europeans and Americans alike at the present day is probably the one who featured in the French comic strip Asterix, created by René Goscinny and Albert Uderzo in 1959. Thirty-three books have now been based upon it, translated into a hundred different languages and dialects. The context of the tales, which are partly a parody of nineteenth-century French nationalist history, is that the village of their hero, Asterix himself, has become the only one in ancient Gaul (the future France) successfully to resist the Romans. Its Druid is Panoramix (in English translations, Getafix) who brews the potion that enables its people to defeat the Romans, as well as curing all their ills. He is a wholly benevolent, and indeed admirable, character. The same pattern is shown when the focus moves onto American culture. In the novels of Marion Zimmer Bradley, about a (barely historic) Roman and post-Roman Britain; in those by Terry Brooks, set in the imagined world of Shannara; and in that of Norman Spinrad, about the Roman conquest of Gaul, Druids feature very much on the side of good.

This contrast remains true even of writers who settle in Britain from abroad. It may be no coincidence that Peter Timlott, whose portrait of Druids was so unusual in its unequivocal admiration, spent much of his career in Australia. When a fully Australian writer, Jules Watson, came to Britain in the 2000s, she chose as the subject for her first novel the Roman invasion of Scotland. She portrayed native society as divided between a small, dark, aboriginal race, who venerate only a great goddess served by priestesses, and taller, fairer Celts who believe in a pantheon of deities. This is a reproduction of the late Victorian interpretation of prehistory as characterised by invasions by different races, abandoned by professional archaeologists in the 1970s. Its gendering, however, is that of 1970s feminist spirituality, and the book projects into the past other aspects of recent Western counter-cultural mysticism such as the Hindu concept of the third eye and the Native American use of vegetable hallucinogens to produce visions. The Druidic religion, that of the Celts, is represented as slightly less politically correct than the older one, because more male-centred, but not otherwise unpleasant: the true villains are the Romans, portrayed as a people, culture and religion so alien to Britain that their defeat is essential for the good of the land itself as well as of its peoples (Watson 2004).

The same decade has seen yet another popular string of novels about the Roman conquest of Britain, illustrating once more the importance of this event to the contemporary creative imagination, as an opportunity to explore the relationship between civilisation and barbarism; social control and social freedom; and mainstream society and its critics. This is the work of Manda Scott, who is both British-born and resident in Britain (Scott 2004a, 2004b, 2005 and 2006). As such, it is highly significant that her sympathies are completely on the side of the natives, whose religion is portrayed as wise and benign. It is focused on a pantheon of different deities representing aspects of the natural world, and is led by spiritual experts, both female and male, who advise tribal councils made up of 'grandmothers'. Women and men likewise have an equal role as warriors. The religious leaders possess effective psychic powers, but these can only slow down and soften the Roman conquerors, who win because of superior technology and numbers. The model for the British society shown in these books comes from far outside Britain: it is a combination of highly idealised representations of Native American and Australian aboriginal cultures, filtered through feminism. We have here at last, therefore, a fictional image of religion in Iron Age Britain which is entirely benevolent and produced by a non-Welsh British author. The truly significant aspect of it is that Druids are never mentioned. The religious leaders who play their part are termed 'dreamers', a name derived ultimately from native Australian tradition: it seems that an English or Scottish author can only write admiringly about the ancient Druids by putting them under a different label.

This should not necessarily condemn modern Druids to the same treatment. Since 1772 there have been societies in Britain which have taken the name of Druid, inspired by the view of the original Druids as patriotic sages, based on the more favourable ancient accounts and dominant in the Georgian period. Most functioned as social, philanthropic and benefit clubs, but from the nineteenth century, first in Wales and then in England, some came to embody an avant-garde spirituality (Hutton 2009: 125–45, 252–86, 348–73). These include the people who have held regular ceremonies at Stonehenge, scorned by Simon Scarrow. The number of this kind of Druid has greatly multiplied since 1985, and one such society, the Order of Bards, Ovates and Druids, has emerged as especially large and influential (Hutton 2007:193–204 and 2003: 239–58). It might be expected that the influence of this movement – in which the name of Druid is attached to practitioners of a nature-based mysticism – would have some impact on fiction, and it has. In 2006 Barbara Erskine, who had given ancient Druids such a hard time eight years before, published a new novel (Erskine 2006).[2] It contains an expression of gratitude to the Order of Bards, Ovates and Druids for friendship and guidance, and its hero is a modern Druid of that sort, who possesses genuine psychic powers as well as wisdom, compassion, knowledge and sound judgement. The plot depends on an interaction of past and present, linked by both reincarnation and the enduring presence of spirits. Ancient Druids are also quite well treated, being dignified and sophisticated figures among whom both sexes hold equal honours in the now expected modern manner which has little basis in ancient sources. Another recent trope is repeated in the crediting of complete sexual freedom to native British women, both inside and outside marriage, with methods of contraception of a reliability not recorded before the 1960s. Once more the context of the ancient dimension of the story is the Roman conquest, and the classic Victorian cultural stereotyping is repeated, with the British (as 'Celts') being heroic, romantic, magically gifted and in harmony with the natural environment, and the Romans dourly, brutally and unstoppably efficient. The sympathy of the author is now, however, completely with the Britons, and the Romans are credited with an atrocity – the slaughter of the entire population of Anglesey, down to children – not recorded in any historic text.

The story therefore seems to break dramatically with the previous tradition of Anglo-Scottish hostility to Druids; but it does not. The religion of Iron Age Britain is still shown as including a regular component of both animal and human sacrifice, producing frightful scenes. More significant is the fact that the Druids' deities are shown as hungry for blood, even at the present day. The villainess of the tale turns out to be a modern feminist pagan, who is transformed by her contact with these old divinities into a homicidal and suicidal maniac, and is only thwarted by an alliance between the Druid and the local Church of England clergyman. It is emphasised that modern Druidry is a philosophy entirely compatible with Christianity, while both ancient and modern paganism are essentially evil. The author's prejudices have remained constant, and she has merely enlisted modern Druidry in their service.

The Order of Bards, Ovates and Druids has itself recently produced a novelist, Penny Billington, who is genuinely innovatory in her approach because her hero is a modern Druid detective who investigates cases that require occult solutions. Like Malcolm Pryce, Billington parodies the classic Chandler stories, and the result is similarly to create a hilarious and surreal parallel world. In the process, many aspects of modern 'alternative' spirituality are both celebrated and sent up, much as Pryce treats modern Welsh culture. Her hero's powers, however, operate in their own right and without any reference to Iron Age predecessors (Billington 2007 and 2008).[3]

As yet, therefore, there seems to be no cessation of the established tradition whereby English and Scottish writers of fiction treat Druids with a hostility not found among others, even in the rest of Britain. This is not a consequence of the ancient and medieval sources, which are, as has been said, ambivalent. Nor is it a pattern that was established when modern Europeans first began to take an interest in Druids, from the sixteenth century: as said, the Georgian English were generally admiring of them (and the Scots had lauded them for two hundred years before that). Nor is it a result of any consensus among experts in Iron Age archaeology or the history of Roman Britain, for apart from the fact that no such consensus exists over the nature of ancient Druidry, none of the authors considered above show any sign of having paid close attention to the work of professional scholars. What these works seem to show instead is how much of an influence over recent British culture, even in an age of late modernity or postmodernity, is still exerted by attitudes adopted under Queen Victoria.

Notes

1 I am grateful to Nick Freeman and Joanne Pearson for the gift of this book.
2 I am grateful to Philip Carr-Gomm for drawing my attention to this work.
3 I am very grateful to the author for the gift of both.

Bibliography

Berresford Ellis, Peter (1994) *The Druids*. London: Constable.
Billington, Penny (2007) *Gwion Dubh: Druid Investigator*. Westcliff on Sea: Appleseed Press.
—— (2008) *Beauty and the Brats*. Westcliff on Sea: Appleseed Press.
Burnett, David (1984) *Priestess of Henge*. London: Hamlyn.
Caesar, Julius. *De Bello Gallico*.
Cornwell, Bernard (1995) *The Winter King*. London: Penguin.
—— (1996) *Enemy of God*. London: Penguin.
—— (1997) *Excalibur*. London: Penguin.
—— (1999) *Stonehenge*. London: Penguin.
Chadwick, Nora (1966) *The Druids*. Cardiff: University of Wales Press.
Erskine, Barbara (1998) *On the Edge of Darkness*. London: Harper.
—— (2006) *Daughters of Fire*. London: Harper.
Green, Miranda J. (1997) *Exploring the World of the Druids*. London: Thames & Hudson.
Hutton, Ronald (1999) *The Triumph of the Moon: A History of Modern Pagan Witchcraft*. Oxford: Oxford Paperbacks.
—— (2003) *Witches, Druids and King Arthur*. London: Hambledon Continuum.
—— (2007) *The Druids*. London: Hambledon Continuum.
—— (2009) *Blood and Mistletoe: The History of the Druids in Britain*. London: Yale University Press.
Kendrick, T. D. (1927) *The Druids*. London: Methuen & Co.
Lucan. *Pharsalia*.
Mills, Pat, Mike Mahon and Glenn Fabry (2000) *The Collected Sláine*. London: Titan.
Owen, A. L. (1962) *The Famous Druids: A Survey of Three Centuries of English Literature*. Oxford: Oxford University Press.

Piggott, Stuart (1968) *The Druids*. London: Thames & Hudson.

Pliny. *Historiae naturalis.*

Pratchett, Terry (1986) *The Light Fantastic*. London: Corgi.

—— (1994) *Soul Music*. London: Corgi.

Pryce, Malcolm (2001) *Aberystwyth Mon Amour*. London: Bloomsbury.

Rathbone, Julian (1997) *The Last English King*. London: Abacus.

Rutherfurd, Edward (1987) *Sarum*. London: Arrow.

Sammes, Aylett (1676) *Britannia antique illustrate*. London.

Sampson, Fay (2003) *The Silent Fort*. London: Robert Hale.

Scarrow, Simon (2002) *When the Eagle Hunts*. London: Headline.

Scott, Manda (2004a) *Boudica: Dreaming the Eagle*. London: Bantam.

—— (2004b) *Boudica II: Dreaming the Bull*. London: Bantam.

—— (2005) *Boudica III: Dreaming the Hound*. London: Bantam.

—— (2006) *Boudica IV: Dreaming the Serpent Spear*. London: Bantam.

Smith, Guy N. (1983) *The Druid Connection*. Sevenoaks: New English Library.

Sutcliff, Rosemary (1954) *The Eagle of the Ninth*. Oxford: Oxford University Press.

—— (1977) *Sun Horse, Moon Horse*. London: Bodley Head.

—— (1978) *Song for a Dark Queen*. London: Knight.

Thomas, Dylan (1954) *Under Milk Wood*. London: New Directions.

Timlott, Peter (1976) *The Power of the Serpent*. London: Corgi.

—— (1977) *The Twilight of the Serpent*. London: Corgi.

Tranter, Nigel (1987) *Columba*. London: Hodder & Stoughton.

—— (1993) *Druid Sacrifice*. London: Hodder & Stoughton.

Treece, Henry (1952) *The Dark Island*. London: Gollancz.

—— (1956a) *The Golden Strangers*. London: Random House.

—— (1956b) *The Great Captains*. London: Random House.

—— (1958) *Red Queen, White Queen*. London: Random House.

Watson, Jules (2004) *The White Mare*. London: Orion.

Williams, Emlyn (1944) *The Druid's Rest*. Cardiff: William Heinemann.

2

OLD DEITIES, NEW WORLDS

The return of the gods in fiction

Marion Gibson

This chapter examines, in two different eras, a selection of re-imaginings of the entities who are thought to have been ancient British deities – and some of the implications of those re-imaginings for constructions of the national, tribal and racial identity of authors and readers. The focus is on some of the deities who might variously be described as 'Celtic', 'Iron Age' or 'Romano-British'. These are easily the most popular deities to be reinvented in fictions long after they had ceased to be worshipped. The chapter suggests that re-imaginings of Iron Age British paganism began in the Middle Ages by facilitating literary innovation and fostering subversive thought, that they played an important part in stimulating British Renaissance writing and that they can still be seen as challenging generic, sexual and political boundaries in contemporary writing. In fiction of the postmodern period they can offer a flexible but emotively satisfying way to imagine British identities, combining contemporary multiculturalism with the surprisingly inclusive discourses of nationhood that writings about paganism created in the late Medieval and Renaissance periods.[1]

The attempts to recreate imaginatively ancient British pagan modes of thought start with Geoffrey of Monmouth, the Welsh secular canon who wrote a history of the monarchy in the 1130s, in the process giving Britain the foundation-myth of Trojan descent from the hero Brutus. There are of course earlier references, most notably in Bede's *On the Reckoning of Time* (c. 721; 1999) and *Ecclesiastical History of the English People* (c. 731; 1968). But Bede's work, like others' of the early Medieval period (e.g. Gildas, *The Ruin of Britain* c. 540; 2002) is a disapproving documentary account of paganism rather than an imaginative recreation. Bede has no empathy with pagans and no desire to detail their beliefs or cultural activities – hence his tantalisingly sketchy reportage of their calendar customs. Geoffrey, meanwhile, industriously imagines his early Britons as transplanted worshippers of classical deities, whom the Trojans (now Britons) had adopted during their exile in Greece and Italy. Unlike earlier writers, he often includes details of temples, feast-days and pagan ceremonies. The first story to be set in Britain itself, after Brutus' flight from his homeland and travel to the island, is that of his friend Corineus and the giant:

> Corineus experienced great pleasure from wrestling with the giants... Among the others there was a particularly repulsive one, called Gogmagog... Once, when Brutus was celebrating a day dedicated to the gods... this creature, along with twenty other giants, attacked him and killed a great number of the Britons... [Corineus] challenged Gogmagog to a wrestling-match... and hurled this deadly monster... far out into the sea.
>
> (Geoffrey 1966: 72–3)

In this account, setting the attack on a religious holiday, even though it is a Romanised pagan one, makes the giants' behaviour seem more shocking and uncivilised – we must care about the pagan Trojans, for when set against the blasphemous giants they must be seen as pious human beings just like the implied British reader. But at the same time, as a good Christian, Geoffrey is implicitly undermining any faith we might have in pagan prophecy: during his travels Brutus had been told by the goddess Diana that Britain *used* to be peopled by giants but was now empty and his for the taking. Clearly, it was not. Geoffrey, then, presents us with ambiguities: a vividly imagined colonial contest between the new, exotic settlers who are 'us' and the diminished but still mighty original inhabitants, set in the context of pagan worship and prophecy of equally doubtful but fascinating nature. He details Brutus' meeting with the goddess in surprisingly positive terms and identifies all Britons with their pagan ancestor Brutus with persuasive charm and verve. Geoffrey's refusal to provide a pejoratively judgemental framework for the interpretation of his pagan culture offers the reader largely unfettered pleasures of imagination – a highly significant pioneering moment in the British imagination of the pagan past.

Few of Geoffrey's literary followers were so empathetic towards paganism, where they mentioned it at all. Laȝamon, a Worcestershire priest who wrote his *Brut* around the turn of the twelfth century, repeatedly condemns pagan gods as devils and their prophecies as witchcraft. Yet in describing Brutus' visit to Diana's temple ('dedicated to the Devil' as a modern translation snappily puts it) Laȝamon cannot help giving him a beautiful prayer to speak:

> Leafdi Diana; leoue Diana; heȝe Diana, help me to neode.
> Wise me & wite me...
>
> (Lady Diana, beloved Diana, lofty Diana, help me in my need. Guide me and govern me...)

In response:

> His lauedi Diana; hine leofliche biheolde.
> Mid wn-sume leahtren; wel heo him bi-hihte,
> & hendiliche hire hond; on his heued leide…
>
> (Diana his lady gazed lovingly towards him; / With an attractive smile, she amicably promised [to help him], / Graciously laying her hand on his head)…
>> (British Library MS Cotton Caligula A.IX; Allen, ed., 1992: 4, 15–16)

What are readers expected to make of this loving, attractive, amicable, gracious devil, who sounds remarkably like the Virgin Mary?[2] Here we see again a fruitful area of slippage between Christian and pagan, official and unofficial, text and subtext, British and other. Laȝamon's approach, as the Brut's form begins to ossify into orthodoxy, is less positive and bold than Geoffrey's – he provides an unimpeachably Christian linguistic framework within which he can put words into his characters' mouths and takes care to identify himself with condemnation of the ways of devils. In Laȝamon, Geoffrey's re-imagined pagans must speak for themselves – their author is wary of appearing to endorse their views, however tacitly. Yet the very fact that they are allowed to speak so lyrically opens up a negotiable space in the text for poetic play with identity.

The tempting opportunities of re-imagined paganism continued with amplification into the Renaissance, and shaped it decisively. Yet in each version there was hesitancy and concern. Robert Fabyan's chronicles of 1516, for example, are part of the new humanist movement, which took as its starting point the need to explore all the history and operation of human experience, even (and perhaps especially) the history of pagan cultures. And we can see Fabyan struggling with the latest variant of the paganism problem in the very early sixteenth century as he offers a prayer to whichever deities can help him in his work:

> In this prayer, I thynke nat to be used,
> As dyddyn these Poetis in theyr olde days,
> Whiche made theyr prayers to goddes abused,
> As Jupiter and Mars, that in theyr olde laws
> Were named Goddes, and fayned in theyr sawes
> That they were Goddes of Batayll and rychesse,
> And had in theym great virtue and prowesse.
>
> For what may helpe these fayned goddess all…?
> Wherto shuld I calle unto Calliope…?
>
> Syne all these were Mynystris of god in mortall,
> And had in theym no power dyvynall
>> (Fabyan 1811: 6)

For Fabyan, in pre-Reformation certainty, there were self-evidently no other gods than the Christian God, so that when Fabyan's Brutus meets Diana the author dismisses her with the lofty addition 'a Goddesse of mysbyleved people' – people very unlike the British (Fabyan 1811: 9). But still, his list of pagan deities and description of some of their attributes suggests pleasure in rehearsing exotic names and demonstrating ungodly knowledge. And as the sixteenth century went on, a positive delight in being able to think like a pagan, however briefly or furtively, became a widespread habit of mind that facilitated the Reformation to flourish in the Renaissance.

It was a deeply troubling habit in its wider implications. The ability to think in two different imaginative worlds – that of, say, Cicero and St. Augustine – offered, I think, a model of empathy for other situations. If one could think like a celebrant of Apollo and a subject of Jesus Christ, what if one could think as both a Catholic and a Lollard/Protestant, or an Italian and an Englishman, or a man and a woman…? The possibilities were both seductive and frightening. Thinking like a pagan was one of the most deeply challenging things that an early modern person could do, and we might argue that the flowering of the British Renaissance began at the moment when that way of thinking became normal, indeed expected, among the creative writers and scholars following in Geoffrey's wide wake. We can see that duality of thinking in almost all great Renaissance writers – certainly in Spenser (the pioneer of such writing in an explicitly British mythopoeic context), Shakespeare, Donne and Marlowe. With this explosive potential, pagan-inspired humanism revolutionised every kind of British writing from around 1590 onwards.

By the end of the reign of Elizabeth I the possibilities offered by a walk on the pagan wild side were thus clear.[3] What is perhaps surprising is how strongly these possibilities continue to haunt literary texts today. Remarkably little has changed. I want to move on in part two of the chapter to exploring some other examples of thinking like a pagan and its anti-Establishment implications in the late twentieth and early twenty-first centuries.

The first godsmith in this second discussion is T.C. (Tom) Lethbridge (although equally I could have chosen Harold Bayley, Margaret Murray, Alfred Watkins, William Flinders Petrie or one of many others – the invention of deities was a popular vice in the first half of the twentieth century). Lethbridge was Director of Excavations for the Cambridge University Museum of Archaeology and Ethnology and the Cambridge Antiquarian Society (Lethbridge 1957: vii). By the 1920s, he was reading about chalk hill figures, like the Cerne Giant and the Uffington White Horse, and – to return to where we began the chapter – he began to connect them with stories circulating in medieval literature. He was especially struck by a story from the thirteenth century, told by Gervase of Tilbury, about Wandlebury hill near Cambridge. Gervase reported that on the hill there was an ancient earthwork, which had been the camp of a pagan horde of invaders who had come to ravage Britain and murder the Christians there – Vandals or 'Wandali'. These attackers seem likely to have been situated, in his imagination, in the period after the Romans left. Their camp was now, Gervase said, the site of a popular legend. If a warrior entered the camp alone at night and called out 'Knight to knight, come forth!' he would meet a mounted opponent who appeared from nowhere to fight him until either the challenger or the apparition was knocked from his horse and conceded victory. Gervase had heard a particular story about a knight named Osbert who had fought the ghostly warrior fairly recently, defeated him and taken his horse. But Osbert had been wounded and the horse had vanished at cockcrow.

Lethbridge was excited by the story as what he called 'a genuine piece of traditional folk-lore', as opposed to an invention by a Medieval romancer whom he disliked as 'a thoroughly beastly person' on the strength of Gervase's biography in the *Encyclopaedia Britannica*. Gervase was a monkish Norman hypocrite, for Lethbridge (who began his career as an Anglo-Saxonist) (Lethbridge 1957: 1–3). But his story could be read against itself if it was connected with the name of the hills around Wandlebury, the Gogmagog Hills. Gogmagog, remember, was the name of the giant whom Geoffrey of Monmouth's Corineus threw into the sea. Lethbridge thus wondered if the knight of Gervase's tale and the giant of myth had become conflated. In 1936 he wrote to *The Times* laying out some of the evidence, in a letter that appeared as part of a silly season correspondence about why the Gogmagog Hills had their name. Noting that in the Elizabethan period university students had been forbidden from attending some unspecified festivities at Wandlebury, Lethbridge finally suggested that there had been a 'survival of fertility rites' at the site of the giant figure. Surely this made both the giant and the knight relics of belief in a pagan god? Lethbridge had got this idea from Harold Bayley's book *Archaic England*, where Bayley artlessly, brilliantly suggested that if Gog was a male god then perhaps Magog (Ma Gog) was his wife, the goddess. Lethbridge thought this 'very sound reasoning' (Lethbridge 1936 and 1957: 4–5, 13–14; Bayley 1919).

Of course, Lethbridge's idea of sound reasoning was not everyone's (anon. 1971; Hawkes 1971; Murray 1957; Newman, Whitlock, The Sons of T.C. Lethbridge, Stout 2006 and Welbourn 2010 and 2011 offer a range of opinions). But the discovery of a lost god was a deeply alluring prospect. Symbolically, it would mean reclaiming Wandlebury from the ravening Wandali of the Norman Gervase's imagination, and making it and its heritage older, more peaceful and more inclusively European. Unlike many others of his wartime generation, Lethbridge did not hate Germans – he described the First and Second World Wars as 'the Kaiser's war' and 'the Hitler war' respectively, showing that he thought war-guilt lay with Germany's rulers, not the German people. So he was satisfied that as builders of the 'camp' and makers of any hill-figures, imagined Germanic hostiles such as the Vandals might be replaced by prehistoric British peoples of mixed Germanic and/or Belgic and/or Celtic origin ('Celticized Germans or Germanized Celts' as he put it – whatever such confusing terminology means).[4] The friendly European creators of both camp and hill figure were thus, in his imagination, battling other, less welcome, invaders well into post-Conquest times and despite losing to the Norman, the ghost-knight had still sent him home with a spear wound and a limp. If Gervase's story were re-read in this way, then, the story would be deeply satisfying to Lethbridge: older, more Celtic, suggesting a collaboration of waves of immigrants until the advent of the Norman 'ruling caste' that he detested (Lethbridge 1957: 8, 60, 69, 17, 61, 71, 105, 128–9).[5] The story would become one of open-minded British pagans rather than tyrant French Christians.

And it is perhaps no coincidence that by the 1950s, Lethbridge had fallen out decisively with his own 'ruling caste', the archaeological establishment, which he saw as dominated by dry, scientific professionals who had forgotten the relevance of folklore, literature, landscape and local knowledge to archaeology. Obsessed with stratigraphy and technical jargon and almost deifying Sir Mortimer Wheeler and Vere Gordon Childe (respectively the founder and contemporary director of University College London's Institute of Archaeology), these diggers seemed to Lethbridge to be unthinking automatons.[6] Instead of digging a trench, Lethbridge used 'a stainless steel bar', graduated in feet and nearly six foot long, with which he prodded the ground that he wished to explore. If the bar went down more than usual, he thought that he 'was probably hitting some artificial hollow', and an upright stick might be placed there as a marker. After the area had been fully prodded, it might be expected that a pattern of markers would be seen (Lethbridge 1957: 22–4).

Lethbridge recounts his proddings in *Gogmagog: The Buried Gods*, published in 1957. Having selected a hillside, he slogged away with the bar, using hundreds of artichoke sticks as markers, and then went home and produced a number of drawings of the patterns of sticks which suggested some curved and straight ditches under the ground surface. These he sent to Sir Thomas Kendrick at the British Museum, and Sir Cyril and Lady Aileen Fox at Exeter.[7] Both replied, suggesting what the patterns that they had seen might represent, as if the exercise were a game of charades. Maybe they were just trying to be helpful – and Kendrick's reply does suggest some possible irony (or concern for Lethbridge's reputation?): 'Rear quarters of an animal. Walking (not galloping) white horse. May the Lord be with you'. But the Foxes went further, explicitly endorsing both the theory of the 'buried god' (except that they thought she was a goddess) and hailing his find: 'Female with two horses probably Epona congratulations'. Epona was a Celtic horse-goddess.[8] Lethbridge, a fair-minded man, wondered sensibly 'how could anyone know that the figure was female?' but he was delighted by his friends' reaction and was soon to conclude that their 'skilful… identifications' were quite correct. Happily, when he carried out some more 'soundings', he found two more male figures and a horse and chariot (Lethbridge 1957: 29–39).

On this basis, Lethbridge argued that Gervase's thirteenth-century story was shaped by the figures, rather than being simply a vague general allusion to supernatural goings-on at the fort. What if the knight *was* the warrior figure, the goddess represented (in a bizarre sex change) the knight's squire, and the Celtic sun-god figure Helith, a favourite of Flinders-Petrie, represented the Norman challenger (Flinders Petrie 1926)? Thus the group told metaphorically the story of the annual triumph of the old sun-god, the warrior of the hill, over darkness and winter, which Lethbridge linked to an obscure piece of folklore about a god called Wandil who he claimed represented winter. Now Gog, Ma Gog and Wandil were all named and their meanings clear for all to see. Lethbridge, the outsider, was sufficiently empowered by this vision to change his entire life and writing, moving from Cambridge's academic orthodoxy to a life of mystic exile in Devonshire, where he experimented with dowsing and ESP and began to publish popular manuals of both. He became a hero of the counter-culture of the 1960s (Lethbridge 1957: 60–4, 72; Welbourn 2011).

It is this story of rebellious desire and its fulfilment that, more than any other, made me want to trace the histories of re-imagined British paganisms back to their Medieval roots. Lethbridge's 'buried gods' are a literal, material re-enactment of the subversive unearthings of pagan cultures being practised by Geoffrey of Monmouth, Spenser, and later on John Dryden, Thomas Gray, William Blake, Henry Rider Haggard, Ted Hughes, T.H. White, Jean M. Auel and others. Yet, for all the importance of this long subversive poetic tradition in British culture, it was still surprising to find Lethbridge's hill figures returning to literature again at the heart of the British fantasy novelist Mark Chadbourn's *Age of Misrule* series, begun in 1999.

Chadbourn's primary sources are Medieval Irish texts such as the Fenian and Ulster cycles, as filtered through popular books and websites about Celtic myth (Chadbourn 1999: 439–41, 189). He uses them to debate the issues raised by non-Christian cosmologies and theodicies in his own time: late twentieth- and early twenty-first-century issues of class, spirituality, sexuality and power relations of all kinds. In *World's End*, the first of the series, the old gods begin to break through from another dimension into British modernity. And the best example of their re-emergence is what Chadbourn does with Lethbridge's *Gogmagog: The Buried Gods*. In the third book of the *Age of Misrule*, Ryan Veitch (one of the five human heroes who are to 'save' the world as we know it) visits the Gogmagog Hills with Tom (Thomas the Rhymer, the thirteenth-century Scottish prophet returned from fairy captivity after hundreds of years). Tom's long experience of the world of the gods means that he knows that at Wandlebury T.C. Lethbridge 'had instinctively uncovered a figure that was spiritual in nature, rather than an exact outline on the hillside' and that giants are a metaphor for 'something like men, only greater, stronger, more vital, something to provide awe and wonder, and a little fear too, responsible for great feats of creation' (Chadbourn 2001: 212, 217). The figure, Tom reveals, is in fact a Jungian mandala, enabling reflection and opening a doorway to another world. Like any good epic hero, Tom must undertake an underworld journey to meet one of the old gods.

Slightly bizarrely, the first manifestation he meets under the Gogmagog Hills comes in the form of Jim Morrison, the lead singer of The Doors. The band's name is important, of course – the Morrison figure is a guardian of a gateway in perception, an idea they took from Blake via Aldous Huxley[9] – but Chadbourn is also quite serious about the historical Morrison's role as the prophet of a better world in 'the last time of innocence', the 1960s (Chadbourn 2001: 221). Chadbourn sees this period of political, religious and sexual radicalism as the last chance the world had to redeem itself. The truth that this version of Morrison teaches comes from this time – that 'we are all gods' and manifestations of a greater spirit, whether Witch or Muslim, Christian, male or female, straight, gay or bisexual (Chadbourn 2001: 222).[10] All these character types are represented by Chadbourn as aspects of godhead. Tom meets an avatar of this 'god', the closest the books come to that spirit itself, under the hill. It takes the form of a lava being shaped something like an Easter Island monolith. Here is Lethbridge's Gogmagog equivocally (as so often in these stories of pagan re-imaginings) but firmly made stone. Meanwhile, outside the hill Veitch, detained by fairies, has stayed out after dark and so meets Chadbourn's version of the knight that haunts the hill. This horseman, now imagined as a kind of centaur, announces itself as Machan's creature, a 'totem of Rig Antona, our Great High Queen [here, a pagan British goddess], who made the sky and the stars and the green grass' (Chadbourn 2001: 237).[11] Tom explains that the site was originally sacred to Epona, also known as Rhiannon, Macha and so on, a highly-creative version of an identity taken from the work of W.J. Gruffydd and others on *The Mabinogion*. This composite goddess, Rig Antona, is a patron of underworld journeys like Tom's own. Here is Ma Gog, Lethbridge's horse goddess, as identified by Cyril and Aileen Fox.

As well as being Thomas the Rhymer, Chadbourn's character Tom is clearly Tom Lethbridge, at some level. His is the imaginative vision brought to life here, in a way that challenges notions of truth and fact, suggesting instead that much of what we call knowledge is simply interpretation: a favourite view of Lethbridge's. Mimetically following his lead, the books emphasise this construction of reality in their plot design, since it becomes clear that the old deities and their magical creatures have always been present alongside the modern, material world, despite human failure to perceive them. And as well as their radical postmodern politics, the *Age of Misrule* books also challenge generic convention, mixing discourses of Fortean and post-processual archaeology (Hodder 1992 and 2006) with ethnography, Medieval myth and chorography, the *bildungsroman* and fantasy novel. Once again, imagining paganism offers an opportunity for subversive innovation, both politically and aesthetically.

Chadbourn's fiction presents a new age blurriness that is actually very helpful in taking seriously fictions about old deities long since swept aside by scholarship, fictions dating back to the twelfth century at least.[12] Just as paganism fired the imagination of Geoffrey of Monmouth, allowing him and his literary descendants to imagine worlds beyond the Christian and British identities that were deliciously malleable and exotic, so Chadbourn's text – haunted by Gervase of Tilbury channelled by T.C. Lethbridge – offers a hippy, postmodern relativism to contemporary readers. We can read this back onto Geoffrey and his ilk to demonstrate that thinking and writing like a pagan is one of the most important drivers of literary subversion and innovation, whichever period of literary history one chooses to explore.[13]

Notes

1 This chapter is part of the AHRC-funded 'Mysticism, Myth and Celtic Nationalism' project. I'm very grateful to the AHRC for funding this work.
2 Thanks to Adam Stout for this last insight.
3 They are discussed in my forthcoming *Imagining British Pagan Worlds* (London: Routledge, 2013), which also examines the Medieval and Renaissance context in more depth, bridges the gap between ancient and modern in this chapter and explores further contemporary fictions.
4 See the Introduction to this book for a discussion of the term 'Celt' and its conflicting associations, as well as Manias' chapter on race: 'Uncovering the deepest layers of the British past, 1850–1914' in particular.
5 Lethbridge was immune to the temptations of racial theory more generally, too: 'of course no one knows exactly who, or what, Aryans are or were. The term has no real racial value… [it] is still wrongly connected in men's minds with the term 'Nordic', which is under a cloud owing to the unfortunate behaviours of Adolph [*sic*] Hitler. The difficulty is that few anthropologists can agree as to what constitutes a race, or even whether there is such a thing at all' (1957: 88). Nevertheless, he did believe in skull shape as important in determining origin, even positing a 'Beaker type' (1957:106).
6 These were the precursors of processualism, an archaeology founded on precise digging controls and scientific testing. See Wheeler 1955 for an outline of his practice and its difference from more traditional work.
7 Kendrick was an authority on both Celtic and Anglo-Saxon art and culture: as for example Kendrick 1927 and 1938. Cyril Fox had been Director of the National Museum of Wales (1926–48) and, with his second wife Aileen, was an authority on the Neolithic and Bronze Ages, especially in south west Britain: on both see Scott-Fox 2002.
8 She was worshipped in Britain by legionaries but it is not clear whether she was naturalised or remained exotic: see RIB 1777, an altar to 'Deae Eponae' from Carvaron Fort, Northumberland. RIB catalogue entry at: http://www.roman-britain.org/places/magnis_carvetiorum.htm
9 The band's name is explained in the documentary *When You're Strange* as being drawn from the line in Blake's 1793 *Marriage of Heaven and Hell*: 'If the doors of perception were cleansed everything would appear to man as it is, infinite' (plate 14). It was used as by Huxley as the title for a book about mescaline in 1954.
10 The books' characters represent a selection of sexualities, ethnic and social backgrounds and religious stances to further Chadbourn's inclusive vision, which he discusses at: http://www.markchadbourn.net/books.htm
11 Rigantona is a version of Brigantia (see RIB 1053, an altarstone from Arbeia Fort, Northumberland: http://www.roman-britain.org/places/arbeia.htm) mixed with *Y Mabinogi/The Mabinogion*'s Rhiannon, thought by some, on the basis of her First Branch story, to be a character based on a horse-goddess like Epona or on the 'Celtic' Mothers. For this mythic complex's most forceful statement see Gruffydd 1953 and, as its survival and popularisation as fact, http://www.rigantona.net/
12 In focusing on this neglected and often scorned or feared material I'm particularly indebted to the work of Hutton (1999, 2007, 2009) including his chapter 'Druids in modern British fiction: the unacceptable face of Celticism' in this collection; Stout 2008; and, for its discussion of religion and atheism in twentieth-century archaeological myth-making, Hauser 2008.
13 For some related examples of the recycling of ancient British deities in popular fiction see: Keene 2008, Durgin 2001, Gemmell 1999, Caldecott 1998, Fisher 1997, Erskine 1994 and Herbert 1988 among many others.

Bibliography

Allen, Rosamund (1992) *Lawman: Brut*. London: J.M. Dent.

Anon (1971) Obituary for T.C. Lethbridge. *The Times* 2 October. 14.

Bayley, Harold (1919) *Archaic England: An Essay in Deciphering Prehistory from Megalithic Monuments, Earthworks, Customs, Coins, Place Names and Faerie Superstitions* 2 vols. London: Chapman and Hall.

Bede (1968) *A History of the English Church and People*. Trans. Leo Sherley-Price. Rev. ed. New York: Dorset.

Bede (1999) *On the Reckoning of Time*. Ed. and trans. Faith Wallis. Liverpool: Liverpool University Press.

Blake, William (1793) *The Marriage of Heaven and Hell*. London.

British Library MS Cotton Caligula A.IX at: http://quod.lib.umich.edu/cgi/t/text/text-idx ?c=cme;cc=cme;rgn=main;view=text;idno=LayCal

Caldecott, Moyra (1998) *The Waters of Sul*. Originally published 1997 as *Aquae Sulis*. Bath: Bladud Books.

Chadbourn, Mark (1999) *World's End*. London: Gollancz.

—— (2001) *Always Forever*. London: Gollancz.

—— (n.d) http://www.markchadbourn.net/books.htm

Durgin, Doranna (2001) *A Feral Darkness*. Riverdale, NY: Baen.

Erskine, Barbara (1994) *Midnight is a Lonely Place*. London: HarperCollins.

Fabyan, Robert (1811) *The New Chronicles of England and France*. Ed. Henry Ellis. London.

Fisher, Catherine (1997) *Belin's Hill*. London: The Bodley Head.

Flinders Petrie, William (1926) *The Hill-Figures of England*. London: Royal Anthropological Institute.

Gemmell, David (1999) *Sword in the Storm*. London: Corgi

Geoffrey of Monmouth (1966) *Historia Regum Britanniae, The History of the Kings of Britain*. Ed. and trans. Lewis Thorpe. London: Penguin.

Gildas (2002) *The Ruin of Britain and Other Works*. Trans. Michael Winterbottom. Chichester: Phillimore.

Gruffydd, W. J. (1953) *Rhiannon: An Inquiry into the Origins of the First and Third Branches of the Mabinogi*. Cardiff: University of Wales Press.

Hauser, Kitty (2008) *Bloody Old Britain: O.G.S. Crawford and the Archaeology of Modern Life*. Cambridge: Granta.

Hawkes, Christopher (1971) Obituary for T.C. Lethbridge. *The Times* 6 October. 16.

Herbert, Kathleen (1988) *Bride of the Spear*. London: Corgi.

Hodder, Ian (1992) *Theory and Practice in Archaeology*. London: Routledge.

—— (2006) *The Leopard's Tale: Revealing the mysteries of Çatalhöyük*. London: Thames & Hudson.

Hutton, Ronald (1999) *The Triumph of the Moon: A History of Modern Pagan Witchcraft*. Oxford: Clarendon.

—— (2007) *The Druids*. London: London and Hambledon.

—— (2009) *Blood and Mistletoe*. London and New Haven: Yale University Press.

Keene, Brian (2008) *Dark Hollow*. New York: Dorchester Publishing.

Kendrick, Thomas Downing (1927) *The Druids*. London: Merchant.

—— (1938) *Anglo-Saxon Art to AD 900*. London: Methuen.

Lethbridge, T.C. (1957) *Gogmagog: The Buried Gods*. London: Routledge and Kegan Paul.

—— (1936) Letter. *The Times* 12 June. 17

Murray, Margaret (1957) Letter. *The Times* 10 May. 13

Newman, Paul (1997) *Lost Gods of Albion: The Chalk Hill Figures of Britain*. Stroud: Sutton.

RIB catalogue. http://www.roman-britain.org/epigraphy/rib_index.htm

Rigantona. (n.d.) http://www.rigantona.net/

Scott-Fox, Charles (2002) *Cyril Fox: Archaeologist Extraordinary*. Oxford: Oxbow.

Sons of T.C. Lethbridge, The (2003) *A Giant*. Lincoln: Aegir Recording Company.

Stout, Adam (2006) *What's Real and What is Not: Reflections Upon Archaeology and Earth Mysteries in Britain*. Frome: Runetree.

—— (2008) *Creating Prehistory: Druids, Ley-Hunters and Archaeologists in Pre-War Britain*. Oxford: Blackwell.

Welbourn, Terry (2010) 'The Buried Gods of Gogmagog', *British Archaeology* 112 (May– June) at http://www.britarch.ac.uk/ba/ba112/feat3.shtml

—— (2011) *T.C. Lethbridge: The Man Who Saw the Future*. Alresford: O Books.

Wheeler, Mortimer (1955) *Still Digging*. London: Michael Joseph.

When You're Strange (2009) Dir. Tom DiCillo, Rhino Entertainment/Wolf Films.

Whitlock, Ralph (1979) *In Search of Lost Gods*. Oxford: Phaidon.

3

UNCOVERING THE DEEPEST LAYERS OF THE BRITISH PAST, 1850–1914

Chris Manias

In Victorian Britain, reflections on the past played an important role in conceptualizing national politics, empire and social development (Bowler 1989 and Burrow 1981). Yet understandings of the movement of history, and particularly its most ancient phases, were frequently subject to debate and uncertainty, with a strong tension between two narrative models. The first saw a sequence of migratory invading peoples, each with their own specific characters and qualities: in the earliest history of Britain, these followed successions of Celtic, Roman, Saxon, Norse and Norman dominance in various configurations across the constituent nations. This was a view which presented progress as driven by the conquest of the inferior, the undisciplined, or the decadent by superior forms. The most studied aspect of this, the mid-nineteenth century upsurge of 'Teutonism', as displayed in the histories of John Mitchell Kemble, J. R. Green and E. A. Freeman, presented virtues drawn from the Anglo-Saxon migrations as emblematic of the best constituents of the national character (Faverty 1951, MacDougall 1982 and Brundage 1994). Yet this interrelated with a second model, defined by what Peter Mandler has termed the 'civilizational perspective' (Mandler 2000), inherited from the conjectural histories of the Scottish Enlightenment and the traditions of political economy. This saw the growth of commercial society, material prosperity and liberty through stages of savagery, barbarism and settled life as universal phenomena – which had reached their apogee in the institutions and society of modern Britain.

These two models – one of ethnocentric and historicist migration and the other of a universal material ladder – were far from mutually exclusive. Yet integrating them into a coherent system required some intellectual effort. John Burrow has examined how this was attempted in history-writing (Burrow 1981: 11–35), but it must be remembered that discourses on the past, and especially the most ancient preliterate past, frequently drew on other methods and sources. As the century wore on, a range of 'historical sciences' attempted to illuminate areas which had been made obscure through a lack of textual records. This chapter will examine a range of means through which nineteenth-century scholars attempted to uncover the deepest and most ancient layers of British history and prehistory. It will pay particular attention to the problems and inconsistencies which were brought up in these studies, as contemporary scholars attempted to reconcile their concepts of race, culture, progress and history into comprehensible systems. This will be with the aim of demonstrating two important features of contemporary discourse: first, the diverse range of influences from across national and disciplinary boundaries which converged on understandings of the past in this period; and second, how concepts of migration and development interacted to build a layered and diverse account of the national past.

Reconfigurations of ancient history in nineteenth-century Europe were driven by shifting relationships between methodologies, approaches, institutions and source material. The works of classical writers, which described the ancient peoples of northern and western Europe, such as Tacitus' *Germania* and *Agricola*, Caesar's *Gallic Wars* and the geographical writings of Pliny, Strabo and Pomponius Mela, were highly significant textual sources, as were early medieval chroniclers, such as Bede and Saxo Grammaticus. Various other texts were also frequently used. Colin Kidd has demonstrated how crucial Biblical ideas were for understandings of human diversity in this period (Kidd 2006). Pagan (or at least pagan-derived) literature, such as the Beowulf epic, Norse Eddas, Welsh Triads and Irish mythological cycles, were also seen as valuable openings to the worldviews of the ancient ancestors, and potentially akin to mediated historical records, with legends of giants, trolls or elves taken as vague memories of ancient adversaries, or gods such as Odin as recollections of historical figures.

However, developments across the century moved beyond texts towards comparisons and analyses of objects, body parts and things. The growth of comparative philology in the early part of the century was one of the earliest aspects of this trend. The need to explain how the majority languages of Europe and Asia were genealogically related to one another fed into stereotypes of history being driven by nomadic horse-warriors from central Asia (Olender 1992 and Arvidsson 2006). Meanwhile, archaeologists and antiquarians engaged in waves of barrow-digging – greatly spurred from the 1830s onwards by major urban renovation projects and the building of railways – and unearthed vast numbers of objects which could be ascribed to peoples, periods and stages of development (Levine 1986 and Sweet 2004).

Another growing subject was racial anthropology. This tied studies of ancient populations to the sharpening biological discourses of the period, but also to statistical and positivistic surveys derived from medicine and anatomy (Stepan 1982). Key works, such as John Barnard Davis and John Thurnam's compendious *Crania Britannica* of the 1850s, combined anatomical studies with other historical methods, lamenting that 'arms, personal ornaments and other relics deposited with the dead have generally engrossed attention, to the exclusion of the tender and fragile bones of their possessors' (Davis and Thurnam 1855–6: I, 2). Meanwhile, others, like the anthropologist John Beddoe, went out into the countryside to note and record local differences in complexion and physical form in a systematic typological manner, and constructed ethnic genealogies through comparisons with archaeological and textual accounts (Beddoe 1885).

However, as should perhaps be expected from a field which mixed so many traditions and methodologies, a crucial and persistent point was that there always remained a great deal of uncertainty in these investigations. When the prominent ethnologist Robert Latham published an *Ethnology of the British Islands* in 1852, the best he could conclude after a survey of over 250 pages was that:

> Kelts, Romans, Germans, and Scandinavians, then, supply us with the chief elements of our population, elements which are mixed up with each other in numerous degrees of combination; in so many, indeed, that in the case of the last three there is no approach to purity.
>
> (Latham 1852: 259)

Likewise, ascribing clear physical features to ancient peoples was often problematic. Beddoe, in his preliminary ethnological investigations in Scotland in the early 1850s, noted that, 'if it is difficult for us to ascertain the complexional peculiarities of the Celts of 2000 years ago, it appears to be a no less puzzling task to determine those of their representatives at the present day' (Beddoe 1853: 3). Davis and Thurnam had similar misgivings about the reliability of classical descriptions:

> those who saw the various peoples of ancient Gaul, for they were not homogenous, must have perceived difference among them; yet they described them carelessly, from insufficient examination, or perhaps fell into some popular prepossession which gave to them certain prescriptive characters, as all Australians and Tasmanians, at the present day receive the appellation of 'Blacks', however much they depart from a negroid hue, and however much they vary.
>
> (Davis and Thurnam 1855–6: I, 163)

In this way, hardening and sharpening notions of racial difference, and a desire to subdivide peoples, often played into the creation of increasingly complex models.

The connection of ancient European populations with those of modern colonial regions suggested by Davis and Thurman was ingrained even further with the development of the field of human prehistory from the 1860s. This began to weave these threads together into a more coherent structure – although one still defined by varied interpretations, methodological division of labour, and interchange between specialists (Van Riper 1993 and Bowler 1989). A key work was John Lubbock's massively popular *Pre-Historic Times*, which went through multiple editions from 1865 to the end of the century as a general survey of knowledge of human antiquity. Lubbock believed, as the subtitle of the volume went, that prehistory was best 'Illustrated by Ancient Remains, and the Manners and Customs of Modern Savages' (Lubbock 1865), and presented the Stone, Bronze and Iron Age Europeans, revealed through archaeology as being equivalent to modern peoples judged to be in similar social states. This therefore placed Europe's ancient development onto a much wider, possibly universal, plane. This reinforced ideas that the progressive condition of all peoples, across both time and space, could be placed on the same ladder of civilization.

Understandings of the most ancient past of the modern nation were therefore highly complex. It could be seen to exist simultaneously in the layers of the ground, traces of language, and the physical features of the modern population. In some respects, it depended on the conceived shifts and alterations in different 'peoples', 'nations' and 'races' (terms which frequently belied some ambiguity as to their characteristics and definitions), but also on continuity across a broader developmental scale. The character of particular eras could be inferred and linked to each other through the relation of methodologies and interdisciplinary approaches. This simultaneously built into an idea that race, language, art, politics, culture, technology and civilization formed a single complex in each epoch, but that these were layered upon one another, and moved according to a single logic of progress. Tracing how these accumulated periods built into a wider historical and national structure thus required disciplines, races and peoples to be linked within a single narrative. This depended on the assertion of an ongoing trajectory of progress and civilization, which gave continuity and comprehensibility to the chaos and diversity of the past.

The deepest and most submerged layers were those of the Palaeolithic Stone Age, itself only recently discovered with the 'establishment of human antiquity' in the 1860s. A wide variety of forms were postulated for these ancient periods, through material records, suppositions on the general character of Ice Age man, and comparative analogies with the modern peoples of the Arctic. The geologist and prehistorian William Boyd Dawkins argued for the existence of a mysterious 'River-drift man, who most probably is as completely extinct at the present time as the woolly rhinoceros or the cave-bear', but linked the slightly more advanced 'Cave-man with the Eskimos' (Dawkins 1880: 233) through judged similarities in artistic styles, tool-forms, association with animals such as reindeer and bears, and cranial forms. Lubbock also hinted at something similar, noting 'that all the animals which are associated with the Lapps once inhabited Great Britain. Was man the only exception?' (Lubbock 1903: 19–20). However, generally, these were all quite tentative judgements. Palaeolithic humanity had existed so deep in the past that it had to all intents and purposes disappeared or been driven to extinction in a similar manner as was often thought to be happening to modern 'primitive' peoples (Brantlinger 2003). Some scholars claimed to have come across physical specimens deriving from these periods in their travels, particularly to explain regionally problematic results or to build into discourses of recapitulation and atavism. Beddoe for example claimed that 'I have myself, once and again, encountered in the flesh the man of Neanderthal' (Beddoe 1912: 31) but broadly, these were felt to have disappeared as a recognizable type.

The next peoples, those of the softened climate of the Neolithic Stone Age, were considered to have left a much more pronounced mark. Boyd Dawkins, Lubbock and others argued that the prehistoric Europeans of the Ice Age had been forced out of their regions by climatic change and the migration of short, dark long-skulled peoples in the onward march of a racial vision of progress. A clear population transfer was indicated in material culture: chipped arrowheads were replaced by polished stone axes, caves were abandoned in favour of fortified camps, carved representations of prehistoric creatures was superseded by abstract geometric designs, and the fauna was no longer dominated by wild Pleistocene beasts but domesticated pigs and oxen. In short, this had seen the advent of a settled society, but marked by barbaric and warlike features.

The ethnological affiliations of the Neolithics were classed, as was often the case, through craniology and interaction with continental debates. European scholars such as Paul Broca had argued for the existence of a short, dark-complexioned, long-skulled Ligurian or Aquitanian population in ancient Gaul in the period prior to the invasion of the Celtic speakers, which was argued to survive in a relatively pure form among the non-Indo-European Basques. These ideas impinged in Britain, where John Thurnam analysed the 'remarkably long and narrow' skulls found in Neolithic barrows to argue that this illustrated the presence of a related population (Thurnam 1869: 198). Beddoe and Dawkins agreed, and also stated that these forms were still present as recognizable types in peripheral regions of the country: 'in Scotland the small dark Highlander, and in Ireland the black Celts to the west of the Shannon, still preserve the Iberian characteristics in more or less purity' (Dawkins 1880: 330). This linkage of the pre-Aryan Neolithics with the modern Basques, and, with it, this new 'Iberian fringe', was often contested, but it raised the issue that those regions regarded as most politically troublesome and primitive retained traces of this primeval period.

Interpretations of what the Neolithic traces could further signify however were diverse. Despite their evident barbarism, Dawkins saw their settled lifestyle as having laid the foundations of modern society, noting that 'the progress of civilisation in Europe has been continuous from the Neolithic age down to the present time, and in that remote age the history of the nations of the west finds its proper starting point' (Dawkins 1880: 341). Not only this, but they 'had contributed to the national character the romantic element, an appreciation of natural beauty, and a tenderness which, united with the severe and stem qualities of the English, have found their noblest fruits in the immortal works of William Shakespeare' (Dawkins 1889: 42). They had thus made valuable contributions to the coalesced modern nation, and 'without them we should not be in the prominent position in which we find ourselves in at the present time' (Dawkins 1879: 105–6).

However, others preferred to portray them as archetypal 'dark-skinned savages'. In the 1890s, the folklorist George Lawrence Gomme argued that 'in South Wales the physical characteristics of this non-Aryan race survive, and why not, therefore, the remnants of their beliefs, especially those attached to definite local objects?' (Gomme 1892: 81). Drawing on global comparisons, he noted that 'pre-Aryan uncivilization' was still extant in many local British folk-rituals, and echoed analogous barbaric practices in Europe and India. This meant that the 'non-Aryan races have brought down survivals of savage culture in our folklore, and this has not been accomplished without other marks of their savagery' (Gomme 1892: 177), with violent and brutal behaviour still characterising these fringe regions, and with memories of the spiteful and war-like pre-Aryans forming the basis for legends of elves and fairies. That they were now found in pure forms only in regions which were already enshrined in national and polemical discourse as backwards and peripheral seemed to exaggerate their distinctiveness by giving it a racial edge. However, whether this racial persistence was the cause of backwardness was rather less clear, and many saw the combination of racial purity and primitive survival as simply a marker that these regions had never been subjected to the forces of progress. William Zebina Ripley, an American ethnologist reflecting on these issues, noted how:

> the ethnic type is still pure for the very same reason that social pheno-mena are primitive. Wooden ploughs pointed with stone, blood revenge, an undiminished birth rate, and relative purity of physical type are all alike derivatives from a common cause, isolation, directly physical and coinci-dentally social.
>
> (Ripley 1900: 529)

Rather more agreement however existed for the Celtic periods. The Celtic languages were usually held to have been introduced 'in the Bronze age, [when] a tall, round-headed, rugged-featured race occupied all those parts of Britain and Ireland that were worth conquering' (Dawkins 1874: 197–8). Significantly though, most scholars did not argue that they had completely exterminated the Neolithics. Thurnam noted numerous mixed cranial forms in the Bronze Age round-barrows, indicating a degree of interbreeding following the conquest (Thurnam 1867–9: 77). This was echoed in Greenwell's *British Barrows*: the Neolithics 'were probably intruded upon and conquered by the more powerfully made round-headed folk, who … would in course of time become intermixed with them, and with whom in the end they would become identified as one people' (Greenwell 1877: 122). Beyond this, archaeology showed the Bronze age to certainly be a period of progress, introducing superior tools, weaponry, pottery styles, domesticated animals and agricultural practices. However, in its development and ethnological constituents, it continued along the same trajectories as the Neolithic, being the next progressive wave to work upon national development.

There was however a potential controversy in the distinctions within the Celtic languages. That these were divided into two branches, alternately called P-Celtic, Brythonic or Kymric, and Q-Celtic, Goidelic or Gaelic, had been noted since the eighteenth century. There were frequent attempts to ethnologize these distinctions arguing that they reflected two streams of Celtic migrants, each with their own physical forms, cultural practices and religious systems. This was an idea with a long pedigree: the French historian Amédée Thierry, in his *Histoire des Gaulois* (first published in 1828), had stated that these represented two Celtic races, with distinct physical features and mental characters, and this concept continued to be expressed in French discourse throughout the century (Blanckaert 2003). Similar ideas were also present in Britain: the Welsh philologist John Rhys argued from his mythological studies that the Brythons had been a second wave of Celtic migrants after the earlier invasion of the Goidels (Rhys 1890–1: 15). While Rhys was cautious about characterizing their physical features, the concept of two distinct Celtic migrations deep in the past was often given a more racial tinge: the Gaels were frequently taken as the round-headed ruddy form, and the Belgic Kymri as a tall, blonde, long-skulled form, possibly connected to Nordic types. Beddoe, on weighing his evidence, argued that 'the natives of South Britain, at the time of the Roman conquest, probably consisted mainly of several strata, unequally distributed, of Celtic-speaking people', some of whom 'partook more of the tall blond stock of Northern Europe', but with various Bronze age and 'long-headed dark races' (Beddoe 1885: 29). As such, even in these earliest periods, racial diversity was a major feature of the British population.

Moving sequentially on, the Romans were usually felt to be an irrelevance in the story of ethnological development: long traditions held that they had only formed a narrow and thin superstructure over what had existed previously, before collapsing into decadence. As a result, Roman rule, 'as indeed might be expected, does not appear to have sensibly affected the character of the population' (Greenwell 1877: 126). At most, it was seen as a time of more pronounced racial intermixture, as urban centres, roads and commerce extended social intercourse between regional populations. Some scholars would argue for the Roman foundations of many towns (Wright 1852), but broadly these were simply pockets within a much deeper racial hinterland that was barely touched.

The Germanic migrants from the fifth century onwards were however taken as having much greater significance. As noted above, prominent Teutonistic discourses saw an English nation – in language, customs, institutions and blood – being carried across the North Sea from the 'forests of Germany' and displacing whatever had been in Britain before. Yet this was a view which still needed to engage with the ideas of racial amalgamation and the stubborn rootedness of many ethnological strains which had become pronounced in anthropological and archaeological discourse. Many certainly regarded the Germanic types as 'more highly endowed, invading races' (Davis and Thurnam 1855–6: I, 238), being more vigorous, larger-bodied, larger-brained, and still existing in relatively pure forms in areas of eastern England and southern Scotland – the places most exposed to

Germanic invasions and the historically-documented first areas of settlement. However, this worked with assumptions that, as the Saxons moved further inland, the conquest became either less violent, that the overwhelmingly male Germanic conquerors needed to intermarry with the local population or retain large populations of native slaves and serfs, or even that the racially-Celtic elites of particular areas adopted Saxon language and habits. Beddoe in *The Races of Britain* (1885: 38–71) and Davis and Thurnam in *Crania Britannica* described this more variegated form of conquest, with the latter arguing how a 'great mixture of races took place during the Anglo-Saxon conquest' (Davis and Thurnam 1855–6: I, 185). This could therefore allow a traditional vision of the swamping or 'rooting out' of the Britons in the east, but then subordination and interbreeding as one moved west across the country. While this did quite neatly tie the pure German regions with some of the most economically and financially dynamic parts of the country, it nevertheless accentuated that the nation itself was mixed and diverse.

A significant point in favour of this was that western parts of England in particular were seen as having the rugged, round-headed type in large numbers, and also retained extensive place names of Celtic derivation. This indicated that Celtic peoples there had been incorporated within an 'English nation' over the course of history. This was even enlarged upon in the quite virulent anthropological writings of the 1860s, which were dominated by the thoroughly unrespectable and often polygenist Anthropological Society of London: its journals noted how 'the best representative of the British Celt is not the little Cardiganshire peasant, with his Amazonian wife ... but the normal Englishman, the well-amalgamated result of Roman, Saxon, Scandinavian, and Norman infusion' (Anon. 1867: 159). In this way, the nation was seen as being founded by a merger of stocks, with the disciplined and stalwart Teuton regulating the unruly Celtic elements, and gaining a degree of creativity and dynamism through it. The implications of this were of course that unruly Ireland, presently gripped by Fenian agitation, should be subjected to the same processes – and that these were completely possible agents of civilization.

Additionally, there were other points which destablized ideas of unitary descent from migrating Teutons. That historical records indicated that large areas of northern England had been depopulated and settled by Scandinavians often led to greater valuations of Norse descent in some regions, even if this tended to be expressed in a quite localized matter. Beddoe noted a variety of Norse 'types' in northern England, and Thurnam and Davis (who were from Yorkshire, an area they characterized as having been particularly affected by this Viking influence), noted how 'the representatives of the vigorous conquerors and colonists from the Scandinavian north ... appear, wherever they have been congregated in numbers, to have impressed their character and features on the population in a very decided manners' (Davis and Thurnam 1855–6: I, 213). Again, local diversity and distinction were highlighted even where clear racial valuations were being made.

Not only this, but the Belgic or Kymric Celts were often argued to be physically very similar to the 'Germanic' Anglo-Saxons and Scandinavians, displaying the same general qualities: blonde, tall and long-skulled. Some scholars attempted to get around this by postulating tiny differences between Danish, Norse, Jutish, Belgic, Saxon, Angle and Frisian forms (Mackintosh 1866), but others sort to break down the barriers even further. Thomas Henry Huxley for example simply classed all darker types as 'Melanchronoi' and all light forms as 'Xanthochroi', regardless of their period of migration, using the notion to further disprove racial separation in the British Isles. Not only did modern peoples 'owe their national names not to their physical characteristics, but to their languages, or to their political relations' (Huxley 1871: 263), but 'Ireland, at the earliest period of which we have any knowledge, contained, like Britain, a dark and fair stock, which, there is every reason to believe, were identical to the dark and the fair stocks of Britain' (Huxley 1871: 268). This ensured that the whole of the United Kingdom was racially mixed in the same manner, and any racial edge could be taken out of modern disputes.

Later historically-documented infusions were also taken as noteworthy: Normans, Flemings and Huguenots were often seen as complementary and assimilatible elements within the national mix, while more recent large-scale Irish and Jewish migrations were regarded more distastefully. Broadly however, the story which these ethnologists and anthropologists attempted to present was 'the Fusion of Races into one Nation' (Dawkins 1889: 45). Lubbock made the point that, 'in my part I submit that the correct terminology is to speak of Celtic race or Teutonic race, of the Irish people or the Scotch people; but that the people of England, Scotland, and Ireland – ay, and of the Colonies also – constitute one great nation' (Lubbock 1903: 18). While different qualities were certainly identified between different racial types and peoples, the national body as a whole depended upon these patterns of unification. Beddoe noted that:

> there are assuredly diversity of gifts pertaining to diverse breeds of men; and unless we are all reduced to the dull dead level of socialism, and perhaps even in that case, for the sake of relief, we shall continue to stand in need of all those gifts. Let us hope, then, that blue eyes, as well as brown eyes, will continue to beam on our descendants, and that heads will never come to be formed all upon one and the same pattern.
>
> (Beddoe 1912: 189)

This all ensured that the scholars engaged in the uncovering of the deep past of the nation and asserting its modern significance saw the eras of ancient history as providing an important series of precedents. While frequently internally problematic and with the individual elements difficult to discern and define, the controversies between the scholars over the significance of particular ethnic periods overlay a common vision of ethnicity, nationality and their relationship to history. They all saw the nation as having been built up over a long trajectory of ancient development as a fused and progressive entity, which had bound together the diverse peoples of the British past in various combinations across the modern national territory. Whatever the turbulences, antagonisms and variations between these forms in ancient history, these were now considered as becoming increasingly irrelevant in the face of the integration, formation and expansion of the progressive British nation.

These were far from exceptional sets of views, and were in fact indicative of over half a century of study, debate and discussion within scientific institutions on how to characterize the races and development of Britain. A number of leading scholars had engaged in a variety of attempts to classify the ancient layers of the British population, and their historical and modern relevances. They drew off distinct disciplines, approaches and understandings of the past, and related them to modern concepts and debates. This occurred in a manner which was often contentious and controversial, and had a variety of ideological tinges. However, common across these syntheses and interpretations was the idea that Britain shared the same racial elements in various proportions across its territory, and that a range of historical processes had interrelated them into a single national community. This was also not something which had ended: in many respects, the development of the fringe regions of the country and the impact of modern technology and commerce upon racial compositions represented their continued working out in the modern age. The solutions presented across these discourses were also the same: progress moved towards unification, binding and incorporation within a stronger, accreted national civilization.

Bibliography

Anon. (1867) 'The Roman and the Celt', *Anthropological Review* 5: 151–175.

Arvidsson, S. (2006) *Aryan Idols: Indo-European Mythology as Ideology and Science*, Chicago: University of Chicago Press.

Beddoe, J. (1853) *A Contribution to Scottish Ethnology*, London: H.K. Lewis.

Beddoe, J. (1885) *The Races of Britain: A Contribution to the Anthropology of Western Europe*, Bristol and London: Arrowsmith.

Beddoe, J. (1912) *Anthropological History of Europe*, Paisley: A. Gardner.

Blanckaert, C. (2003) 'Of Monstrous Métis: Hybridity, Fear of Miscegenation, and Patriotism from Buffon to Broca' in S. Peabody and T. Stovall (eds) *The Color of Liberty: Histories of Race in France*, Durham: Duke University Press, 42–70.

Bowler, P. (1989) *The Invention of Progress: The Victorians and the Past*, Oxford: Blackwell.

Brantlinger, P. (2003) *Dark Vanishings: Discourse on the Extinction of Primitive Races, 1800–1930*, Ithaca, NY: Cornell University Press.

Brundage, A. (1994) *The People's Historian: John Richard Green and the Writing of History in Victorian England*, Westport, CT: Greenwood Press.

Burrow, J. (1981) *A Liberal Descent: Victorian Historians and the English Past*, Cambridge: Cambridge University Press.

Davis, J. B. and Thurnam, J. (1855–6) *Crania Britannica: Delineations and Descriptions of the Skulls of the Early Inhabitants of the British Islands*, London: 2 vols.

Dawkins, W. B. (1874) *Cave Hunting: Researches on the Evidence of Caves Respecting the Early Inhabitants of Europe*, London: Macmillan.

Dawkins, W. B. (1879) 'Our Earliest Ancestors in Britain' in *Science Lectures for the People*, Manchester: 95–106.

Dawkins, W. B. (1880) *Early Man in Britain and His Place in the Tertiary Period*, London: Macmillan.

Dawkins, W. B. (1889) *The Place of the Welsh in the History of Britain*, London: Simpkin, Marshall and Co.

Faverty, F. (1951) *Matthew Arnold: The Ethnologist*, Evanston, IL: Northwestern University Press.

Gomme, G. L. (1892) *Ethnology in Folklore*, New York: D. Appleton and Co.

Greenwell, W. (1877) *British Barrows: A Record of the Examination of Sepulchral Mounds in Various Parts of England*, Oxford: Clarendon Press.

Huxley, T. H. (1871: rpt. 1929) 'On Some Fixed Points in British Ethnology 1871', in *Man's Place in Nature and Other Anthropological Essays*, New York and London: D. Appleton.

Kidd, C. (2006) *The Forging of Races: Race and Scripture in the Protestant Atlantic World, 1600–2000*, Cambridge: Cambridge University Press.

Latham, R. G. (1852) *The Ethnology of the British Islands*, London: Van Voorst.

Levine, P. (1986) *The Amateur and the Professional: Antiquarians, Historians and Archaeologists in Victorian England, 1838–1886*, Cambridge: Cambridge University Press.

Lubbock, J. (1865) *Pre-Historic Times, as Illustrated by Ancient Remains, and the Manners and Customs of Modern Savages*, London: Williams and Norgate.

Lubbock, J. (1903) 'Huxley's Life and Work', in John Lubbock, *Essays and Addresses*, London: B. Tauchnitz: 7–45.

MacDougall, H. A. (1982) *Racial Myth in English History: Trojans, Teutons, and Anglo-Saxons*, Hanover, NH: University Press of New England.

Mackintosh, D. (1866) 'Comparative Anthropology of England and Wales', *Anthropological Review* 4: 1–21.

Mandler, P. (2000) '"Race" and "nation" in mid-Victorian thought', in S. Collini, R. Whatmore, and B. Young (eds) *History, Religion, and Culture: British Intellectual History, 1750–1950*. Cambridge: Cambridge University Press: 224–244.

Olender, M. (1992) *The Languages of Paradise: Race, Religion, and Philology in the Nineteenth Century*, Cambridge MA: Harvard University Press.

Rhys, J. (1890–1) *Early Ethnology in the British Isles*, Edinburgh: Llanerch Press.

Ripley, W. Z. (1900) *The Races of Europe: A Sociological Study*, London: Kegan Paul, Trench Trubner and Co.

Stepan, N. (1982) *The Idea of Race in Science: Great Britain, 1800–1960*, Hamden, CT: Archon Books.

Stocking, G. (1987) *Victorian Anthropology*, New York: Free Press.

Sweet, R. (2004) *Antiquaries: The Discovery of the Past in Eighteenth-Century Britain*, London: Hambledon and London.

Thurnam, J. (1867–9) 'Further Researches and Observations on the Two Principal Forms of Ancient British Skulls' in *Memoirs Read Before the Anthropological Society of London* 3: 41–80.

Thurnam, J. (1869) 'On Ancient British Barrows, especially those of Wiltshire and the adjoining Counties Part I. – Long-barrows', *Archaeologia* 42: 161–244.

Van Riper, A. B. (1993) *Men Among the Mammoths: Victorian Science and the Discovery of Human Prehistory*, Chicago: University of Chicago Press.

Wawn, A. (2000) *The Vikings and the Victorians: Inventing the Old North in Nineteenth-Century Britain*, Cambridge: D.S. Brewer.

Wright, T. (1852) *The Celt, the Roman, and the Saxon: A History of the Early Inhabitants of Britain, down to the Conversion of the Anglo-Saxons to Christianity*, London: Arthur Hall, Virtue and Co.

4

DREAMS OF CELTIC KINGS

Victorian prehistory and the notion of 'Celtic'

Rebecca Welshman

In 1851, in *The Archaeology and Prehistoric Annals of Scotland,* the archaeologist and ethnologist Sir Daniel Wilson stated that archaeology had become 'an indispensable link in the circle of the sciences' (Wilson 1851: xii). Prehistory, a new branch of archaeology, became popular in the 1860s after the discovery of ancient human remains at sites in France and England, and captured the imagination of the Victorian public. In light of its broad appeal to enthusiasts, thinkers and artists alike, archaeology became one of the most popular topics in the periodical press. An anonymous article in the *Academy* notes that:

> the popularity of archaeology … is afforded by the number and excellence of the departments of local notes and queries in various newspapers … and in some cases the matter has received greater permanence by being reprinted in book form.
>
> (Anonymous 1878: 553)

Academic and public interest in the subject led to the launch of the *Antiquary: a Magazine devoted to the Study of the Past* in 1880.

Consonant with the rise of archaeology was the development of ethnology: a desire to trace the ancestry of British people through the archaeological record. 'Celtic' races were those who had existed before the Romano-British and Saxon periods, and were thought of as tribal communities, still traceable in characteristics of the inhabitants of Scotland, Wales and Cornwall. The term 'Celtic', first introduced in the eighteenth century, achieved widespread popularity during the Victorian era, inspiring a Celtic revival in literature towards the end of the century.[1] The qualities of the Celts, which intrigued and mystified the Victorians, were recounted in an anonymous article titled 'Celtic

Characteristics', published in 1863 in *Duffy's Hiberian Magazine* – a journal of legends, tales and antiquities. The author states that the word 'Celt' was, to the Greeks and Romans, synonymous with 'Galatian' and 'Gaul', and that the name had even been fancifully traced to Galates, the son of Hercules. The author writes that Celtic means 'battle' and 'armour', and describes a Celt as 'a valiant man armed for combat' (Anonymous 1863: 124).

For authors writing in the southwest of England – an area particularly rich in archaeology, with Avebury the 'megalithic centre' (Huxley 1954: 241) at its heart – the turbulent history of Celtic societies being invaded by the Romans, and their retreat to the southwest, was an intriguing and beguiling idea; one which fostered connections between the lone author wandering these ancient landscapes and the tribal activities of past communities. Richard Jefferies, a Wiltshire author and naturalist, and Thomas Hardy both recognised the imaginative significance of ancient landscapes in their work. Both authors were involved in their local archaeological societies, and gave papers on excavations which they attended in the 1870s and 1880s.[2] Intrigued by the lingering presence of Celtic societies in the landscape in the forms of barrows, stone circles and ancient monuments, both authors used these landscapes as settings for some of the most poignant and dramatic events in their work.

For late Victorian society, still coming to terms with the irrefutable evidence of the antiquity of man, perceived continuities between past and present cultures offered a form of reassurance amidst the spiritual uncertainty of an increasingly secular world. Antiquaries – many of whom were clergymen – saw these continuities in the very forms of human habitation and in the landscape itself, as expressed in an article by Thomas Wright, eminent author and antiquarian and founder of the British Archaeological Association:

> Our modern country cottage is a copy, of course on a small scale, of the mansion of the Anglo-Saxon chieftain, and if the only remains of the cottager's residence were reduced to the bank and ditch which had surrounded the garden, we should have a diminutive example of those earthworks which formed the wall or walls of the dwelling-place of the Saxon chieftain, and which now puzzle eager antiquaries, and give rise to dreams of Celtic kings and prehistoric peoples belonging to very mythic ages.
>
> (Wright 1867: 464)

For late Victorian authors, whose work was deeply grounded in their native landscapes, the imagined lives of ancient communities was a fertile and popular line of inquiry. An anonymous article in the *Pall Mall Gazette* titled 'Beside the Cromlech' describes a visit to a megalithic monument in Wales known as 'The Fairy's Grave'. The author speculates on the construction and age of the megaliths, identifying them to be 'modern' in terms of late nineteenth-century 'geological or even anthropological estimate[s]':

Hither, some day five thousand years [ago] – perhaps ten thousand for all that science can say – a crowd of brown-skinned, short-statured tribesmen bore up the body of their chief from the village in the clearing on the little stream below. Here with wooden levers and round logs for rollers they toilfully brought together by sheer force of straining sinews these four great ice-worn boulders [...] they hewed them into rough symmetry [...] in the hut they placed the dead body of their chief, with his weapons, his ornaments, and his household goods, that his ghost might eat, drink, and fight in the world of ghosts as it had done in the valley below. Then they piled up the great mound of earth above it, to keep the body safe from beasts or birds; and around the fresh heap they performed I know not what barbaric orgies of dancing and sacrifice and human massacres. [...] Since then the rain has washed down every particle of soil that formerly covered the dead chieftain's grave. But still the memory of what it all once meant lives on uninterruptedly in the minds of the Ancient Britons around the spot. While the doctors of the eighteenth century were talking learned nonsense about Druidical temples and Arkite worship, the Welsh peasants were speaking correctly every day of The Fairy's Grave. For fairies and goblins and all such Keltic superstitions are mainly based upon stories about the ghosts of these Neolithic people, whom the Keltic Welsh overcame and enslaved. But they would not touch the graves of their chieftains lest harm should come upon them. Many of the Neolithic people lived on as serfs under the Kelts, and much of their blood may be noted in the Llanfair villages at the present day. [...] When we remember that in all popular tradition the fairies are said to live inside the green grass-grown hills and that their names are always connected with the prehistoric Neolithic monuments [...] The Fairy's Grave, gains in our eyes a double interest. For while on the one hand it is the burial place of a Euskarian chief, on the other hand it is the almost certain birthplace of a Keltic fairy tradition.

(1881: 515)

Here the archaeological setting affords imaginative connections between the individual mind in the present and the grander sequence of past human life. In what the author terms the 'peaceful industrial nineteenth century' the archaeological imagination at once conceives of the 'loss' of prehistory, and the 'birth' of Celtic tradition; an observation which connects the mind to the landscape in a more grounded form than the Romantic ideal of achieving synthesis between man and nature. The author considers the stones under what he calls 'the softening and romantic influence of time' seeing them as the 'titanic, archaic, immemorial temples of a forgotten creed'. Yet despite this loss of insight into the real events which happened here, the stones' endurance through time, and the myths associated with them, 'always connect' the local people with their ancestors, creating a powerful regional identity, which transcends time.

Yet consonant with the imaginative potential of archaeology were negative implications for the disturbance and removal of material remains. Although barrows held a sepulchral charm that contributed to the popularisation of archaeology, superstition still very much surrounded the removal of burial treasures from the tomb or body. For example, the author of an article on 'The Folk-Lore of Barrows' in 1866 records watching a barrow opening with 'high strung nerves', noting that it was not easy to find labourers who were willing to break into 'the old men's houses' as tumuli were sometimes called in Cornwall, and that 'whoever breaks into them is certain, according to a widely spread piece of folk-lore, to do at least as much mischief as an unhappy whistler at sea' (King 1866: 693). That labourers could be encouraged to open barrows using any convenient means (usually with a pickaxe), in order to obtain the treasures within, is indicative of the vast amount of grave theft that occurred during the nineteenth century, when thousands of barrows were opened by antiquarians who had no systematic approach to their excavation and no concern to categorise their finds.

The mystery and ambiguity of prehistory motivated the late-Victorian inclination to identify and, as far as possible, reconstruct a picture of how previous cultures lived and died. For late Victorian authors the new dimension to human history afforded by archaeology was potentially less alienating than considering human life in the context of geological or astronomical time. In Thomas Hardy's *The Return of the Native,* the heroine Eustacia Vye first appears on top of the Rainbarrow on Egdon Heath, and is almost thought to be one of the 'Celtic' builders of the Rainbarrow:

> As the resting man looked at the barrow he became aware that its summit, hitherto the highest object in the whole prospect round, was surmounted by something higher. It rose from the semiglobular mound like a spike from a helmet. The first instinct of an imaginative stranger might have been to suppose it the person of one of the Celts who built the barrow, so far had all of modern date withdrawn from the scene. It seemed a sort of last man among them, musing for a moment before dropping into eternal night with the rest of his race. There the form stood, motionless as the hill beneath. Above the plain rose the hill, above the hill rose the barrow, and above the barrow rose the figure. Above the figure was nothing that could be mapped elsewhere than on a celestial globe.
>
> (Hardy 1959: 19—20)

The image of a map connects the limited topographical knowledge of the mind of man with the larger unknown space of the sky above, similarly linking the grounded experience of the human being, lodged in the present, with the ambiguous activities of his Celtic ancestors. Hardy describes the barrow as occupying the 'loftiest ground of the loneliest height that the heath contained', suggesting that, for the individual mind 'adrift on change' in the late nineteenth century, and seeking to secure itself, this height afforded greater potential for imaginative insight than the lower lying heathland. This distinction between low and high ground was something widely appreciated by prehistoric societies, who engineered earthworks of great heights as a means of protection from attack, but also, as in the case of Hardy's Rainbarrow, for prominence – the visibility of a barrow in a landscape keeping alive the memory of the ancestor interred within it.

For Hardy, prehistory afforded a point of reconciliation between the individual human life and the natural world – all the more significant in light of the increasing estrangement from landscape encouraged by the industrial revolution. Frank Giordano notes that this appearance of Eustacia Vye on the Rainbarrow immediately associates her with 'pre-Christian paganism' (1984: 58). Away from her contemporary community, in the death-world of prehistoric ancestors, Eustacia embodies an otherworldliness that is achieved through her engagement with her native landscape. The Rainbarrow, more than just a feature of the landscape, is a phenomenological point of contact between mankind and the natural world; an embodiment of past human cares and desires carried through time to impact upon the modern mind in new and unpredictable ways. In his interpretation of this passage Giordano recognises that the land itself, 'so nearly resembling the torpor of death' causes Eustacia to seem 'alien in a world inimical to her temperament' (Ibid.). Hardy suggests that Eustacia is one of the last upholders of what he terms in *The Well-Beloved* 'the last pagan stronghold' of south Dorset, referring to her as 'a sort of last man among them, musing for a moment before dropping into eternal night with the rest of his race'.

Hardy's desire to align imaginative human experience with the material reality of the landscape is most poignantly addressed in *The Well-Beloved,* the last of his novels, published in 1897. In this novel Hardy combines his knowledge of Celtic and Roman societies in the south Dorset area with his interests in geology. The Island-bred sculptor Pierston is described as a 'native of natives', directly descended from pagan societies in the region. The gradual accumulation of strata within the 'single rock' that is the Isle of Portland is mirrored within the emotional make-up of Pierston, whose powerful native instinct causes him to search for the human embodiment of an illusive feeling that he terms his 'Well-Beloved' – in three generations of women from the same family. Pierston refers to his love of beauty as something transcendental, beyond philosophical, and beyond his own conception: 'of no tangible substance; a spirit, a dream, a frenzy, a conception, an aroma [...] a light of the eye, a parting of the lips' (Hardy and Hetherington 1998: 16).

Pierston's sculpted figurines of Greek and Roman goddesses are symbolic of his young emotional impulse to seek the embodiment of his desires. Creations of his father's own quarried Portland stone, these symbols become obsolete once Pierston reaches old age and finally marries. What Hardy terms the 'many embodiments' of Pierston's fantastical imagination are directly associated with the 'infinitely stratified walls of oolite' stone. As the human affinity with a landscape develops over time and is passed on through generations, albeit modified by evolutionary and cultural variants, so the character of a landscape, such as Portland, is sculpted and shaped by the changing chemical states of its rock, variations in weather and climate, and the human impact of quarrying. By the late nineteenth century it had been established that the clays and shale of the Portland area, used in prehistoric and Roman pottery manufacture, were unique for their strength and durability; a quality attributed to their slow stratified formation over many thousands of years. In the *Well-Beloved,* Pierston's profession as a sculptor of Purbeck stone suggests that Hardy, writing from an archaeologically-informed perspective, perceived significant continuity between the manufacturing and sculpting practices of pre-Roman and nineteenth-century communities living and quarrying in the same area.[3] This continuity, kept alive through the landscape itself, is reflected in Hardy's description of Pierston and his first fiancée, walking along the coast to the old churchyard:

> The evening and night winds here were, to Pierston's mind, charged with a something that did not burden them elsewhere. They brought it up from that sinister Bay to the west, whose movement she and he were hearing now. It was a presence — an imaginary shape or essence from the human multitude lying below: those who had gone down in vessels of war, East Indiamen, barges, brigs, and ships of the Armada — select people, common, and debased, whose interests and hopes had been as wide asunder as the poles, but who had rolled each other to oneness on that restless sea-bed. There could almost be felt the brush of their huge composite ghost as it ran a shapeless figure over the isle, shrieking for some good god who would disunite it again.
>
> The twain wandered a long way that night amid these influences — so far as to the old Hope Churchyard, which lay in a ravine formed by a landslip ages ago. The church had slipped down with the rest of the cliff, and had long been a ruin. It seemed to say that in this last local stronghold of the Pagan divinities, where Pagan customs lingered yet, Christianity had established itself precariously at best. In that solemn spot Pierston kissed her.
>
> (Hardy 1998: 18)

In this remote spot, exposed to the erosive winds, Celtic customs 'linger' and become tangible through the turbulent character of the landscape; stronger than the precarious Christian church which has slipped away into the ravine. Hardy uses the ancient place as a setting in which the couple are temporarily freed from the restrictions of late-Victorian marriage laws, suggesting an inherited identification between the spiritual freedom of pre-Christian societies and the two 'native' islanders. Throughout the book, Pierston's unrelenting search for his ideal woman – which he only understands in glimpses and flashes of insight – echoes the driven idealism of Celtic communities whose idea of deity was associated with the hunter's qualities of endurance and the ability to conquer.[4]

Richard Jefferies, writing in the 1880s, also perceived close affiliation between the beauty of the human form and the transcendent potential of the imaginative mind. In his 1883 spiritual autobiography, *The Story of My Heart,* set partly on the Wiltshire and Sussex Downs, he writes of the human body:

> that the cartilage and sinews may be more enduring, and the muscles more powerful, something after the manner of those ideal limbs and muscles sculptured of old, these in the flesh and real. That the organs of the body may be stronger in their action, perfect, and lasting. That the exterior flesh may be yet more beautiful; that the shape may be finer, and the motions graceful. [...] I believe in the human form; let me find something, some method, by which that form may achieve the utmost beauty. Its beauty is like an arrow, which may be shot any distance according to the strength of the bow. So the idea expressed in the human shape is capable of indefinite expansion and elevation of beauty.
>
> (1905: 25)

Writing in 1867, Jefferies described his Wiltshire landscape as a 'mine for an antiquary', noting that the 'Roman and British coins, arrow-heads, tumuli, and camps' made the country seem 'alive with the dead' (cited in Thomas 1909: 49). In his notebooks Jefferies records that it was near the Bronze and Iron Age hill fort, Liddington Castle, by the burial mound of an ancient warrior, where he began to forge a deeper spiritual relationship with the natural world. In *The Story of My Heart* he writes:

> There were grass-grown tumuli on the hills to which of old I used to walk, sit down at the foot of one of them, and think. Some warrior had been interred there in the ante-historic times. The sun of the summer morning shone on the dome of sward, and the air came softly up from the wheat below, the tips of the grasses swayed as it passed sighing faintly, it ceased, and the bees hummed by to the thyme and heathbells. I became absorbed in the glory of the day, the sunshine, the sweet air, the yellowing corn turning from its sappy green to summer's noon of gold, the lark's song like a waterfall in the sky. I felt at that moment that I was like the spirit of the man whose body was interred in the tumulus; I could understand and feel his existence the same as my own. He was as real to me two thousand years after interment as those I had seen in the body. The abstract personality of the dead seemed as existent as thought. As my thought could slip back the twenty centuries in a moment to the forest-days when he hurled the spear, or shot with the bow, hunting the deer, and could return again as swiftly to this moment, so his spirit could endure from then till now, and

the time was nothing. […] Resting by the tumulus, the spirit of the man
who had been interred there was to me really alive, and very close. This
was quite natural, as natural and simple as the grass waving in the wind,
the bees humming, and the larks' songs.

(1905: 28−9)

After researching the prehistoric archaeology of his local area in the early
1870s Jefferies went on to use archaeological sites in his work as settings
where the mind was free to imagine back through time, and into the future.
In this passage the spirit of the prehistoric ancestor is as alive to the author as
the natural landscape which surrounds him. Although physically separated by
death, the conceptual distinction between the warrior and the civilised Victorian
gentleman is bridged through their inhabiting the same landscape. The identity
of the interred warrior – what Jefferies conceives of as 'the abstract personality
of the dead' – is known to him through the swaying grasses which grow on the
same soil as thousands of years before, the warmth of the same sun, and the
singing of the same generations of larks, all of which transcend ordinary time to
connect the living with the dead. This late-Victorian thought echoes ideas from
the older Celtic paganism, which believed in spirits existing in natural objects
such as trees and rocks (Davidson 1988: 111), but seeks to inhabit a new form.
The courage of the warrior interred in the tumulus echoes the Celtic 'daring'
and what was recognised as the Celtic 'indifference to death' (Anonymous?
1863: 124) fortifying the imagination to conceive of otherworldly states which
transcend life and death.

The author of 'Celtic Characteristics' describes a Celtic identity which has yet
to be fully realised, and which withholds significant imaginative implications.
The author writes:

see in the Celt one who pants for excitement, who is whirled from
extreme to extreme, but to whom the abyss of anguish, into which he so
often sinks, unfolds divine truths hidden from the sage. The Celt is an
idealist; he was an idealist both in his good and in his evil, far back in the
dim centuries.

(Ibid.)

The courageous and adventurous Celtic instinct to seek beyond the territories
of the known, into the unknown, captured the minds of late nineteenth-century
thinkers. In *The Story of My Heart* Jefferies refers to the idea of a traditional
Christian deity being superseded by new forms of belief; what he terms a
'fourth idea'. The author of 'Celtic Characteristics' identifies the Celts to have
fostered the 'solemn' and 'metaphysical' Druidism, describing the religion as
'based on contemplation, surrounded by the awful, [which] held commune
with the stars, and beyond the stars sought immortality', an inclination echoed
in Jefferies' visionary desire to seek what he termed 'immortality of the soul'.[5]

A key figure of the Celtic revival in literature at the end of the century was William Sharp, who wrote under the female pseudonym Fiona Macleod, and who corresponded with Richard Jefferies. Sharp defined the movement as an effort to discover rather than reconstruct the past, writing in an article titled 'Celtic' in 1900 for the *Contemporary Review*, that he 'seeks in nature and in life, and in the swimming thought of timeless imagination, the kind of beauty that the old Celtic poets discovered and uttered' and that to do so was a 'spiritual need' of the late nineteenth century (Macleod 1900: 669). Sharp's interpretation of the Celts focused on their strength, courage and appreciation of beauty, which they believed could lead to higher forms of spiritual realisation. For Sharp, and for Jefferies, the Celts were a connection between historic and prehistoric times, bridging the gap between the known and the unknown. In his article, Sharp echoes Jefferies' belief that past societies were more closely affiliated with their native landscapes and that − even amidst the anxieties at the turn of the century− this affiliation may yet be realised in modern society:

> If one can think with surety but a little way back into the past, one can divine through both the heart and mind. I do not think that our broken people had no other memories and traditions than other early people had. I believe they stood more near to ancient forgotten founts of wisdom than others stood: I believe that they are the offspring of a race who were in a more close communion with the secret powers of the world we know and the secret powers of the world we do not know, than were any other people. I think their ancient writings show it, their ancient legends, their subtle and strangely spiritual mythology. I believe that, in the East, they lit the primitive genius of their race at unknown and mysterious fires: that, in the ages, they have not wholly forgotten the ancestral secret: that, in the West, they may yet turn from the grey wave that they see, and the grey wave of time that they do not see, and again, upon new altars, commit that primeval fire.
>
> (Ibid.)

Anticipating the 'grey wave' of an increasingly industrial and secular twentieth century, Sharp saw − through the study of Celtic societies − potential for the twentieth-century mind to repair a lost connection with the natural world. The Celts' close identification with the landscape spurred the Victorian mind to conceive of a more grounded form of spiritual experience; connecting the present to a dynamic and mysterious past.

Notes

1   The Celtic revival was led by authors such as W. B. Yeats, who published *The Wanderings of Oisin and Other Poems* (1889), and William Sharp, who wrote under the pseudonym Fiona Mcleod. Gregory Castle discusses the Celtic Revival in detail in *Modernism and the Celtic* Revival (2001) Cambridge: Cambridge University Press.

2 Jefferies presented a paper 'Swindon: its History and Antiquities' to the Wiltshire Natural History and Archaeological Society in 1873. In 1884 Hardy attended a meeting of the Dorset Natural History and Antiquarian Field Club where he spoke about the Romano-British human remains and grave goods found when laying the foundations to his home, Max Gate.
3 See Patrick Tolfree and Rebecca Welshman (2010) *Thomas Hardy and the Jurassic Coast*. Dorset: The Thomas Hardy Society. 13–14.
4 Cf Sharon Paice MacLeod (2011) *Celtic Myth and Religion: A Study of Traditional Belief, with Newly Translated Prayers, Poems and Songs*. Jefferson: McFarland. 42–3.
5 The Roman poet Lucan, writing in the first Century AD, noted the Celtic belief in immortality: 'If what you sing of is true, death is but the mid-point of a long existence' (MacLeod 2011: 69).

Bibliography

Anonymous (1863) 'Celtic Characteristics' *Duffy's Hibernian Magazine: a monthly journal of legends, tales, and stories, Irish antiquities, biography, science, and art*, 3 14: 124–7.
Anonymous (1878) 'Notes and News', *Academy* 320 (June 22) 553.
Anonymous (1881) 'Beside the Cromlech' *Pall Mall Gazette* Aug. 5: 515. Castle, G. (2001) *Modernism and the Celtic Revival*. Cambridge: Cambridge University Press.
Davidson, H. R. E. (1988) *Myths and Symbols in Pagan Europe: early Scandinavian and Celtic religions*. Manchester: Manchester University Press.
Giordano, F. R. (1984) *I'd Have My Life Unbe: Thomas Hardy's self-destructive characters*. Tuscaloosa: University of Alabama Press.
Hardy, T. (1959) *The Return of the Native*. New York: Signet Classic.
Hardy, T. and Hetherington, T., ed. (1998) *The Well-Beloved*. Oxford: Oxford University Press.
Huxley, J. (1954) *From an Antique Land: ancient and modern in the Middle East*. London: M. Parrish.
Jefferies, R. (1905) *The Story of My Heart: my autobiography*. Portland, ME: Thomas B. Mosher.
King, R. J. (1866) 'Folk-lore of Barrows', *Once a Week*, 1:25 (June 23): 693–5.
Macleod, F. (1900) '"Celtic"', *Contemporary Review*, 77 (May): 669–676.
MacLeod, S.P . (2011) *Celtic Myth and Religion: a study of traditional belief, with newly translated prayers, poems and songs*. Jefferson, IA: McFarland.
Thomas, E. (1909) *Richard Jefferies: his Life and Work*. London: Hutchinson.
Tolfree, P. and Welshman, R. (2010) *Thomas Hardy and the Jurassic Coast*. Dorchester: The Thomas Hardy Society.
Wilson, D. (1851) *The Archaeology and Prehistoric Annals of Scotland*. Edinburgh: Sutherland and Knox.
Wright, T. (1867) 'Up the Valley of the Oney', *Once a Week* 3:68 (April 20): 464–7.

5

'THE TRUTH AGAINST THE WORLD'

Spectrality and the mystic past in late twentieth-century Cornwall

Carl Phillips

Introduction

This chapter aims to analyse the production of a particular Cornish subjectivity through a series of contemporary engagements with Cornwall's mystic past that can be grouped under the umbrella term of 'alternative archaeology'. In doing so, it builds on work in cultural and historical geography around the nature of the subjects of such engagements (see, for example, Pile and Thrift 1995, Thrift 1996, Matless 1997) while, at the same time, focusing at least as much on the cultural products of such engagements as on the geographical subjects themselves. In doing so, it connects to another set of debates around, on one hand, such cultural objects as representations (Cosgrove and Daniels 1988; Duncan 1990; Daniels 1993) and, on the other hand, the non-representationality of spatio-temporal experience (Thrift 1996, 1997, 2000). This chapter does not directly address these issues of intra-disciplinary demarcation, instead following Matless in 'considering words, pictures, voices in terms of the geographical enfolding of subject and object'. By considering cultural objects as 'one significantly congealed state within a wider field of relations of which it is an effect' (Matless 2000: 335), this approach:

> can take us into various dimensions of the geographical self: the production of identity through the internalization of wider spatio-temporal relations, the moral geographies of conduct in place, the constitution of the human through relations with the animal, vegetable and mineral non-human, and the historicity and spatiality of experience.
>
> (Matless 2000: 336)

Recent work on cultural and geographical engagements with the prehistoric past has also connected them to a certain version of the spectre (Derrida 1994) in which it is not a figure, either literal or metaphorical, but is instead an often visionary and always unsettling spatial formation (Matless 2008a, see also Matless 2008b, 2009; cf. Nash 1998; Wylie 2007). Similarly, this chapter additionally aims to map the spectropolitics of the particular Cornish subjectivity that constitutes its primary concern. It follows Luckhurst in his contention that the spectral turn in the social sciences is limited by the belief that 'the breaching of limits is itself somehow inherently political' (Luckhurst 2002: 542), and reminds us that to fetishise the liminality of the spectre is 'to forget the other cultural convention about ghosts: that they appear precisely as *symptoms*, points of rupture that insist their singular tale be retold and their wrongs acknowledged' (Luckhurst 2002: 542, original italics). Where the cultural objects in question, and their associated Cornish subjectivity and spectral topography, can be understood as being in some way transgressive, then, this chapter is prepared 'to risk the violence of *reading* the ghost, of cracking open its absent presence to answer the demand of its specific symptomatology and its specific locale' (Luckhurst 2002: 542, original italics). It is, in other words, unafraid to foreground precisely the Cornishness of alternative spatialisations of Cornwall, and alternative ways of being Cornish.

Though the cultural objects in question emerge from different socio-cultural backgrounds, the argument here is that, through them, one can identify a process of convergent subjectification around the trinomial of archaeology, language and politics, around which the rest of this chapter is structured. This Cornish alternative archaeological subject, it will be argued, exists in a paradoxical – indeed, spectral – space between 'official' and 'alternative'; the associated linguistic culture exists in a similarly spectral space between 'authentic' and 'inauthentic', and the associated political culture exists in the space between 'orthodoxy' and 'opposition'. Caution over Luckhurst's foregrounding of the ghost-in-context as explanatorily and politically confining can thus be seen to be misplaced; the ghost-in-context, as Matless observes, is 'liable to break narrow frames, indeed the deconstructed ghost becomes a creature of precise if not necessarily linear geographies, histories, temporalities, spatialities, all contributing to its make up. Precision here can release as much as restrain' (Matless 2008a: 338).

Archaeology

Cornwall County Council established the Cornwall Archaeological Unit, the professional field section of the Historic Environment Service, in 1975. Prior to then, the preservation and development of the archaeological record depended, to a large degree, upon the voluntary works of the Cornwall Archaeological Society, established in 1961. One such work – *West Penwith Survey* (Russell 1971), a catalogue checklist of prehistoric sites – inspired Craig Weatherhill to develop his early interest in Cornish place-based myths and legends. 'I thought, well, the catalogue list is great', says Weatherhill (interview 5 July 2002), 'but without having plans, sections, elevations, you don't know what the hell is there to be preserved'. With his background in draughtsmanship, architecture and surveying, he took it upon himself to fill in this gap in the archaeological record, publishing the results of his project as *Belerion* (Weatherhill 2000a) before expanding his focus from the Land's End peninsula to encompass a survey of the prehistoric sites of Cornwall in *Cornovia* (Weatherhill 2000b).

Belerion functions as a gazetteer. The sites are divided into sections by archaeological time period, and listed in alphabetical order. For most sites, the entry includes a photograph and a hand-drawn plan view of the sites themselves, accompanied by a short description. Mên-an-Tol , for example, 'consists of four stones; one fallen stone, two uprights 4½ft (1.3m) high and, between these and in direct line with them, a wheel-shaped slab set firmly on its rim. This is 4ft (1.2m) across and is pierced by a large round hole 20in (51cm) in diameter' (Weatherhill 2000a: 24). A similar format is followed by Cheryl Straffon, a practising pagan and co-founder of the Cornwall Earth Mysteries Group, in the first of her *Earth Mysteries Guide* series, in which she describes Mên-an-Tol as 'a holed stone some 3½ft high, with a hole of 1½ft diameter,' with 'an upright of about 4ft high' on either side, along with an accompanying photograph and sketch map (Straffon 1998: 19). In these terms, Cornwall is a series of sites of archaeological interest, engagement with which could be defined as 'amateur' though not necessarily 'alternative' archaeology, proceeding as it does through the draughtsman's hand and the surveyor's eye, mediated by a tape measure, a pencil and paper, and a camera.

Both works also include an Ordnance Survey (OS) grid reference for the respective sites (Weatherhill 2000a; Straffon 1998), adding a map to the list of mundane technologies through which engagement with the prehistoric past is mediated. They also present a brief set of directions for would-be visitors to the sites, placing them in the context of their proximity to present-day transport links. Ian McNeill Cooke, owner (until his recent retirement) of the Mên-an-Tol Studio, goes a stage further, organising some of the sites into 'an approximately 4 mile (6½km) long walk' (Cooke 1997: 3) of his own devising, starting and finishing at the Studio itself. In *Journey to the Stones*, he explains: 'The idea of structuring the book around a series of walks stems from my belief that it is only by experiencing the local landscape on foot that a deep and intimate acquaintance with this unique peninsula can be attained' (Cooke 2000: 5). Straffon agrees: 'The beauty and the power' of West Penwith is that most of its sites of alternative archaeological interest:

> are free and open, not fenced in with special opening hours, nor given tarmaced access and tourist shops. You have to walk to find them, across the wild moors, through boggy farms, down overgrown lanes. Finding them is part of the joy; it is a spiritual pilgrimage.
>
> (Straffon 1998: 51)

There are several points to be made here. Most obviously, we must add walking boots to the list of mundane technologies through which engagement with the prehistoric past is mediated (see Macnaghten and Urry 1998; Edensor 2000; Michael 2000). Additionally, the draughtsman's eye is now mobilised, with the sensory geographies of a moving body with endorphins in the bloodstream passing through changeable atmospheric conditions becoming part of this particular Cornish subjectivity. There is a cultural authority at work too; local knowledge, earned by time and effort spent learning to navigate one's own archaeological landscape, is privileged above the Cornwall of brown road signs. It is from within this nexus of eyes, map, feet and landscape that a specifically mysticised version of Cornishness also begins to emerge – for Straffon, getting to the sites is as much a part of the engagement as being at the sites themselves that it becomes 'a spiritual pilgrimage' (Straffon 1998: 51; compare this to the normative phenomenological approach to archaeology proposed in Tilley 1994). 'The eye', writes Matless (2000: 353) in a similar context, 'is here given transhistorical capacity, with looking ultimately the same the world and history over, part of a human phenomenological place in the world'. In a walking body, the eye 'can thus function as a gnostic device' (Matless 2000: 353), allowing the modern re-creation and re-enactment of the ritual practices of an eco-feminist megalithic landscape (see Trower 2009).

Among the practices of this megalithic landscape are those pertaining to John Michell's reworking of Alfred Watkins' theory of ley lines. For Watkins (1970), ley lines were prehistoric trackways, and the various sites that studded their length were navigational aids. Through Michell (1974, 2001), the megalithic landscape was reconceived as a complex repository of numerological, geometric and astronomical knowledge wherein lay the essence of the true human spiritual condition. In *The Old Stones of Land's End*, seeking evidence to support his theory, Michell (1974) revealed a regional geography to ley hunting. Claiming Cornish descent on his father's side of his family, he sought confirmation in Cornwall, writing that 'West Penwith is the most suitable for the study of megalithic alignments, being almost an island, relatively undisturbed and containing more ancient stones than any other district of comparable size' (Michell 1974: 111). Michell located sites by means of an eight-figure OS grid reference, seeking out possible ley lines with a pencil and ruler. It is at this stage, once possible ley lines have been identified, that the ley hunter replaces their pencil and ruler with binoculars and a camera, and confirmatory fieldwork ensues (Williamson and Bellamy 1983).

Ley hunting is thus one of the most attractively open aspects of alternative archaeology; as Williamson and Bellamy acknowledge, a ley line 'can easily be found and confirmed in a weekend, so the ley hunters can feel themselves to be pushing forward the boundaries of knowledge without giving up an enormous amount of time' (Williamson and Bellamy 1983: 202). However, while alternative archaeology continues to gain impetus from its questioning of established knowledge, the relationship between academic and alternative archaeology is by no means oppositional. 'The two approaches to the past', write Williamson and Bellamy (1983: 25), 'the conventional and the "fringe", are certainly not divided by the kind of gulf which many academics would like to believe exists'. On the one hand, alternative archaeologists freely draw upon academic archaeological knowledge in order to inform and support their theories; on the other, for Straffon, the two 'have in many ways come closer together in recent years' so that 'archaeologists are now freely talking about ritual sites, ceremonial monuments, and patterns in the landscape' (Straffon 1995: 2). Refusing to adhere to definitional gridlines, the Cornish alternative archaeological subject instead emerges from the cultural spaces between the 'official' and the 'alternative', so that we can begin to speak of the spectropolitics of alternative archaeology.

Indeed, there is also a politics of disciplinary knowledge within the field of ley hunting, as the spectral Cornish alternative archaeological subject and the similarly spectral Cornish landscape refuse even to adhere to their own definitional gridlines. On the one hand, there are those for whom, after Michell (2001), ley lines are invisible lines of earth energy. As Straffon writes:

> Our prehistoric ancestors were probably much more in tune with the earth and its place in the cosmos than we are today, surrounded as we are by so much artificial electricity, light and other energies. They could probably sense or dowse minute changes in the patterns of power and energy that flow through this earth. They were aware of changes in the radiation, the electromagnetic fields, the light anomalies, and the strange sounds that sometimes can be found in certain rocks and stones, and manifest in particular places. At these places they built their monuments.
>
> (Straffon 2004: 82)

It is not necessary for the modern ley hunter to pick up a pair of dowsing rods, though; Straffon suggests that megalithic sites 'are best visited in ones and twos and threes, places to deeply connect with the earth spirit, to perhaps sit and meditate awhile, perhaps even in an altered state of consciousness' (Straffon 1994: 20).

In contrast, there are those like Paul Devereux – the Penzance-based editor of *The Ley Hunter* between 1976 and 1996, who encouraged Straffon to form the Cornish Earth Mysteries Group – for whom ley lines might instead be ritual landscapes of more recent origins: church ways, straight or near-straight pathways marked by stone crosses from isolated farmsteads to churches, and from churches along the route by which coffins would be carried to graveyards, similar to the *Geisterwege* of Germanic north-western Europe (Devereux 1994). Danny Sullivan, Devereux's successor as editor, wrote that Devereux 'attempted to fashion the subject into one worthy of serious study' (Sullivan 1997: 45). Devereux's conclusions were that, 'apart from variable and rare anomalous features in the earth's geomagnetic field, natural background radioactivity and ultrasound there was no evidence at all for an unknown earth force' (Sullivan 1997: 46). This is not to suggest that Devereux dismissed dowsing as a field of enquiry outright, though. He allows for the dowsing of 'tangible, accountable targets such as lost objects or water', but argues that the dowsing of earth energies 'is not only not ley hunting, it is not true dowsing either. In the end, it harms both fields of valid endeavour' (Devereux 1994: 75–76).

Language

Williamson and Bellamy observe that, as well as 'astronomy, geometry, prehistory, history, [and] mathematics', alternative archaeologists are able to mobilise, to varying degrees, a working knowledge of 'etymology' and 'the analysis of folklore' (Williamson and Bellamy 1983: 11). Thus, as well as observing that Boscawen-Ûn stone circle consists of 19 stones 'from 3 to 4½ft (0.9–1.4m) high', arranged in 'an ingeniously constructed ellipse with diameters of 80ft (24.4m) and 71ft (21.7m)' (Weatherhill 2000a: 20; cf. Cooke 1997; Straffon 1998) with an single off-centre stone of 8 feet (2.4m) in height, Weatherhill also traces the origins of the name to the middle Cornish *bos*, 'dwelling', and the late Cornish *scawan an oon*, 'elder tree on the downs' (Weatherhill 2000c: 26). In addition, he uses his children's fantasy novel, *The Lyonesse Stone*, to present a distinctively alternative archaeological description of Boscawen-Ûn, having one of the characters describe how 'ancient power, older, greater and beyond all mortal wizardry, was locked within this stone circle. We call it the Breath of the Dragon and it is a secret of the Earth Mother herself' (Weatherhill 1991: 30). The connections between the practices of alternative archaeology and Cornish linguistic culture, and their role in the production of a particular Cornish subjectivity, are the concern of this section.

Weatherhill (2000a), Cooke (1997) and Straffon (1998) all raise the spectral landscape of folk religion, recounting how, according to Cornish folklore, the ritual of crawling through Mên-an-Tol hole nine times [for adults] or three times [for children] was said to cure rickets and scrofula (see also Lowerson 1992). Cooke adds that the ritual could also enhance adult fertility, though 'it was generally appreciated that such rituals would only be effective at particular times of the lunar month' (Cooke 1997: 5), in keeping with his historical narrative of 'a sophisticated ancient culture coexisting harmoniously with earth through a feminine principle' (Matless 2000: 352) that gave way to a patrilineal and property-oriented society based, out of the increasing necessity of population pressures, on political and environmental conflict – or, in Cooke's own words, an historical narrative of British prehistory as being the story of the movement of society from 'commune' to 'kingdom', based on his reading of Engels' *The Origin of the Family, Private Property and the State* (Cooke, interview, 19 April 2005; Engels 1972).

Furthermore, all three authors refer to an additional folk belief associated with Mên-an-Tol that 'if two brass pins were placed crosswise on the stone, questions would be answered by a mysterious movement of the pins' (Weatherhill 2000a: 24, cf. Cooke 1997, Straffon 1998). This belief is brought to life in *The Lyonesse Stone*, in a sequence in which Jack the Tinner – a giant-killer from Cornish folklore – helps John Trevelyan, the main protagonist, locate his abducted sister, Penny. In order to achieve this, Jack places two pins atop Mên-an-Tol, and turns his thoughts to the missing girl:

> One of the pins was indeed moving; at first, an almost imperceptible motion, then, jerking slightly as though it were steel and reacting to the pull of a magnet, the other began to stir. The tinner's face was lined and strained as he fought to meld his mind to the power of the holed stone and keep it there; the invisible forces flowed back and forth between rock and man.
>
> (Weatherhill 1991: 100)

Although a children's fantasy novel, there are obvious parallels with Straffon's argument that our prehistoric ancestors 'could probably sense or dowse minute changes in the patterns of power and energy that flow through this earth' (Straffon 2004: 82). Within this particular subjectivity, alternative archaeologists do not passively receive sensory impressions of megalithic sites. Instead, active participation – through meditation, or deliberate induction of altered states of consciousness, is required in order to achieve and maintain the necessary state of mind, so as to open up a dialogue with the prehistoric landscape.

Another central plot point in *The Lyonesse Stone* is John's participation in the ancient Gorsedd of the Bards of Cornwall. This sequence is foreshadowed in an earlier passage, in which Ben Trevelyan, John's uncle, makes a connection between speaking the Cornish language and participating in bardic rituals:

> People who've done a lot for Cornwall in some way are made bards. You see, in spite o' what some people d'think, Cornwall edn no more a part of England than Wales or Scotland are. Tes a Celtic land an' we're Celtic people, who've been in Britain thousands o' years longer than the English. We even had our own kings once, an' lots o' the old traditions are still carried on. We've even got our language, as I've told 'ee. It near died out a century or so back, but tes growing ago. Quite a few people can speak 'en.
>
> (Weatherhill 1991: 24)

He goes on to describe the Gorsedd itself as:

> a sight to see. All the bards in long blue robes, p'raps a couple o' hundred of 'en, all in a big circle. There's harp music, an' a huge sword which represents King Arthur's sword. The whole thing's conducted in the language.
>
> (Weatherhill 1991: 24–25)

In the preface to *Myths and Legends of Cornwall*, Weatherhill and Devereux provide the historicity of Cornish folklore and the revived Gorsedd:

> The bardic traditions of the Celtic lands, in which such tales were committed to memory and retold to a gathered host, lasted in Cornwall well into the 19th century. By this time, the accompaniment of the harp had gone and the bard – or, in Cornwall, the 'droll' – had become the man who told tales by the fireside in return for a meal. The demise of the droll should have signalled the end of Cornwall's myths and legends which would have died with them had it not been for dedicated Victorians intent on recording them for posterity.
>
> (Weatherhill and Devereux 2001: iii)

The drolls, then, become the inheritors of a body of knowledge within which, 'behind the giants, small people, faerie folk, demons and witches are shadows of ancient Celtic gods and goddesses, or heroes from a time before writing' (Weatherhill and Devereux 2001: iv) so that, through the pen of the Cornish folklorist and the robes, harps and sword of the neo-druidic revivalist, the Cornish alternative archaeological subject might open up the same kind of transhistorical dialogue with prehistoric landscape as they might through ley hunting.

As with alternative archaeology, there is also a politics to Cornish linguistic culture. 'The mythology and legends of ancient Kernow are', for Weatherhill and Devereux, 'a vital part of Cornwall's cultural heritage', and *Myths and Legends of Cornwall* exists in print 'at a time when the commercial forces of tourism seeks to alter, trivialise and deface that legendary heritage for its own advantage' (Weatherhill and Devereux 2001: v). Weatherhill (interview, 5 July 2002) and Cooke (interview, 19 April 2005) both reserve particular criticism for Peter de Savary and his 1987 purchase and subsequent development of Land's End. This single development, for Cooke, has since been responsible for bringing 'a different kind of tourist' (Cooke, interview, 19 April 2005) to the Land's End peninsula, a tourist who rarely, if ever, strays from established tourist traps and the beaten trails between them. Such an alignment of the local with the authentic, in opposition to a certain version of tourism, was partly the inspiration for Cooke's series of walking guides to sites of archaeological interest, as discussed above. These guides are not anti-touristic, though; recognising the importance of tourism to the Cornish economy, an approved tourist-subject emerges in Cooke's guides from within the familiar alternative archaeological nexus of eyes, maps, feet and walking boots.

There is an internal politics within Cornish linguistic culture, too. Straffon (interview, 5 July 2002) expresses a cautious sympathy with such groups as the Gorsedd of Cornwall, largely because of the possible negative connotations of cultural nationalist movements; while Weatherhill, himself a Bard of *Gorseth Kernow*, expresses sympathy with neo-pagan movements but makes the Cornish-speaking tongue central to opening up a transhistorical dialogue with prehistoric pagans, opining that 'if you're going to be a true druid, speak Celtic' (Weatherhill, interview, 5 July 2002). Through these political questions, we can again speak of the spectropolitics of the Cornish alternative archaeological subject as it emerges from the cultural spaces between the definitional gridlines of 'local' and 'tourist', 'authentic' and 'inauthentic', and 'insider' and 'outsider'.

Politics

The catalyst for the events of *The Lyonesse Stone* is the rediscovery of the crown of the lords of Lyonesse, which prompts the political question of where the characters should send such a valuable historical artefact for safe keeping:

> 'We've got some hard-headed thinking to do,' said Ben. 'I doubt we'll be able to keep it. Tes too old an' valuable. It'll probably have to go to a museum; maybe the County one in Truro. The British Museum may want 'en, but I'll put my foot down if they do. It shouldn't be allowed to leave Cornwall, it b'longs here, not up there in London. I'll give Truro a ring in the mornin'. They'll want to date'n but, if the legend is right, it'll date from the sixth century.
>
> (Weatherhill 1991: 17)

The politics at work here operates partly through spatial distinctions between 'here' in Cornwall and 'up there in London,' but also partly through the spatialities of *Cornwall at the Crossroads* (Deacon, George and Perry 1988), which relates the county's socio-economic problems not to Cornwall's distance from London but to London's distance from Cornwall, and with which Weatherhill explicitly aligns himself (Weatherhill, interview, 5 July 2002).

This political stance derives, in part, from Weatherhill's position as Conservation Officer at Penwith District Council, a position that Weatherhill lost after a series of disputes with English Heritage at the end of 1998. In the late 1980s, one of the roofing stones of the *fogou* at Chysauster became unstable and English Heritage quoted a five-figure sum for repairs that, according to Cornish Heritage – a politically-oriented pressure group that was formed in 1984 to oppose the management of Cornwall's historical environment by English Heritage – local archaeologists knew merely required 'a block and tackle to raise one end of the stone, a competent local stone hedger to consolidate the wall beneath and careful re-lowering of the stone' (Cornish Heritage, undated). English Heritage counter-claimed that labour costs would account for most of the quoted five-figure sum, 'to which one local archaeologist replied that labour costs could be eradicated by using volunteers from the Cornwall Archaeology Society and the West Cornwall Conservation Volunteers' (Cornish Heritage, undated). A London spokesman for English Heritage allegedly did not even know the meaning of the word *fogou* (literally 'cave'; used to refer to stone-walled and -roofed passages of uncertain functions associated with Iron Age settlements). For English Heritage, the preferred alternative was to bury the *fogou*. Weatherhill's ensuing decade-long period of public criticism of English Heritage culminated at Christmas 1998, when he 'received a letter from his employers accepting a resignation he had never tendered' (Cornish Heritage, undated).

Clearly, for Weatherhill, the politics of land ownership operate through the privileging of the local land management practices of the Cornish volunteer-subject, acquired through time spent in the field. These stand in a rather ambivalent position relative to the politics of *The Old Stones of Land's End*, which carries a dedication to Prince Charles, Duke of Cornwall. Beneath the dedication is an untitled poem in which Michell declaims the 'Scorn for the Law', the 'consequent contempt for human kind / Its ways, its marks, its native cast of mind', and the 'impious hand that felled the antique stone' (Michell 1974: vi). He goes on to second Prince Charles – 'heir to a throne restored' – to the defence of a more spectral version of the Cornish landscape, prevailing upon him to 'See how in Cornish stones a sign remains / Of ancient, mystic rule, by none abhorred / Save by the godless tyrant, 'gainst whose hand / Our cross, our Crown, our customs rock-like stand' (Michell 1974: vi). Michell (interview, 14 April 2005) explains that the politics of this dedication were derived from his opposition to the Darwinian and Marxist social theories that informed the archaeology of the time. For Michell:

> archaeology has contributed virtually nothing to the study of megalithic science, nor has it been much inclined to take the matter seriously, regarding prehistoric structures as necessarily the work of men inferior to ourselves in intellect and knowledge, and of interest only as relics of their primitive culture.
>
> (Michell 1974: 108)

Recognising that his work was 'going against the orthodoxy of the time' – a social evolutionary orthodoxy in which the prehistoric past was teleologically subordinate to the present – Michell, by dedicating his work to Prince Charles, 'tried to claim a higher orthodoxy' (Michell, interview, 14 April 2005). Michell's work is not unorthodox in an absolute sense; rather, as his aim is to help bring about the restoration of one orthodoxy – a once-universal system of knowledge to which he refers as geomancy – to replace another, that of:

> the modern European with his European with his materialistic philosophy and science as the highest product of an evolutionary process, in the course of which the human race has supposedly been led through stages of bestiality, unreason and superstition to modern enlightenment.
>
> (Michell 1974: 107)

His work represents instead his intervention in a debate between complex rival sets of alignments of certain cultural, historical, political and intellectual orthodoxies. That said, Michell describes *The View over Atlantis* as 'a product of its time – the middle '60s,' a time during which the boundaries of thought and experience were being challenged, for Michell, at least – by 'new music, new drugs' (Michell, interview, 14 April 2005; cf. McKay 1996). There thus remains a spirit of counter-cultural protest in Michell's work, although not so much related to 1960s drop-out culture and a refusal to participate in political discourse as to an active political opposition to modern progressive orthodoxies.

Related to the moral geographies of land ownership are those of land access, and of conduct in place while visiting the various sites of alternative archaeological interest, especially since many of the sites are on privately owned farmland. Weatherhill (2000a), Cooke (1997) and Straffon (1998) all make at least passing reference to the Countryside Code. 'The average Cornish farmer is friendly and helpful', says Weatherhill:

> but not if his gates are left open, if dogs are let loose among his livestock, if litter is left on his land or if his crops are trampled. If no footpath exists, keep to the very edge of fields and always ask the farmer's permission to cross his land. His hospitality is both generous and genuine. Please don't abuse it.
>
> (Weatherhill 2000a: 4)

Similarly, when giving directions to Mên-an-Tol, Cooke directs the would-be visitor to turn off the road 'by the farm lane directly opposite the Studio', but warns them not to 'cause danger and inconvenience to walkers' by driving their car up the lane as 'it is a public footpath only, with no right of access for unauthorised vehicles' (Cooke 1997: 2).

In respect of contemporary debates over public rights of access to private land, Devereux – perhaps recognising that the discipline of alternative archaeology depends upon maintaining amiable relations with landowners on whose land a number of megalithic sites are located – is notably cautious, urging that 'respect be accorded to landowners, whatever personal opinions may be held (Devereux 1994: 51). However, for Straffon, megalithic sites 'are always under pressure... from those indifferent or antagonistic landowners (thankfully the minority) who would like to get rid of them' (Straffon 1998: 2). It was partly for this reason that Cooke (2000), a member of the West Cornwall Footpaths Preservation Society, sought to publicise the existence and locations of as many sites as possible, so as to help maintain a critical mass of walkers on public footpaths and customary rights of way that might otherwise be lost to landowners and encroaching vegetation. Footpaths thus become as much a part of the landscape heritage as the prehistoric sites themselves, and the Cornish walking–looking subject can simultaneously open up a series of transhistorical dialogues, not only with prehistoric pagans but with all those who have walked the footpaths before them.

Conclusion

In his conclusion to *The Pagan Religions of the Ancient British Isles*, Hutton reflects upon the difficulty in drawing any conclusions on the nature of pre-Christian paganism from the historical and archaeological sources of evidence available to the contemporary researcher:

> part of our uncertainty derives from our discovery of a tremendous diversity of ritual practice and architecture, over both space and time, which may reflect an equal diversity of belief and which almost defies generalisation. The peoples of our remote past have emerged as more creative, more dynamic, more fascinating and more baffling.
>
> (Hutton 1991: 340–341)

Hutton has since described *The Pagan Religions...* as 'essentially a pessimistic work', not 'because we would never know the objective truth about large areas of the subject' but because he 'doubted whether our culture was capable of taking advantage of the opportunities for freedom of imagination and for pluralism that this situation presented' (Hutton 1996: 6) by enhancing the status of alternative viewpoints and thereby making them potentially more effective agents for change in a modern democratic state.

This chapter has argued that, by considering the production of a particular Cornish subjectivity through a series of contemporary engagements with Cornwall's mystic past, and the cultural products of those engagements (see Matless 2000), one can identify a process of convergent subjectification around the trinomial of archaeology, language and politics. While all of these cultural products emerge from different socio-cultural backgrounds, this chapter has also drawn attention to the resulting contradictions within this subjectivity which, in turn, result from precisely the opportunities for pluralism that this subjectivity itself provides. It is in the spirit of the politics of pluralism that the chapter concludes by restating its central argument that this subjectivity and the Cornish landscape, as it is variously mobilised as a set of archaeological sites linked by prehistoric trackways, earth energy lines, public footpaths and present-day transport links, existing in a spectral space between absence and presence, past and present, vision and the visionary, conscious and unconscious, and reality and imagination, and animated through measuring, preserving, speaking, performing and re-enacting, represents one localised, culturally- and historically-specific [though no less liminal] manifestation of the spectral.

Acknowledgements

An earlier version of this chapter was presented at the 'Mysticism, Myth, Nationalism' conference at the University of Exeter (Cornwall Campus) on 23 July 2010. I would like to thank David Matless for his comments on a subsequent draft of this chapter.

Bibliography

N.B. This chapter also builds on primary research undertaken in the course of my postgraduate research project (Phillips 2006).

Cooke, I. M. (1997) *Antiquities of West Cornwall and How to Get There Without a Car – Guide One: the Men-an-Tol holed stone and other nearby ancient sites*, Penzance: Men-an-Tol Studio

—— (2000, orig. 1987) *Journey to the Stones: ancient sites and pagan mysteries of Celtic Cornwall*, Penzance: Men-an-Tol Studio

Cornish Heritage (undated) 'The Saga of Craig Weatherhill, the Cornishman and Inheritor of the Tradition of Joseph Angoff and Thomas Flamank, who dared Oppose and Expose the Grim Reality', http://www.cornish.heritage.care4free.net/page14.htm (accessed 14 June 2002)

Cosgrove, D. E. and Daniels, S. (eds) (1988) *The Iconography of Landscape: essays on the symbolic representation, design and use of past environments*, Cambridge: Cambridge University Press

Daniels, S. (1993) *Fields of Vision: landscape imagery and national identity in England and the United States*, Cambridge: Polity Press

Deacon, B., George, A. and Perry, R. (1988) *Cornwall at the Crossroads?*, Redruth: Cornwall Social and Economic Research Group

Derrida, J. (1994) *Spectres of Marx: the state of the debt, the work of mourning, and the new international*, trans. P. Kamuf, New York: Routledge

Devereux, P. (1994) *The New Ley Hunter's Guide*, Glastonbury: Gothic Image

Duncan, J. S. (1990) *The City as Text: the politics of landscape interpretation in the Kandyan kingdom*, Cambridge: Cambridge University Press

Edensor, T. (2000) 'Walking in the British Countryside: reflexivity, embodied practices and ways to escape', in P. Macnaghten and J. Urry (eds) *Bodies of Nature*, London: Sage, 81–106

Engels, F. (1972, orig. 1884) *The Origin of the Family, Private Property and the State*, London: Lawrence and Wishart

Hutton, R. (1991) *The Pagan Religions of the Ancient British Isles: Their Nature and Legacy*, Oxford: Blackwell

—— (1996) 'The Past and the Post-Modern Challenge', *The Ley Hunter* 125: 5–8

Lowerson, J. (1992) 'The Mystical Geography of the English', in B. Short (ed.) *The English Rural Community: image and analysis*, Cambridge: Cambridge University Press, 152–174

Luckhurst, R. (2002) 'The contemporary London gothic and the limits of the "spectral turn"', *Textual Practice* 16 (3): 527–546

McKay, G. (1996) *Senseless Acts of Beauty: cultures of resistance since the sixties*, London: Verso

Macnaghten, P. and Urry, J. (1998) *Contested Natures*, London: Sage

Matless, D. (1997) 'The Geographical Self, the Nature of the Social and Geoaesthetics: work in social and cultural geography, 1996', *Progress in Human Geography* 21 (3): 393–405

—— (2000) 'Five Objects, Geographical Subjects', in I. Cook, D. Crouch, S. Naylor and J. R. Ryan (eds) *Cultural Turns/Geographical Turns: perspectives on cultural geography*, Harlow: Prentice Hall, 335–358

—— (2008a) 'A Geography of Ghosts: the spectral landscapes of Mary Butts', *Cultural Geographies* 15 (3): 335–357

—— (2008b) 'Properties of Ancient Landscape: the present prehistoric in twentieth-century Breckland', *Journal of Historical Geography* 34 (1): 68–93

—— (2009) 'East Anglian Stones: erratic prehistories from the early twentieth century', in J. Parker (ed.) *Written on Stone: the cultural reception of British prehistoric monuments*, Cambridge: Cambridge Scholars Publishing, 66–81

Michael, M. (2000) 'These Boots are Made for Walking: mundane technologies, the body and human–environment relations', in P. Macnaghten and J. Urry, (eds) *Bodies of Nature*, London: Sage, 107–126

Michell, J. (1974) *The Old Stones of Land's End: an enquiry into the mysteries of the megalithic science*, London: Garnstone Press

—— (2001, orig. 1983) *The New View over Atlantis*, London: Thames and Hudson

Nash, C. (1998) 'Visionary Geographies: designs for developing Ireland', *History Workshop Journal* 45: 49–78

Phillips, C. (2006) 'Mystical Geographies of Cornwall', unpublished PhD thesis: University of Nottingham

Pile, S. and Thrift, N. (eds) (1995) *Mapping the Subject: geographies of cultural transformation*, London: Routledge

Russell, V. (1971) *West Penwith Survey*, Truro: Cornwall Archaeological Society

Straffon, C. (1994) *The Earth Mysteries Guide to Mid Cornwall and the Lizard*, St Just: Meyn Mamvro

—— (1995) *The Earth Mysteries Guide to Bodmin Moor and North Cornwall including Tintagel*, St Just: Meyn Mamvro

—— (1998) *The Earth Mysteries Guide to Ancient Sites in West Penwith*, Penzance: Meyn Mamvro

—— (2004) *Megalithic Mysteries of Cornwall*, St Just: Meyn Mamvro

Sullivan, D. (1997) 'Ley Lines: dead and buried – a reappraisal of the straight line enigma', *3rd Stone* 27: 44–49

Thrift, N. (1996) *Spatial Formations*, London: Sage

—— (1997) 'The Still Point: resistance, expressive embodiment and dance', in S. Pile and M. Keith (eds) *Geographies of Resistance*, London: Routledge, 124–151

—— (2000) 'Still Life in Nearly Present Time: the object of nature', in P. Macnaghten and J. Urry (eds) *Bodies of Nature*, London: Sage, 34–57

Tilley, C. (1994) *A Phenomenology of Landscape: places, paths and monuments*, Oxford: Berg

Trower, S. (2009) 'Supernatural Nationalism and New Age Ecology', in J. Parker (ed.) *Written on Stone: the cultural reception of British prehistoric monuments*, Cambridge: Cambridge Scholars Publishing, 111–127

Watkins, A. (1970, orig. 1925) *The Old Straight Track: its mounds, beacons, moats, sites and mark stones*, London: Garnstone Press

Weatherhill, C. (1991) *The Lyonesse Stone*, Padstow: Tabb House

—— (2000a, orig. 1981) *Belerion: ancient sites of Land's End*, Tiverton: Cornwall Books

—— (2000b, orig. 1985) *Cornovia: ancient sites of Cornwall and Scilly*, Tiverton: Cornwall Books

—— (2000c) *Cornish Place Names and Language*, Wilmslow: Sigma Leisure

Weatherhill, C. and Devereux, P. (2001) *Myths and Legends of Cornwall*, Wilmslow: Sigma Leisure

Williamson, T. and Bellamy, L. (1983) *Ley Lines in Question*, Kingswood: World's Work

Wylie, J. (2007) 'The Spectral Geographies of W. G. Sebald', *Cultural Geographies* 14 (2): 171–188

PART II

Gothic, romance and landscape

6

'CONFINED TO A LIVING GRAVE'

Welsh poetry, Gothic and the French Revolution

Elizabeth Edwards

In May 1799, the *European Magazine* printed a poem written at Bangor, north Wales by a young woman who had recently escaped the 'horrors and turbulence' of revolutionary France:

> 1
> From civil feuds and bloody fields,
> The rebel pike and trumpet's clangor;
> The exil'd fair to fortune yields,
> And finds a short relief at Bangor.
>
> 2
> Ye verdant rocks! ye peaceful floods!
> To turbulence unknown, as languor;
> Save, then the wild winds bow your woods,
> The sole annoyance felt at Bangor!
> […]
>
> 5
> Accept these thanks – here care and pain
> Subsided first, that wont to pang her;
> For Bath, and pleasure's varying train,
> Can ne'er efface the spells of Bangor!

('A Lady' 1799: 331)

By coming to Bangor, the unnamed emigrant had exchanged the shocks of French wartime violence for scenes of peace; soothing 'spells' that favourably compare with the hurried sociability of eighteenth-century Bath as well as the horrors of war. And yet at the same time the traces of mysterious enchantment lingering at the close of 'Bangor Ferry' breach the poem's central impression of calm, suggesting a world beyond the peaceful or picturesque.

The notion that apparently serene, undisturbed Welsh landscapes sometimes carried more unsettling messages can clearly be seen in poems written by Welsh writers in the same period. To give just one example, David Hughes, Master of Ruthin School in north-east Wales between 1795 and 1800, described another location very near Bangor in quite different terms in a manuscript poem dating from around the same time as 'Bangor Ferry'. Hughes depicted Wales as a nation in chains and benighted by colonial conquest in an untitled work equally written in the shadow of the French Revolution. The poem is set in Arvon on the banks of the river Conwy, a scene best known in the eighteenth century as the site of Thomas Gray's poem *The Bard* (1757), a text that will become important later in this chapter. Hughes's poem centres on the ragged and despairing figure of Merlin, his 'prophetic lyre' lying helplessly unstrung beside him, while 'sprites and demons' cling to him and join his laments. Merlin's anguish stems, we learn, from the occupation of Wales, a nation compromised in all sorts of ways by foreign oppression:

> His country's wounds his wounded soul opprest;
> His bleeding country wrung his bleeding breast.
> The generous Britons weigh'd with foreign chains,
> And torn by force from Anglia's fruitful plains,
> To barren rocks and Cambrian wilds confin'd –
> This, this the pang that tears his lab'ring mind.
>
> (Hughes 1798)

Hughes seems to be speaking here of mythical and ancient affairs: the figure of Merlin, or the displacement of the Welsh, the original or aboriginal Britons, from the lands that now make up England ('Anglia's fruitful plains'). But his poem is also very clearly located in the 1790s, when Britain was engaged in a lengthy war with revolutionary France that had terrible consequences for people in Wales (Jones 1973), as well as for those fighting abroad, and to which Hughes is referring when he notes how 'War and Famine, with an iron hand, / Now scatter ruin thro' this victim-land'. Suffering the consequences of conquest *and* the miseries of an ongoing war, Wales becomes a doubly victimised nation in this poem.

Hughes was not alone in linking the events of the French Revolution both to the history of Wales and to its current situation. This essay discusses below the ways in which the revolution also prompted the poet Richard Llwyd to represent his nation as enduring its own form of *ancien régime* in the late eighteenth century, existing under various forms of political and cultural repression. Both of these poets invoke dark visions of Wales as damaged, brutalised and dispossessed – a bleeding country (Hughes), or a living grave (Llwyd). However the response of Hughes or Llwyd was, of course, only one of many possible reactions to events in France from 1789 onwards. Ongoing research carried out within the AHRC-funded 'Wales and the French Revolution' project shows that virtually all responses to the Revolution were possible in Wales, and largely existed there in one form or another. A whole spectrum of viewpoints on the Revolution can be seen in Wales, from a hardline loyalism that readily supported English anti-revolutionary measures (Davies 2001), to radical responses that presented rebellious, pro-reform messages, remodelling them where necessary to fit Welsh contexts and audiences (Löffler 2012). At a popular level, the response to the revolution and the war that followed it was often shaped by local affairs, such as episodes of famine, recruiting for the revolutionary and Napoleonic wars (much resisted in some parts of Wales), or periodically heightened fears of a French invasion.

Although the Welsh response to revolution is a complex subject, it is clear that the 1790s was a period of sustained trauma in Wales for writers of all political persuasions, whether that trauma took the form of social distress, repressed civil rights (especially among religious dissenters), or the persistence of threats that the French would launch an invasion attempt somewhere in Britain, as they did near Fishguard in Pembrokeshire in 1797. As Hughes's Merlin poem suggests, Wales has long been linked with myth, folklore and the supernatural. However, this chapter argues that the events of the post-revolutionary period led to the emergence of an historically-grounded form of the Gothic that some Welsh poets used to articulate the traumas and terrors of these years. Gothic literature has more often than not been synonymous with prose fiction, but taking into account Welsh verse written in English in this period considerably broadens the scope of late-eighteenth-century Gothic. Pre-twentieth-century anglophone Welsh writing is a negelected field in general (Aaron 2010: 289) but the concept this essay outlines – a national Gothic for Wales – does not yet really exist at all for the period around the French Revolution. And yet it should exist, since national Gothic is a sign of the devolutionary times. Studies of the Gothic have recently turned to Scottish and Irish contexts (Gibbons 2004; Killeen 2005; Wright 2007), but attention is also beginning to move more generally beyond Ireland and Scotland to Wales, the north-west of England, or Devon and Cornwall: to the provincial in detail, where regional difference emerges in sharper and more precise terms (Moore 2008; Navickas 2009). For my purposes in this chapter, the most important aspect of national Gothic is its tendency to foreground contested histories. In Welsh poetry written after 1789, past events merge with contemporary ones, mixing the historically marginal and ruptured with present-day anxieties surrounding revolution and war. Central in this convergence of past and present is a sense of Wales as an injured or oppressed nation.

The Gothic has often been seen as a disorderly concept, a literary category that is difficult to define. This is particularly true of the 1790s when contemporary events meant that the resources of the Gothic could be used to illustrate virtually any political perspective, from revolutionary Jacobinism to the numerous and now little-known loyalist Gothic romances that appeared in the 1790s (Watt 1999: 42–69). But as several critics of the Gothic have noted, the violent and sometimes confusing events of the 1790s transformed the significance of terror, making the strains of fear and unease that characterise the Gothic particularly relevant for writers responding to current affairs in this period (Botting 1996: 40). My discussion of Welsh Gothic also draws on the historical turn of Gothic studies in the past decade or so in which critics have emphasised the literal meanings of the term, especially its historical and geographical specificities (Clery 1995; Watt 1999; Mighall 1999). As Robert Mighall has put it, the Gothic is 'a "mode" rather than a genre, the principle defining structure of which is its attitude to the past and its unwelcome legacies' (Mighall 1999: xix). Mighall's sense of the Gothic as a means of dealing with history is an important starting point for the following account of anglophone Welsh poetry written in the aftermath of the French Revolution.

Elements of the Gothic appear in virtually every genre in which Wales was represented after 1789, from published and manuscript travelogues, to fiction, drama (performed and unperformed) and poetry. Wales becomes increasingly visible in the literature of this period at least partly because the Revolutionary War with France meant that continental travel became largely impossible in the 1790s. Tourists visited Wales instead in ever-increasing numbers, and travel writings from the period present a distinctive tourist Gothic for Wales, a register of transcendent horror or fear most often linked with the north-west, especially Snowdonia and its surroundings. Although Wales seemed 'Gothic' enough to many of these travellers, the version of the Gothic they created was largely anglocentric, sometimes quite obviously derived from the contemporary Gothic novels that offered visitors to Wales a language with which to describe the unfamiliar landscapes and people they encountered. Touring Wales in 1799, the painter Robert Ker Porter recorded his simultaneous sense of terror and pleasure in the awesomely inhospitable environment of Snowdonia:

> a quarter of a mile brought us to a scene perfectly opposite to the calm and delightful one we had so recently beheld. a very narrow pass amidst masses of rock enormous to the sight and terrible to the mind led to the end of that days [sic] exertions. this spot presents to the traveller so desolate, so dreary, so aweful [sic], and so terror striking a view, that every discription [sic] will give but a sorry idea of its sublimity.
>
> (Porter 1799: 73)

Time and again travellers mention the nervousness with which they approach Wales – a sublime, wild, even dangerous region in the eyes of many tourists. Gothic fictions actually set in Wales offer similar viewpoints. In Sarah Lansdell's *The Tower; or the Romance of Ruthyne* (1798), a story of two sisters banished to Wales by their wicked stepmother, the gloomy appearance of Ruthyne Tower seems 'a spot of all others the most calculated to inspire horror and despondence'

(Lansdell 1798: vol 1, 31, quoted in Aaron in press). As Jane Aaron argues, the wildness of Wales in novels such as *The Tower* commonly signals dispossession and entrapment or imprisonment: 'a threatening zone, in which weather, landscape, and surly natives unable to speak English, take their long revenge on the unwary traveller' (Aaron in press). Welsh Gothic also took on a more overtly politicised quality in a number of novels published in this period as it does, for example, in Mary Robinson's *Angelina* (1796), where the eponymous figure of Angelina lives as a recluse in a ruined castle said to have belonged to 'Lewellin [Llywelyn, the last prince of an independent Wales], in the reign of Edward the First'. Playing up the notion of Wales as 'the last preserve of native British virtue' throughout this novel, Robinson's *Angelina* offers a critical perspective on the continuing war and the various forms of greed and corruption that, Robinson argued, were blighting mid-1790s British society (Robinson 1796: xvii).

These two examples illustrate the conflicting sense in which Wales stood for the hostile, uncivilized and irregular *and* the possibility of escaping or rejecting the vitiated tastes of modern life. A number of other English writers taking up the subject of Wales at this point focused more clearly on Welsh history, developing the Gothic directly in the light of the Welsh past. What is only a passing reference in *Angelina* becomes a central feature of other works composed in this period, such as James Boaden's *Cambro-Britons, an Historical Play* (1798), the most popular play staged at the Theatre Royal in the Haymarket in the summer of 1798 (Burling 2000: 173). This work frames the events of the conquest of Wales in the thirteenth century with a series of Gothic shocks: desolate and wild landscapes, deception, betrayal and murder, and a ghost who directs the action of the play at a crucial moment. In William Sotheby's unperformed tragedy *The Cambrian Hero, or Llewellyn the Great* (1800), the conquest of Wales becomes the backdrop to a theatre of the mind, in which the gathering storms that hang over the play are as much psychological as they are physical and political. But just as the landscapes of north-west Wales appear quite different depending on the position of the poet – the French emigrant celebrating safety and peace, or the Welsh schoolmaster lamenting the impoverishment of his incorporated nation – so the subject of the conquest of Wales becomes a question of perspective in these years.

Few subjects summoned up as much feeling in late eighteenth-century Wales as the loss of independence, and poetry written in this period suggests that the bards and brutal conflicts of medieval Wales acquired new resonances in these war-struck years. The new significance of the Welsh past in this period owes much to the fact that the mid- to late eighteenth century was a period of rapid development in terms of the recovery of earlier, especially medieval Welsh literature (Constantine 2008; Jones 2010: 14–48). Just one example of the fruit of this late-century cultural nationalism can be seen in *The Cambrian Register*, an ambitious English-language journal first published in 1796. *The Cambrian Register* vividly depicts the violence and disturbance that characterised the middle ages in Wales through the early Welsh poetry it printed, which was, the *Register* noted, characteristically 'of the harsher kind, formed in scenes of slaughter and desolation' (Pughe 1796: 401), while the period around the time of the conquest of Wales was one of 'terror' for Welsh bards newly under 'the first severe law of strangers' (Pughe 1796: 414).

As Susan Aronstein has explained, '[l]ate medieval Welsh literature tells the tale of a people in search of a national identity within the context of over four centuries of domination, conquest and assimilation' (Aronstein 2003: 541). The literature of Wales of the middle ages offers glimpses of the social and political history of a period of intense uncertainty and instability. And for Richard Llwyd, a labouring-class poet who was also a self-taught scholar of medieval Welsh verse, the middle ages represented a contested history, unresolved and unworked through, that was still shaping national identities in Wales at the turn of the nineteenth century. Without suggesting that events in France map onto poetry written in Wales in any neat or direct fashion, it is possible to see that the political turmoil and violence of this period suggested parallels between the medieval and modern. In poems by Llwyd and Hughes, living in Revolution-era Wales feels, we sense, just a little like living through the disruptions of the middle ages in Wales – a period whose experience of violent conquest becomes if not a foundation myth then certainly a focal point for Wales in the 1790s. The following discussion of Llwyd's poetry suggests that the French Revolution inspired him to see and portray Wales differently, as the Revolution added new dimensions to the legacies of colonial conquest, the version of the past that most often haunts the present in his work. Llwyd outlines a form of national Gothic in his poetry that is strongly linked with the post-conquest status of Wales: a Welsh Gothic with distinctly postcolonial undercurrents. Some of his most powerful Gothic moments focus on monuments and ruins, or objects that 'speak ... of a history that is constantly under the threat of erasure' as David Punter has put it (Punter 2002: 105). Llwyd's use of castles linked with the conquest of Wales (Beaumaris, Rhuddlan) particularly suggests his sense of history as 'inevitably involved in specific modes of ghostly persistence which may occur when ... national aspirations are thwarted by conquest or by settlement' (Punter 2002: 105).

Llwyd celebrated the French Revolution in a New Year ode for 1791, seeing it as France's contribution to 'the gen'rous flame' of liberty and reason that 'Spurns a tyrant's mad decrees'. However, Llwyd sets the Revolution in a Whiggish narrative of progress-as-liberty in which Wales takes centre stage as an ancient place of freedom and peace in this poem published in a provincial newspaper, *The Chester Chronicle*:

> Such as o'er the trackless heath,
> Unharass'd yet in fields of death,
> Unfetter'd freedom ran;
> Ere yet the moated rampart knew
> Oppression's callous steel-clad crew,
> Her foes, and those of man!

(Llwyd 1791)

Llwyd appears to be fitting the Revolution into a wider account of Wales's lost liberty in this poem, or, by late 1790 or early 1791, viewing Welsh history in the context of events in France.

This moment belongs to a larger discussion of the situation of Wales that takes place across his poems. Around a decade later, having published the long topographical poem that made his name, *Beaumaris Bay* (1800), Llwyd's depiction of Wales is altogether darker and more complex. 'Ode of the Months', published in 1804, is an adaptation of a fourteenth-century poem by the bard Gwilym Ddu. Gwilym Ddu's poem had been subject to a mainly very faithful, literal translation by the cleric and poet Evan Evans in *Specimens of the Poetry of the Antient Welsh Bards* (1764), a work that Llwyd used as a template for his version (Johnston in press). However, Llwyd also made a number of significant changes to 'Ode of the Months', which is a bard's lament for the capture of his lord by the English and his imprisonment in Rhuddlan Castle in north Wales. Drawn from Evans's translation is a sense that Wales has become a sort of prison:

> No ray of hope pervades our woes,
> No trait of mercy, marks our foes;
> 'Britain's sons, in vain, are brave,
> Immur'd within a living-grave!

> (Llwyd 1804: 63–4)

New in Llwyd's version is an anguished, Gothicised sensibility that turns on images of blood, crisis, gloom, sorrow and pain, which is explicitly linked with the conquest of Wales ('a nation falls … Oppression's plan, at length succeeds, / At every pore, my Country bleeds'). The poem concludes with a suicidal sense of dejection:

> Affliction wild, with piercing cry,
> And dark Despair, with downcast eye;
> The manly Mind, that scorns to speak,
> The indignant Heart, that swells to break;
> All agonise my breast to close,
> At once – existence and its woes!

> (Llwyd 1804: 64)

The poem seems perfectly to express a more Romanticised strain of the Gothic, characterised by (in Fred Botting's words) a sort of absorption of terror and horror, less a spectacle of villains, persecuted heroines, and ghosts than 'an internalised world of guilt, anxiety, despair' (Botting 1996: 7). This version of the Gothic can clearly be seen in 'Ode of the Months', but with Llwyd's particular reworkings. The castle-prison, for instance, mainstay of eighteenth-century Gothic fiction is still there, but the emotional theatre of the poem transforms the Gothic into a tool of national critique, a means of articulating the predicament of post-conquest Wales, confined to its 'living-grave'.

However much medieval Wales fills the foreground of this poem, the ongoing war with France also plays a minor but significant role. The war on the continent provides a sustained backdrop to events in the poem, most obviously through footnotes referring to developments in the war, which set an early nineteenth-century scene alongside the main fourteenth-century setting of the poem. The overlaying of these two timeframes invites comparisons between the medieval crisis of Gwilym Ddu's poem and the contemporary one of Llwyd's poem, bringing double meanings to his description of 'Ode of the Months' as 'the produce of a period of peculiar calamity' (Llwyd 1804: 50). Llwyd's poem sketches both fourteenth-century struggles over Welsh lands and liberty – what he describes in the preface to the poem as 'suffering in the insolence of conquest, the reluctance of submission, and the unhumanised ferocity of the age' (Llwyd 1804: 50) – and the ongoing 'calamity' of the war with France, just as ferocious and inhumane.

Llwyd also dramatises these issues in other poems, and I want to conclude with a closer look at *Beaumaris Bay*, the work that transformed him from aspiring amateur poet to the 'Bard of Snowdon'. *Beaumaris Bay* is an account of a day around Anglesey, beginning at dawn on Puffin Island just off Beaumaris, and ending at dusk with a trip up the Menai Straits in a fishing boat. Between these two points, Llwyd takes us on a series of excursions into Welsh landscape, literature, history and contemporary life. This chapter has argued for the vital place of history, rather than myth, in anglophone Welsh poetry written after the French Revolution. There is, however, one towering myth in late eighteenth-century Welsh writing that deserves more space in this discussion. This is the myth of the 'bardicide', the idea (popularised by Thomas Gray around the mid-century in *The Bard*) that Edward I had massacred the Welsh bards as part of his attempts to subdue Wales and its people. Although the bardicide was an invented tradition, it acquired a great deal of power by the late-eighteenth century, becoming something of a problem and an opportunity for Welsh writers by this point in time (Prescott 2008: 56–83). Poets translated *The Bard* into Welsh in bardic competitions, while the Glamorganshire stonemason and writer Edward Williams (better known by his bardic pseudonym 'Iolo Morganwg') rubbished its historical inaccuracies and its reliance on what he called 'barbarous Scandinavian Mythology' in his manuscripts:

> Gray's Bard, has been very generally, and extravagantly praised, but notwithstanding of all that has been said, I think it a very inferior thing … the ode is destitute of mythological truth its fictitious names of Bards also violate historic Truth, for of that period we have the real names, as well as the works, of Great Bards who really suffered greatly under the usurpation of Edward Longshanks, and of whom some were put to Death.
>
> (Williams n.d.)

Richard Llwyd would also have known that the bardicide myth was fictional, and yet he set this myth to very different purposes. Part of *Beaumaris Bay* includes a portrait of Beaumaris Castle, built by Edward I in the late-thirteenth century as part of his attempts to secure north-west Wales. Welsh history speaks through the fabric of the nation in various different ways in Llwyd's poem, but it does so with particular intensity in the passage on Beaumaris Castle:

> Here [Beaumaris Castle] earth is loaded with a mass of wall,
> The proud insulting badge of Cambria's fall,
> By haughty Edward rais'd; and every stone
> Records a sigh, a murder, or a groan.
> The Muse of Britain, suff'ring at its birth,
> Exulting sees it crumbling to the earth.
> Ah! what avails it that the lordly *tower*
> Attracts the thoughtless stare and vacant hour!
> If ev'ry Bard with indignation burns,
> When to the tragic tale the eye returns;
> If for his haunted race, to distant times,
> There's still reserv'd a vengeance for his crimes.
>
> (Llwyd 1800: 13–5)

This extract gives a sense of the depth of feeling in Llwyd's account of the 'tragic tale' of the Welsh past, its losses and atrocities. No less revealing are the footnotes Llwyd appends to these lines on the wrongs of Welsh history, where he quotes Gray's very well-known vision of the bards slaughtered by Edward I – 'On dreary Arvon's shore they lie, / Smear'd with gore, and ghastly pale'). In this lengthy footnote, Llwyd explains that killing the bards was the 'most effectual of the means resorted to by Edward, for securing the submission of his new subjects' (Llwyd 1800: 15n).

This version of events seems clear-cut enough, and yet Llwyd's response to Gray is oddly double throughout *Beaumaris Bay*. While Llwyd seems repeatedly haunted by Gray and *The Bard* in *Beaumaris Bay* he also continually writes over Gray in his poem, as though in an attempt to replace *The Bard* with native perspectives on Welshness and Welsh history. And in an unexpected twist, Llwyd ends up reliant on Gray in the footnote just quoted. 'Of late it has become fashionable to doubt [the truth of the bardicide] among other historical facts:' Llwyd comments, 'but what is to become of the testimony of Sir John Wynn, and the strains of the sufferers?' (Llwyd 1800: 15n). For Llwyd, we sense, Gray's version of events folds the fate of a nation into myth. However fabricated it may be – and there is no doubt that Llwyd knew it never happened – the idea of the bardicide brilliantly articulates and memorialises Welsh grievances, packaging the real into the unreal, or into a kind of history imagined beyond history that Llwyd seems unwilling to give up.

This chapter has suggested that the French Revolution brought fresh meanings to the warlike brutality of earlier periods of Welsh history. Some of these meanings fed into new notions of Wales's post-conquest or postcolonial condition and, through these, into new perspectives on national identity in the 1790s. It is important, then, to read David Hughes and Richard Llwyd's portrayals of the Welsh as deracinated and dispossessed in the context of the ways in which the Revolution raised questions far beyond the borders of France about how nations should be structured and governed, or about the rights of men (and usually only men) within those nations. Questions such as these were more politicized and actively contested elsewhere in Europe, notably in Ireland (Curtin 1994). But there is no doubt that early Welsh literature appears newly haunted, and haunting, as a result of being brought into the revolutionary theatre of the period, in which late eighteenth-century Wales appears as a shadow of pre-1789 France, suffering the oppressions of its own particular kind of *ancien régime*, or living death, in an age of sustained distress and insecurity.

Wales has, however, too often been satirised, ignored or subject to the myths of others. This essay draws on research in progress on Revolution-era Wales that is changing the ways in which we understand its history and literature. Long-standing myths about Wales include its redhot artisan radicalism, or its underdevelopment or lack of sophistication, neither of which sufficiently describes Wales in the light of new and ongoing work on these years. There is more to be said, for instance, about Welsh radicalism in the period (a more subtle matter than the fiery version suggests) as well as Welsh loyalism; more to be said about the complicated networks of print and manuscript that criss-crossed 1790s' Wales, and the political cultures that flourished in various public and private settings in Wales in this period (Löffler in press). Welsh Gothic, a category that has hardly been thought to exist until now, is just one aspect of the new, more accurate view of Wales that is currently emerging, re-routing conceptions of Wales from the marginal and mythical towards the mainstream.

Bibliography

'A Lady' (1799) 'Bangor Ferry', *The European Magazine and London Review… From January to June 1799*, London: J. Sewell.

Aaron, J. (2010) 'Twentieth-Century and Contemporary Welsh Gothic Fiction', *Literature Compass* 7 (4): 281–289.

—— (forthcoming) 'Haunted by History: Welsh Gothic 1780–1801', in Stewart Mottram and Sarah Prescott (eds) *Writing Wales from the Reformation to Romanticism*, Aldershot: Ashgate.

Aronstein, S. L. (2003) 'Wales: Culture and Society', in S.H. Rigby (ed.) *A Companion to Britain in the Later Middle Ages*, Oxford: Blackwell, 541–57.

Botting, F. (1996) *Gothic*, London and New York: Routledge.

Burling, W. J. (2000) *Summer Theatre in London, 1661–1820, and the Rise of the Haymarket Theatre*, London and New Jersey: Associated University Presses.

Centre for Advanced Welsh and Celtic Studies (2012) Wales and the French Revolution, Aberystwyth, University of Wales <http://frenchrevolution.wales.ac.uk/en/index.php> (accessed 29 March 2012).

Clery, E. J. (1995) *The Rise of Supernatural Fiction 1762–1800*, Cambridge: Cambridge University Press.

Constantine, M. (2008) 'Welsh Literary History and the Making of "The Myvyrian Archaiology of Wales"', in D. Van Hulle and J. Leerssen (eds) *Editing the Nation's Memory: Textual Scholarship and Nation-Building in Nineteenth-Century Europe*, Amsterdam: Rodopi, 109–28.

Curtin, N. J. (1994) *The United Irishmen: Popular Politics in Ulster and Dublin, 1791–1798*, Oxford: Clarendon Press.

Davies, H. M. (2001) 'Loyalism in Wales, 1792–1793', *Welsh History Review* 20 (4): 65–93.

Gibbons, L. (2004) *Gaelic Gothic*, Galway: Arlen House.

Hughes, D. (1798) Untitled poem ('In a wild cave...'), National Library of Wales MS GB 0210 GARN FL/1/1/12.

Johnston, D. (forthcoming) 'Radical Adaptation: Translations of Medieval Welsh Poetry in the 1790s', in M. Constantine and D. Johnston (eds) *'Footsteps of Liberty and Revolt': Essays on Wales and the French Revolution*, Cardiff: University of Wales Press.

Jones, D. J. V. (1973) *Before Rebecca: Popular Protests in Wales, 1793–1835*, London: Allen Lane.

Jones, F. M. (2010) *'The Bard is a Very Singular Charater': Iolo Morganwg, Marginalia and Print Culture*, Cardiff: University of Wales Press.

Killeen, J. (2005) *Gothic Ireland: Horror and the Irish Anglican Imagination in the Long Eighteenth-Century*, Dublin: Four Courts Press.

Lansdell, S. (1798) *The Tower; or the Romance of Ruthyne*, London: Hookham and Carpenter.

Llwyd, R. (1791) 'Ode for the New Year, Inscribed to Paul Panton, of Plasgwyn, Esq.', *The Chester Chronicle*, 7 January.

—— (1800) *Beaumaris Bay, A Poem*, Chester: J. Fletcher.

—— (1804) *Poems, Tales, Odes, Sonnets, Translations from the British, &c. &c. In Two Vols*, Chester: J. Fletcher.

Löffler, M. (ed.) (2012) *Welsh Responses to the French Revolution: Press and Public Discourse 1789–1802*, Cardiff: University of Wales Press.

—— (forthcoming) 'The Marseillaise in Wales', in M. Constantine and D. Johnston (eds) *'Footsteps of Liberty and Revolt': Essays on Wales and the French Revolution*, Cardiff: University of Wales Press.

Mighall, R. (1999) *A Geography of Victorian Gothic Fiction: Mapping History's Nightmares*, Oxford: Oxford University Press.

Moore, D. (2008) 'Devolving Romanticism: Nation, Region and the Case of Devon and Cornwall', *Literature Compass* 5 (5): 949–63.

Navickas, K. (2009) *Loyalism and Radicalism in Lancashire 1798–1815*, Oxford: Oxford University Press.

Porter, R. K. (1799) National Library of Wales MS 12651B.

Prescott, S. (2008) *Eighteenth-Century Writing from Wales: Bards and Britons*, Cardiff: University of Wales Press.

Pughe, W. O. (ed.) (1796) *The Cambrian Register, for the Year 1795*, London: E. and T. Williams.

Punter, D. (2002) 'Scottish and Irish Gothic', in Jerrold Hogle (ed.) *The Cambridge Companion to the Gothic*, Cambridge: Cambridge University Press, 105–24.

Robinson, M. (1796) *Angelina: A Novel*, ed. S.M. Setzer (2009), London: Pickering and Chatto.

Watt, J. (1999) *Contesting the Gothic: Fiction, Genre and Cultural Conflict, 1764–1832*, Cambridge: Cambridge University Press.

Williams, E. (n.d.) National Library of Wales MS 13159A.

Wright, A. (2007) 'Scottish Gothic', in C. Spooner and E. McEvoy (eds) *The Routledge Companion to Gothic*, London: Routledge, 73–82.

7

FINGAL IN THE WEST COUNTRY

The poems of Ossian and cultural myth-making in the South West of England, 1770–1800

Dafydd Moore

James Macpherson's *Poems of Ossian* (1760–65) were one of the publishing sensations of their age. Reputedly the remains of the third-century Gaelic bard Ossian (they were in fact the result of Macpherson's combination of extant Gaelic balladry and his imagination as inspired by his engagement with that Gaelic tradition), the poems introduced Enlightenment Europe to a world of tragic maidens, melancholy warriors and of dim and mysterious battles played out against a sublime landscape. The aged Ossian reminisces about the reign and deeds of his father Fingal, and laments the loss of all that was dear to him:

> Pleasant is the voice of thy song, thou lonely dweller of the rock. It comes on the sound of the stream, along the narrow vale. My soul awakes, O Stranger! In the midst of my hall. I stretch for my hand to the spear, as in the days of other years.– I stretch my hand, but it is feeble; and the sigh of my bosom grows. – Wilt thou not listen, son of the rock, to the song of Ossian? My soul is full of other times; the joy of my youth returns. Thus the son appears in the west, after the steps of his brightness have moved behind a storm; the green hills lift their dewy heads; the blue streams rejoice in the vale. The aged hero comes forth on his staff, and his grey hair glitters in the beam.
>
> (Macpherson 1762: 219–20)

> I behold my departed friends. Their gathering is on Lora, as in the days that are past. – Fingal comes like a watery column of mist; his heroes are around [...] How are ye changed, my friends, since the days of Selma's feast!
>
> (Macpherson 1762: 210)

The appeal of Napoleon's favourite poet was felt from America to Russia and most parts in between: one hundred years later, Matthew Arnold announced 'when we are unjust enough to forget [our debt to *Ossian*], may the Muse forget us' (Arnold 1886: 371). Yet for much of the twentieth century *Ossian* was known solely for the bad tempered dispute about its provenance. Only in the last 30 years have the poems been considered in broader terms: as an expression of Scottish literary and cultural sensibility in the age of Enlightenment; as an important early Romantic influence; as a key impetus to the dawning of indigenous cultural consciousness across Northern Europe; as a text that reconceived perceptions of the natural world, of the wild places on the map, and of the people who live within them.[1]

Macpherson has been a major beneficiary of the 'four nations' approach to literary studies that has emphasised the polycentric nature of the British Isles and replaced a monolithic, anglo- (indeed London-) centric perspective with one emphasising the nations and regions of the British Isles. Early work focussed on Scotland and Ireland, but over recent years it has spread to Wales, to Cornwall and, still more recently, the regions of England.[2] Nicholas Roe, responding to a 'sharper awareness of the decentred energies of Romantic culture', has suggested that 'regionalism [...] is a key critical dynamic of Romantic studies now' and crucially that 'canonical marginality and regional cultures are in fact most urgently in need of reassessment within England' (Roe 2010: 4, 5). This essay contributes to this reassessment by addressing itself to an area of the far West Country relatively untouched by Roe's volume, and considers some of the ways in which *Ossian* was used in the projection of poetic and cultural consciousness in Devon and Cornwall during the last third of the eighteenth century.

This essay is not a comprehensive account of literary identity building in the area in the period, and, in concentrating on the period 1770–1800, it does not consider at all what might otherwise be thought of as a prime period of regional literature in the early decades of the nineteenth century, encompassing works such as George Woodley's *Cornubia* (1819), Joseph Cottle's 'Dartmoor' (1823), Nicholas Carrington's 'Dartmoor: A Descriptive Poem' (1826) or Felicia Hemans' 'Dartmoor: A Prize Poem' (1839). Instead it directs attention on an earlier, less well known and loosely affiliated group of writers who took significant cues from Macpherson's *Ossian*, or at least from a discourse surrounding an imagined ancient heroic and poetic past that can be associated to a greater or lesser extent with *Ossian*. This qualification is important, but not disabling or disingenuous. As the purpose here is not to establish new significances for Macpherson through simplistic models of influence (that he was responsible for 'inventing' a type of West Country cultural expression), it need not concern us whether this or that image or phrase owes its use to *Ossian*. Rather, in examining the ways in which *Ossian* provided an interpretative framework or vocabulary for certain sorts of literary and broader cultural consciousness in the minds of writers and readers, I am invoking Paul Baines' notion of *Ossian* as a 'literary claude glass', framing a particular literary discourse, in his case surrounding the Highlands of Scotland, in mine a certain sort of heroic poetry (Baines 1997: 54). I am also pursuing Joep Leerseen's suggestion of 'a certain topic and quiddity [...] brought into literary circulation by Macpherson's *Ossian*':

> [the]mode [of Arnold's 'Dover Beach'] is Ossianic, not because it might or might not be possible to register similar imagery more or less verbatim in such-and-such a portion of Macpherson's work, but because of a general imaginative strategy involving the distribution of emotion, space and chosen moment.
>
> (Leerseen 1998: 2–3)

Equally I am also interested in, and will conclude with some discussion of, some of the ways this topic and quiddity is adapted, differentially emphasised and constructed a-new. By not relying on simplistic claims of influence, I hope to remain alive to the complex and myriad ways in which a 'general imaginative strategy' might enter literary discourse.

The clearest register of interest in *Ossian* are versifications of Macpherson's poems. The limited published writings of the Exeter poet Richard Hole are dominated, one way or another, by his abiding interest in *Ossian*, most explicitly his version of the six book epic *Fingal* (1762) in heroic couplets published in 1772. Book 4 of Macpherson's poem opens:

> Who comes with her songs from the mountain, like the bow of showery Lena? It is the maid of the voice of love. The white-armed daughter of Toscar. Often hast thou heard my song, and given the tear of beauty. Dost thou come to the battles of thy people, and to hear the actions of Oscar? When shall I cease to mourn by the streams of the ecchoing Cona? My years have passed away in battle, and my age is darkened with sorrow.
>
> (Macpherson 1762: 49)

Hole's version reads:

> Who seems descending from yon hill on high,
> Bright as the bow that paints the showery sky?
> 'Tis fair Malvina – To thy Oscar's praise
> Shall aged Ossian tune his sounding lays?
> Where Cona's waters wander o'er the plain
> We'll sit, and pour the melancholy strain.–
> Alas my son! For thee my sorrows flow,
> And my heart throbs with ever-during woe.
> When shall I cease to mourn, when find relief?
> My youth in war consum'd, my age in grief!
>
> (Hole 1772: 102)

As this suggests, Hole was not a bad poet as such, and indeed the project of versification was not as idiosyncratic as it might appear to us now. Admiration or validation expressed through verse-rendering was a common feature of the response to *Ossian*. Versions of the *Fragments of Ancient Poetry* were appearing in the London periodical press within a fortnight of their publication in Edinburgh, and a number of the reviews of the *Fragments* in late summer of 1760 were accompanied by versifications. There were six different full versifications of the epic *Fingal* before 1820, while versifications originally published in the 1760s were reprinted as late as the 1850s. Turning Macpherson's prose into couplets was explicitly understood as demonstrating the way in which *Ossian* could be thought of as a classic text, amenable to being rendered into English heroic verse (Anon. 1858: xxiii). Hole's version was well received by reviewers and met with a wide audience: it was, for example, spotted on the bookshelves of Highland libraries by Thomas Hill when he was conducting his Ossianic investigations in the Highlands in 1780 (Hill, 1782/3).

Near-cousin of versification was imitation and poetic appreciation. Again this was a widespread (indeed international) industry, but in terms of the far west of England, the two-volume *Poems Chiefly by Gentlemen of Devonshire and Cornwall* (1792) was graced by its editor Richard Polwhele's 'Ossian Departing to His Fathers' (1780). Modelled on a passage from Macpherson's 'Berrathon' (1762), it extended the original to include a muster of *Ossian*'s greatest tragic heroes and heroines. 'Berrathon' also provided the model for another better-known Devon poet around this time. Samuel Taylor Coleridge's 'Effusion XXIX', an imitation of *Ossian*, written in 1793 and published in 1796 opens:

> The stream with languid murmur creeps
>   In Lumin's flowery vale:
> Beneath the dew the Lily weeps
>   Slow-waving in the gale.
>
> 'Cease, restless gale!' it seems to say,
>   'Nor wake me with thy sighing!
> The honours of my vernal day
> On rapid wings are flying.
>
> Tomorrow shall the Traveller come
>   Who late beheld me blooming:
> His searching eye shall vainly roam
>   The dreary vale of Lumin.'

(1997: 42)[3]

Ossian was not the only ancient Northern poet represented in Polwhele's *Poems* volumes. Various others 'from Northern mythology' were represented: 'The Tomb of Gunnar' by Hole; 'Gram and Gro', 'Hother', 'The Incantation of Herva' and an extract from the old chestnut 'The Epicedium of Regnor

Lodbrog' as rendered by Polwhele. Some of these represent a different strain of ancient heroic verse, a poetry of the 'carnag'd plain', as Polwhele puts it, whose gory details are at some remove from the polite sentiment of *Ossian*. The connection between *Ossian* and the *Epicedium*, between the Celtic and the Teutonic, had begun in terms of precisely such a distinction in Hugh Blair's *Critical Dissertation on the Poems of Ossian* (1763), however by the 1790s and in the hands of imitators, the distinction was not thought of as the ethnic one Macpherson and perhaps Blair had originally implied. Hole's 'The Tomb of Gunnar' suggests the transplanting of the Ossianic effects of mood and scene into a Teutonic setting:

> 'What mean those dreadful sounds that rise
> From the tomb where Gunnar lies?'
> Exclaims the Shepherd in affright,
> As by the Moon's uncertain light,
> Athwart the solitary plain,
> He homeward drives his fleecy train.
>
> *Sarpedine, Hogner*, mark the tale,
> And fearless cross the lonely vale:
> They stand the stately tomb beside;
> Whilst slowly-sailing vapours hide
> In their dun veil night's glittering pride.
>
> A moon-beam, on the cave of death,
> Sudden glanc'd athwart the heath

> (Hole 1792b: 78)

I shall return to the question of promiscuous ethnic identity in the conclusion, but for now move on to a related form of Ossianic admiration: the poem of appreciation. Again Hole offers an important example. His 'Ode to the Imagination' had originally prefixed his version of *Fingal*, and was reprinted in Polwhele's collection (it was a widely admired poem, set to music, for example, by composer and fellow Exonian William Jackson), and offers an insight into the imaginative appeal of Macpherson's world:

> Imagination, mighty power!
>   Where dost thou guide my roving mind?
> By time, by distance unconfin'd
>   On fancy's rapid wings I fly
> To *Morven*'s coast, where mountains tower,
>   And break the clouds that roll on high.
> Before my view the dark-brown heath extends,
>   From reed-crown'd lakes the creeping mists exhale,
> Down the rock bursting, the rude stream descends,

> And foams along the solitary vale.
> Cona, thy waters murmur to my ear!
>> Selma, thy halls unfold!
> There sits FINGAL:– the chiefs of old
> Gaze on the ruler of the war.
>
>> (Hole 1772: 1)

The speaker sounds not unlike Ossian himself, whose evocation of his past and his father's deeds is after all a memorial-cum-imaginative reconstruction of a long dead world. In the retreating hall of mirrors that is the Ossianic narrative set-up, the poet Ossian offers only the first of the representations and mediations of the absent world of Fingal, and as such licences the participatory emphasis within responses to poems, that, in the words of James Mulholland, 'make readers feel like they are participating in the ancient Scottish past and listening in on Ossian's heroic tales' (2009: 408). Overall, Hole's poem is a testament to the kind of imaginative suggestiveness and readerly response that made *Ossian* such a success. Equally, Hole also emphasises the upland coastal landscape of *Ossian*, one of easy applicability to the South West of England.

Indeed, *Ossian* provided a number of writers with a way of understanding the landscape of the South West. Samuel Drewe's 'The Rapt Bard; Written in the Valley of Stones, near Linton in Devonshire' offers one example. Not all bards are obviously or self-evidently Ossianic in the period, but bearing in mind Leersen's call for attention to the 'general imaginative strategy' there is something suggestive of *Ossian* in the way the bard is placed in a (for Devon, perhaps uncharacteristically) barren landscape, a landscape from which the past is envisaged as arising:

> Thus sung the bard, as far from human haunt
>> Where *Devon* spreads her heathy desert wide,
> Reclin'd beneath a frowning rock he lay,
>> Lull'd to soft slumber by the murmuring tide
>
>> (Drewe 1792: 33)

Compare this with Ossian's dedication of a memorial stone in 'Colna-dona':

> Speak to the feeble, O Stone, after Selma's race have failed! Prone, from the stormy night, the traveller shall lay him, by thy side; thy whistling moss shall sound in his dreams; the years that were past shall return.
>> (Macpherson 1763: 220–21)

An emphasis on Exmoor's 'heathy desert' shows how the West can be thought of topographically in Ossianic terms; in Polwhele's 'The Castle of Tintadgel' (1781) it is the setting for storms of Ossianic proportions:

I
High o'er Tintadgel's echoing tow'rs
Flew the Dark Genius of the blast:
Around the scene the tempest lours,
And roars along the spectred waste:
Whilst the blue meteor stream'd with transient light,
The rolling thunder shook the shades of night.

II
Immur'd amidst these dreary walls,
A soliltary Mourner sat,
And, as the shade of sorrow falls
Dark from the hov'ring cloud of fate,
Oft from her eye the silent waters start,
Pale her wan cheek, and cold her flutt'ring heart.

(Polwhele 1781: 330–31)

There is more than Macpherson behind this, but along with everything else there certainly is *Ossian's* meteorological sensibility, a sublime and threatening landscape, in which mournful characters lament and die:

> Roll on, ye dark-brown years, for ye bring no joy in your course. Let the tomb open to Ossian, for his strength has failed. The sons of the song have gone to rest; my voice remains, like a blast, that roars, lonely, on a sea-surrounded rock, after the winds are laid.
>
> (Macpherson 1761: 218)

> Autumn is on the mountains; gray mist rests on the hills. The whirlwind is heard on the heath. Dark rolls the river through the narrow plain. A tree stands alone on the hill, and marks the slumbering Connal, The leaves whirl around with the wind, and strew the grave of the dead. At times are seen here the ghosts of the deceased, when the musing hunter alone stalks slowly over the heath.
>
> (Macpherson 1761: 206–7)

When these writers imaginatively engaged with the fancied heroic past whose traces littered the landscape of their region, one of the ways they did so was through the imagined past of Macpherson's *Ossian*, of miserable warriors and tragic loves, of hauntings and desertings. But *Ossian* would seem to have provided a way of interpreting the ancient landscape of the South West for more than just its poets.

William Stukeley's 1763 letter of congratulations to Macpherson had made clear the usefulness of *Ossian* in corroborating his own antiquarian speculations about Wiltshire, and the reverse applied as well: *Ossian* could be used as a basis for antiquarian theorising, as in John Swete's 'Of Sepulture in General, and Sepulchral Single Stones Erect', which uses *Ossian* as evidence for the ubiquity of marking high status graves with standing stones. Indeed *Ossian* is recruited to a universalist argument associating monuments not otherwise bracketed together, also including memorials to Homeric heroes and Biblical characters, Egyptian obelisks, Roman columns and pillars discovered by Captain Cook on 'LeFooga, one of the Friendly Islands' (Swete 1796a: 307). Swete returned to the subject in his 'On Some of the More Remarkable British Monuments in Devon', though he notes the relative scarcity of 'huge monuments of the first natives of these island' in Devon when compared with 'the mountainous parts of Wales and Scotland, on the plains of Sarum, in the wastes of Derbyshire and Cornwall' (1796b: 110). Swete's combination of empiricist observation, self-conscious historical theorising and fanciful corroboration accords with Joanne Parker's observation that it is 'far too simplistic' to oppose 'sentimental and fanciful engagements with prehistory' with the 'disciplined enquiry and rigorous empiricism' of the emerging discipline of modern archaeology at the end of the eighteenth century (2010: 15). Parker also reminds us that the megalithic remains of the South West were a potential mark of 'cultural prestige', though only when seen through an appropriate interpretative frame – in the case of her examples, druidism. *Ossian* provided another such pseudo-historical lens, and a way of increasing the cultural value ascribed to what might be otherwise considered to be rather disappointing artefacts of past civilisations.

The importance of *Ossian* in validating an historic past is also clear from Hole's most ambitious work, his seven-book romance of 1789 *Arthur; or the Northern Enchantment*, in which a King Arthur fights off Scandinavian invasion from his West Country centre of operations. It was a work of serious poetic endeavour, replete with everything one could wish of in an eighteenth-century national poem (and quite possibly a little more besides), including dream-visions of future British glory and apostrophes to what it identifies as the key British values of liberty, homeliness and hospitality. It also contains anthropological and historical accounts and speculations on a variety of matters, including, but far from limited to, the sacrificial rites of the druids; the veneration of the raven; the origin of Stonehenge; the fact that country of birth plays a small role in the ultimate association of national heroes and saints with particular nations. It may be eclectic, but the poem is also generously spirited, good humoured and rather lively. Hole is working hard to ensure *Arthur* fits within the antiquarian discourses of late eighteenth-century Britain. In other words, the poem represents the earlier eighteenth-century paraphernalia of the patriotic national poem read through the historicising gaze of the later eighteenth-century antiquarian.

Arthur's literary precedents are similarly self-conscious and wide ranging, moving from Homer through Virgil to Ariosto, Spenser and Shakespeare, and on to Thomas Chatterton and Richard Hurd. For example, the poem opens with Arthur's Aeneas-like shipwreck on a foreign shore and, lest the Virgilian inspiration escape the reader, Hole has Arthur virtually quoting Aeneas' response to the temple mural at Carthage when he wonders 'has fame too partial told in distant lands / the deeds of Arthur'. There is no denying the eclecticism of what James Merriman termed Hole's 'cultural potpourri' but it is under a measure of aesthetic control, provided by the consistent presence and use of a world and sensibility drawn from *Ossian* (Merriman 1973: 106). So death in battle, for example, is almost always described in terms of that key Ossianic obsession, heroic aftermath:

> Unconscious of her much-lov'd hero's fall,
> Ithona sits in Thomond's lofty hall,
> And bids the bards to him awake their lays –
> For who like Conal claimed the meed of praise!
> Sudden, ere yet they touch'd the warbling wire,
> Burst mournful sounds instinctive from the lyre:
> And lo! The dogs, companions of the chace,
> In shuddering terror gaze on vacant space.
> Their lord's sad image rises to their view;
> Faint gleam his arms, and pallid is his hue.
> His dimly-rolling eyes on Thomond's fair
> In grief he bends; then borne aloft in air,
> And wrapt in darkness on the gale he flies;
> Deep mourn the faithful train, and howlings wild arise.
> She marks the signs that speak her hero low;
> Rends her dark tresses, beats her breast of snow,
> And gives her days to solitary woe.

(Hole 1789: 143)

Hole acknowledged a debt to Macpherson on the subject of canine premonition, but it hardly stops there: the names, diction and imagery are straight from *Ossian*, as, crucially, is the turning 'away from the military engagement in order to linger among the various half-lights produced by the battle' (deGategno 1989: 79):

> Nina-thorma sat on the shore, and heard the sound of battle. She turned her red eyes on Lethmal the gray-haired bard of Selma, for he had remained on the coast, with the daughter of Torthórma. Son of the times of old! She said, I hear the noise of death. Thy friends have met with Uthal and the chief is low! [...] Art thou fallen on thy heath, O son of high Finthormo! Thou didst leave me on a rock, but my soul was full of thee. Son of high Finthormo! Art thou fallen on thy heath?

(Macpherson 1762: 265)

Hole's only recent biographer has suggested that with *Arthur*, Hole was attempting 'to do for West Britain what Macpherson had done for Scotland' (Radcliffe 2004). What Macpherson had done, of course, was generate massive cultural capital from the home-grown sensibility of *Ossian*, and it is worth considering how this plays out amongst our West Country writers.

In 1763 and at the height of the *Ossian* craze, David Erskine Baker had treated the theatre-goers of Edinburgh to a play based on Macpherson's poems. Its epilogue notes:

> For you must know that I have read romances;
> Have heard of knights, dames, coursers, shields and lances;
> Have read how heroes went, of old, to battle;
> Of trumpet's roar, drum's beat, and canon's rattle –
> But then those writers through strange countries lead ye;
> Idalian groves, and forests of Arcadia:
> But I was told, the author of this piece
> Had fixed on Caledonia, not Greece;
> That he had scorn'd tow'ards foreign climes to roam,
> When he'ad such fair examples here at home.
>
> (Baker 1763: np)

It is possible (though not essential) that this production was seen by a young medical student from Exeter. Hugh Downman returned to his home town to practice medicine and write poetry (activities neatly combined in his most successful work, a Miltonic poem on paediatrics entitled *Infancy* that went through nine editions between 1774 and 1809). On the 18th of January 1781 Downman had his own heroic verse drama, *Editha*, performed in Exeter (it went on to play in Plymouth Dock – now Devonport – on the 15th of February). Set during an imaginary defence of Exeter from Viking invaders, it is dedicated to 'the inhabitants of the city' and opens with a tribute to the martial spirit of the city and its people. And before then, the prologue has made the cultural nationalism of the project apparent in an argument that echoes that of Baker:

> Not through Antiquity's obscurer ways,
> To climes remote our British Author strays,
> Not from th'Italian, or the French translates,
> Alters old plots, or even imitates.
> From your own Annals he his story draws.
>
> (Downman 1784: np)

The play in fact owes little to *Ossian* (*King Lear* is its most obvious inspiration), but the point is the shared logic of cultural value. It is a logic Downman repeats in a congratulatory ode to his friend Hole:

> […] let me haste
> *Enthusiastic Maid!* to taste
> Of thy beloved, deceptive rills,

Which high among the *Gothic* hills
Forth from the well of fiction spring,
And thence their mingled currents fling
O'er rocks whose heads are wreathed with snow,
And thro romantic vales below.

Th'inspiring draught my soul pervades,
I range thro long-deserted glades:
With Hole, companion of my way,
Thro scenes, where Spenser loved to stray,
O'er the wild heath, or trembling sod,
Which Ariosto whilom trod;
Where the free Muse with native charms
Her Votary's panting bosom warms.

(Downman 1790: 195–6)[4]

This recalls, amongst other things, Hole's own poem on *Ossian* quoted above (a comparison with which makes the transferred eroticism of Downman's poem even clearer). It also implies a national and even political dimension to this aesthetic preference: Gothic hills, native charms and the 'free Muse' of Hole. Milton might be behind a good deal of this, but then he is also behind much of *Ossian* as well. There is also a reaching for a certain sort of Ossianic discourse: the past tense of that last stanza, with its 'long-deserted glades' suggests an act of imaginative resuscitation redolent with the Ossianic desire to reanimate an empty scene. Downman demonstrates the importance placed on the literary representation of a home-grown heroic past by these writers. Macpherson was a central part of this not only through the adaptation or and borrowing from the *Ossian* poems, but also in the exemplar they offered, or the possibility they extended, not just of general cultural assertiveness but of a specific cultural identity.

It is now commonplace to assert that *Ossian* gains traction as a cultural myth because it answers one of the more troubling questions of the age: the possibility of warrior epic in an age of politeness. The effort *Ossian* represents to reconcile virtue with power, civic heroism with polite sensibility, is often understood to be the poems' most pressing Enlightenment context.[5] These debates might have been felt in Scotland with particular force as a consequence of political union with England, and rehearsed in Macpherson's time through militia debates, but there are other examples too: Paul Usherwood (2004) has noted the importance of the language of civic humanism within the establishment of important dimensions of the art scene in the North East of England in the early nineteenth century. These South West writers are equally attracted to the heroic possibilities of an Ossianically inflected past. Hole's 'Ode on the Imagination' articulates both the martial valour and the civilising power of feeling he saw in the Ossianic world. On the one hand we are offered the traditional Homeric appeal to heroic posterity:

Again inspir'd with glory's charms,
The dauntless warriors call to arms,
   To snatch the unfading wreath of praise:
Each hopes to gain a deathless name,
To live renown'd, or die with fame,
   The theme of future days

                                         (Hole 1772:10)

On the other, the sentimental reflection encouraged by bardic song:

The melting lay their rage controls,
And calms to peace their furious souls:
Thy charms, destructive fame! Inspire
Their breasts no more with martial fire:
Each hero mourns some breathless friend;
Compassion's tender tears descend:
Their useless arms bestrew the plain;
And the keen falchion thirsts for blood in vain.

                                         (Hole 1772:12)

These two dimensions must be kept in balance: without 'compassion's tender tears' the appeal of 'glory's charms' lead only to 'destructive fame'; without the bracing motivation of the need to earn a 'a deathless name' through heroic acts, we are left with only military defeat or redundancy, a field strewn with 'useless arms' not as the aftermath of battle (the traditional image) but on account of the emasculation of their bearers. Hole's *Arthur* goes on to be animated by precisely this tension, and is never more Ossianic than in its admiration for heroes possessing both an astonishing capacity for violence and what the poem repeatedly terms 'the sympathetic breast'. Thus the opening to the poem is highly Ossianic not only on account of the belatedness it invokes (the physical symptoms of which could come directly from many others as well as Macpherson), but in the models of virtue and heroism it validates:

Those days are past: the vocal strain no more
Is heard, that charm'd our fathers' hearts of yore.
Now, sole memorial of their echoing halls,
Clasp'd by rude ivy, nod the mould'ring walls:
In cumb'rous heaps are stretch'd the stately towers,
While noxious weeds usurp the roseate bow'rs;
And, long enfolded in death's cold embrace,
Silent have slept the minstrel's gentle race.
Yet still his name survives; nor deem it vain,
That one, the meanest of the tuneful train,
Caught by the lofty theme, with feebler lays
Presumes t'unfold a tale of other days.

Such, as of old to Fancy's ear addrest,
Perchance had struck the sympathising breast;
When lovely were our maids, and brave our youth,
When virtue valour crown'd, and beauty truth.

(Hole 1789: 4)

Hole's is a Britain beset, fighting off foreign aggression in the name of national values, notably liberty. His vision of a West Country Arthur can be placed alongside that of friends such as Downman and Polwhele in creating a mythical West Country based upon a warrior virtue imbued with modern politeness. Hole's *Arthur* was published in the year of George III's visit to the region and the fall of the Bastille. Within three years this East Devon *literati* would be an enthusiastic component of the Church and King Movement, and through their publications were eager to project a loyalist identity for their region and history.[6] The interest of these writers in *Ossian* and its sentimental civic heroism are part of a nationwide interest in the creation of an identity that accommodated the values of traditional citizenship within eighteenth-century polite society.

That said, *Ossian*'s utility went beyond being a model of literary and social value upon which a cultural identity could be built. Indeed the malleability of *Ossian* belies the stability any talk of foundational texts implies, since the flipside of the imaginative intervention the text licenses is *Ossian*'s ability to act as a cipher for aesthetic and indeed ethnic characteristics outwith the compass of Macpherson's original. As such it is important to register the ways in which *Ossian*'s sensibility is open to being rewritten in the process of mediating a South West past. I will therefore conclude with two variations discernible in one of the otherwise Ossianic poems already discussed, Polwhele's 'Castle of Tintagel'.

The first reinvention has been touched on previously, that of ethnic identity. With the (albeit significant) exception of Hole's *Arthur*, the heroic past of the South West evoked by these writers was broadly Teutonic. Swete's essay on 'British' monuments ultimately suspected that they were as likely to be the handwork of Saxons as Ancient Britons, and elides the two on the grounds that it was impossible to tell the difference (1796b: 126). Indeed the Cornishman Polwhele, whose seven-volume *History of Cornwall* (1803–1808) is seen by some as a key text of Cornish cultural consciousness, offers a good example of the perils of critical anachronism on our part when we assume the inevitably Celtic nature of Cornwall and Cornish history as it was understood in the period. This is the argument to 'The Castle of Tintagel':

In a battle between the Saxons and Danes, Arvina, the beautiful daughter of Sweno King of Denmark, having been taken prisoner by Odred, Chief of the Saxons, is confined in the Castle of Tintadgel. There the lovely Mourner is represented as surrounded with every circumstance of horror. At length, in fancy, she sees the ghost of her father, and swoons away and dies.

(Polwhele 1781: 330)

Tintagel is of course one of the key sites of the Celtic West. Unusual testimony to the non-anglophone otherness of the name was registered by Polwhele's friend and patron, Edmund Rack (in whose book the poem first appeared), who noted that 'I will take particular care of the copy of Tagtongtidal (what d'ye call it) – your breakteethly Cornish names were never formed for English organs – this is a bad word for poetry' (Polwhele 1826: 1.114). Seen one way, this is an archetypal example of the sanction of the Ossianic idiom, by which the unfamiliar and the strange is brought into mainstream anglophone culture. Yet at the same time, this early account of a mythic history to Tintadgel is a matter between Saxon and Dane, and nothing to do with the 'Celtic Cornish', a point all the more striking considering the linguistic strangeness of Cornish registered by Rack.

Polwhele's argument to this poem contains another difference from the classically Ossianic. Macpherson's sentimentalism is as vulnerable as any other to the charge that it takes an unhealthily vicarious interest in lachrymose scenes of grief, and to R.F. Brissenden's accusation of 'moral defeatism' (1974: 126). Yet it is not notably nasty in its vicariousness. This is the kind of scene that provides the inspiration for Polwhele's poem:

> It is night; – I am alone, forlorn on the hill of storms. The wind is heard in the mountain. The torrent shrieks down the rock. No hut receives me from the rain; forlorn on the hill of winds.

> Rise moon! From behind thy clouds; stars of the night appear! Lead me, some light, to the place where my love rests from the toil of the chace! [...] the stream and the wind roar; nor can I hear the voice of my love.

> [...]

> But who are these that lie beyond me on the heath? Are they my love and my brother? – Speak to me, O my friends! They answer not. My soul is tormented with fears. – Ah they are dead. [...] Dear were ye both to me! What shall I say in your praise? Thou wert fair on the hill among thousands; he was terrible in fight. [...]

> Oh! From the rock of the hill; from the top of the windy mountain, speak ye ghost of the dead! Speak, I will not be afraid. – whither are ye gone to rest? In what cave of the hill shall I find you? No feeble voice is on the wind: no answer half-drowned in the storms of the hill.

> I sit in my grief. I wait for morning in my tears. Rear the tomb, ye friends of the dead; but close it not till Colma come. My life flies away like a dream: why should I stay behind? Here shall I rest with my friends, by the stream of the sounding rock.

> (Macpherson 1762: 210–212)

At first pass, Polwhele's envisaged setting could have been accommodated within *Ossian* quite easily, but on closer examination the differences go beyond the ethnic identity of the suffering maiden. They are best encapsulated in one sentence that finds little sanction in Macpherson's mood piece: 'there the *lovely* Mourner is represented as surrounded with *every circumstance of horror*' (my emphasis). There is little horror in Macpherson, at least not of this sort. In this one sentence, and its slightly queasy juxtaposition of loveliness and horror, Polwhele takes a decisive step in the direction of a Gothic more associated with Matthew 'Monk' Lewis than the sentimental melancholy of Macpherson.

Polwhele had a career-long interest in the history, literature, people and customs of Devon and Cornwall. Yet almost every document of his interest in the past contains a streak of Gothic terror and viciousness one stage removed from Macpherson's ancient sensibility. From his earliest published work (when he was 17) 'The Fate of Lewellyn; or the Druid's Sacrifice' (1777) through to perhaps his most ambitious Cornish romance *Fair Isobel of Cotehele* (1815), which opens with an account of a druidic 'shivering sacrifice of blood', he retained a taste for the bloodthirsty within his evocation of the ancient past. Joanne Parker has acutely noted that Polwhele's *History of Devonshire* represents the 'first concerted and developed endeavour to assert for Devon a Druidical inheritance to rival not only Borlase's Cornwall, but even Stukeley's Wiltshire' (2010: 23). However this was no cosy accommodation and not exclusively an evocation of patriot liberty. It was also the revelation of a buried heart of darkness, of potentially disruptive anti-social energies and primitive forces underlying the settled state of modern Britain that, in the case of the anti-Jacobin Polwhele, it is not hard to read in terms of a post-Terror Gothic and what Philip Connell terms the 'uneasy negotiations with more politicised and refractory representations of the national past' (2006: 192). Further and detailed analysis of the impact of the French Revolution on cultural myth-making by the likes of Polwhele is a matter for another occasion. In the context of the immediate argument about the way in which *Ossian* is operative within this cultural milieu, this difference between *Ossian*'s Highland Gothic and Polwhele's Cornish Gothic is an eloquent example of the way Macpherson's poems were adopted and adapted, were channelled and diverted, and were carried into the bloodstream of English poetry, evolving as they went.

Notes

1   There have been a multitude of essays on Macpherson in recent years, but as a single point of reference for *Ossian* a recent and very useful point of departure is Stafford 2011.

2   Works in this area are now legion, but see as a representative sample on top of various others quoted throughout this essay: Borsay 1989; Brewer 1997; Clark 2000; Kent 2000; Uglow 2003; Berry and Gregory 2004; Davis, Duncan and Sorenson 2004; Jenkins 2005; Stafford 2010; Pittock 2008; Moore 2009; Chandler 2010.

3   Coleridge also wrote 'The Complaint of Ninathoma' and began the libretto for an opera based on the poem 'Carthon'. Macpherson is variously mentioned in the notebooks, usually in connection with music. A fugitive Ossianic voice has been heard in much of his work: see Dunn 1969. Coleridge knew of the activities of the Exeter group central to this essay, may have helped write a paper presented to the

Exeter Society of Gentleman and referred to it as part of his own efforts to set up a literary/philosophical society while at Cambridge.
4 'Ode, On Reading Mr Hole's *Arthur, or the Northern Enchantment*' in Hugh Downman, *Poems*, 2nd edition, (1790).
5 See as a selection: Potkay 1992; Mitchell 1999; Weinbrot 1995; Moore 2003.
6 Such projection went further than mythic history, as one of Sebastian Emmett's contribution to Polwhele 1792 illustrates (Emmett 1792). Lines 'Written on Viewing the Improvements at Pynes-House, the Seat of Sir Stafford Henry Northcote, Bart. Near Exeter. 1789' demonstrate the place of house and garden design in the overall project of regional assertiveness in the cause of national identity (for more on this general point, see Moore 2009).

Bibliography

Anon. (1858) *Ossian, His Principle Poems, Translated into English Verse*, London: Adam and Charles Black.

Arnold, M. (1886) 'On the Study of Celtic Literature'; reprinted in Super, R.H. (ed.) (1962) *The Prose Works of Matthew Arnold*, vol. 3, Ann Arbor: University of Michigan Press.

Baines, P. (1997) 'Ossianic Geographies: Fingalian Figures on the Scottish Tour, 1760–1830', *Scotlands* 4.1: 44–61.

Baker, D. E. (1763) *The Muse of Ossian, A Dramatic Poem in Three Acts*, Edinburgh: for the author.

Berry, H. and Gregory, J. (eds) (2004) *Creating and Consuming Culture in North East England, 1660–1830*, Aldershot: Ashgate.

Borsay, P. (1989) *The English Urban Renaissance: Culture and Society in the Provincial Town 1660–1770*, Oxford: Oxford University Press.

Brewer, J. (1997) *The Pleasures of the Imagination: English Culture in the Eighteenth Century*, London: Harper Collins.

Brissenden, R.F. (1974) *Virtue in Distress: Studies in the Novel of Sentiment from Richardson to Sade*, Basingstoke: MacMillan.

Chandler, D. (2010) '"The Athens of England": Norwich as a Literary Centre in the Late Eighteenth Century', *Eighteenth-Century Studies* 43.2: 171–192.

Clark, P. (2000) *British Clubs and Societies, 1580–1800: The Origins of the Associational World*, Oxford: Oxford University Press.

Coleridge S. T. (1997) *Complete Poems*, ed William Keach, London: Penguin.

Connell, P. (2006) 'British Identities and the Politics of Ancient Poetry in Later Eighteenth-Century England', *The Historical Journal* 49: 161–192.

Davis, L., Duncan I. and Sorenson J. (eds) (2004) *Scotland and the Borders of Romanticism*, Cambridge: Cambridge University Press, 2004.

de Gategno, P. (1989) *James Macpherson*, Boston, MA: Twayne.

Downman, H. (1784) *Editha: A Tragedy*, London and Exeter: Grigg.

Downman, H. (1790) 'Ode, On Reading Mr Hole's *Arthur, or the Northern Enchantment*' in *Poems*, 2nd edn, Exeter: R. Trewman.

Drewe, S. (1792) 'The Rapt Bard; Written in the Valley of Stones, near Linton in Devonshire' in Polwhele, R. (ed.) *Poems, Chiefly by Gentlemen of Devon and Cornwall*, 2 volumes, Bath: R. Cruttwell.

Dunn, J. (1969) 'Coleridge's Debt to Macpherson', *Studies in Scottish Literature* 7: 76–89.

Emmett S. (1792), 'Written on Viewing the Improvements at Pynes-House, the Seat of Sir Stafford Henry Northcote, Bart. Near Exeter. 1789' in Polwhele, R. (ed.) *Poems Chiefly by Gentlemen of Devonshire and Cornwall*, Bath: R. Cruttwell.

Hill, T.F. (1782/3) 'Interesting Light on the Ossian Controversy'; reprinted in Moore, D. (ed.) (2004), *Ossian and Ossianism*, vol.3, London: Taylor and Francis.

Hole, Richard (1772) *Fingal, a poem in Six Books, by Ossian. Translated from the Original Gaelic by Mr Macpherson; and rendered into verse from that translation*, Oxford: Fletcher *et al.*

Hole, Richard (1789) *Arthur; or the Northern Enchantment*, London: G. G. J. and J. Robinson

Hole, Richard (1792a) 'Ode to the Imagination' in Polwhele, R. (ed.), *Poems Chiefly by Gentleman of Devonshire and Cornwall* Bath: R Cruttwell.

Hole, Richard (1792b) 'The Tomb of Gunnar, Imitated from an Ancient Islandic Fragment preserved in Batholine's Danish Antiquities' in Polwhele, R. (ed.), *Poems Chiefly by Gentleman of Devonshire and Cornwall* Bath: R Cruttwell.

Jenkins, G. H. (ed.) (2005) *A Rattleskull Genius: The Many Faces of Iolo Morganwg*, Cardiff: University of Wales Press.

Kent, A. M. (2000) *The Literature of Cornwall: Continuity, Identity, Difference 1000–2000*, Bristol: Redcliffe Press.

Leerseen, J. (1998) 'Ossianic Liminality: Between Native Tradition and PreRomantic Taste' in Stafford, F. and Gaskill, H. (eds), *From Gaelic to Romantic: Ossianic Translations*, Amsterdam: Rodopi, 1–16.

Macpherson, J. (1762) *Fingal and Other Poems*; reprinted in Moore, D. (ed.) (2004) *Ossian and Ossianism*, vol.2, London: Taylor and Francis.

Macpherson, J. (1763) *Temora and Other Poems*; reprinted in Moore, D. (ed.) (2004) *Ossian and Ossianism*, vol. 2, London: Taylor and Francis.

Merriman, J. (1973) *The Flower of Kings: A Study of the Arthurian Legend in England between 1485 and 1835*, Lawrence, KS: University of Kansas Press.

Mitchell, S. (1999) 'James Macpherson's Ossian and the Empire of Sentiment', *British Journal of Eighteenth-Century Studies* 22.2: 155–72.

Moore, D. (2003) *Enlightenment and Romance in James Macpherson's Poems of Ossian*, Aldershot: Ashgate.

Moore, D. (2004) *Ossian and Ossianism*, 4 volumes, London: Taylor and Francis.

Moore, D. (2009) 'Patriotism, Politics and National Identity in the South West of England in the Late Eighteenth Century', *English Literary History*, 76.3: 739–62.

Mulholland, J. (2009) 'James Macpherson's Ossian Poems, Oral Traditions, and the Invention of Voice', *Oral Tradition*, 24.2: 393–414.

Parker, J. (2010) '"More Wondrous Far than Egypt's Boasted Pyramids": the South West's Megaliths in the Romantic Period', in Roe, N. (ed.) *English Romantic Writers and the West Country*, Basingstoke: Palgrave, 15–36.

Pittock, Murray (2008) *Scottish and Irish Romanticism*, Oxford: Oxford University Press.

Pocock, J. G. A. (1973) 'British History: a plea for a New Subject' reprinted in Pocock, J.G.A. (2005) *The Discovery of Islands: Essays in British History*, Cambridge: Cambridge University Press, 24–46.

Polwhele, R. (1777) *The Fate of Lewellyn: Or the Druid's Sacrifice*, Bath: R. Cruttwell.

Polwhele, R. (1781) 'The Castle of Tintadgel; Or the Captive Princess of Denmark', in Rack, E. *Essays, Letters and Poems*, Bath: R Cruttwell.

Polwhele R. (ed.) (1792) *Poems Chiefly by Gentlemen of Devonshire and Cornwall*, Bath: R. Cruttwell.

Polwhele, R. (1815) *Fair Isabel of Cotehele: A Cornish Romance*, London: Cawthorn.

Polwhele, R. (1826) *Traditions and Recollections: Domestic, Clerical, Literary*, 2 volumes, London: Nichols and Son.

Potkay, A. (1992) 'Virtue and Manners in Macpherson's *Poems of Ossian*', *PMLA* 107: 120–131.

Radcliffe, D. H. (2004) 'Hole, Richard (*bap.* 1746, *d.* 1803)', in *Oxford Dictionary of National Biography*, Oxford: Oxford University Press. Online. Available HTTP: <http://www.oxforddnb.com/view/article/135022004> (accessed 30 Nov 2004).

Roe, N. (2010) 'Introduction', in Roe, N. (ed.), *English Romantic Writers and the West Country*, Basingstoke: Palgrave, 1–14.

Stafford, F. (2010) *Local Attachments: The Province of Poetry*, Oxford: Oxford University Press.

Stafford, F. (2011) 'Romantic Macpherson', in Pittock, M. (ed.) *The Edinburgh Companion to Scottish Romanticism*, Edinburgh: Edinburgh University Press, 27–38.

Stukeley W. (1763) 'A Letter from Dr Stukeley to Mr Macpherson on his Publication of Fingal and Temora. With a print of Cathmor's Shield' reprinted in Moore, D. (ed.) (2004) *Ossian and Ossianism*, vol.3, London: Taylor and Francis.

Swete J. (1796a), 'Of Sepulture in General, and the Sepulchral Single Stones Erect', in *Essays by a Society of Gentlemen at Exeter*, Exeter: R. Trewman.

Swete J. (1796b) 'On Some of the More Remarkable British Monuments in Devon', in *Essays by a Society of Gentlemen at Exeter*, Exeter: R. Trewman.

Uglow, J. (2003) *The Lunar Men: the Friends who Made the Future*, London: Faber.

Usherwood, P. (2004) 'Newcastle's First Art Exhibitions and the Language of Civic Humanism', in Berry, H. and Gregory J. (eds) *Creating and Consuming Culture in North East England, 1660–1830*, Aldershot: Ashgate, 141–51.

Weinbrot, H. (1995) *Britannia's Issue: The Rise of British Literature from Dryden to Ossian*, Cambridge: Cambridge University Press.

8

GEOLOGICAL FOLKLORE

Robert Hunt and the industrial, aesthetic and racial composition of 'Celtic' Cornwall

Shelley Trower

Robert Hunt was a mine surveyor who wrote geological works, such as *On Mines and Mining*, as well as poetry and folklore, from the late 1820s until the 1880s. He was employed as the Keeper of Mining Records at the Museum of Practical Geology in London from 1845 to 1883. His employer, Henry de La Beche, was the director of the Geological Survey, a government-funded project set up to examine and map the geology of Britain in detail, and Hunt's role was to gather and to consolidate information such as statistics about mineral production.

De La Beche's project was typical of the growing professionalisation of geology. He wanted paid employees to carry out the work of the project in provincial surveys rather than to leave this work in the 'amateur' hands of local men (see Secord 1986: 238 and 244). In the process of establishing its status as a modern scientific profession, during the nineteenth century, geology at times struggled to distinguish itself from literary works in order to promote itself as objective, as uncorrupted by imagination, but historians and critics have also observed their continuing connections and inseparability (see, for example, Wyatt 1995; O'Connor 2007; Buckland 2010; Heringman 2010). Noah Heringman argues that while geology begins to declare its separateness from unscientific 'sensational narratives' early in the nineteenth century, both geology and poetry shared the same historical conditions – namely cultural preoccupation with landscape aesthetics and demand for mineral resources – an argument that I will here develop and extend into the later nineteenth century.

Hunt's work in this context is an interesting example of how geology and literature continued to be intertwined. This chapter demonstrates the significance of this geologist-poet, whose work in contrast to other writers such as the 'Romantic scientist' Humphry Davy has as yet received almost no critical attention (his *The Poetry of Science* is an exception due mainly to Charles Dickens' review of it in *Household Words*, the review normally being quoted rather than Hunt's work itself).[1] It will bring together Hunt's various forms of narrative – namely his mining treatises, poetry and folklore collection – to illustrate how particular rocks are used to ground regionalist claims about the distinctiveness of particular places and peoples. In this case the focus is specifically on how granite has served to distinguish 'Celtic' Cornwall – with its mineral wealth and sublime landscapes – from a more 'sedimentary' England, and, further, to distinguish the 'primitive' Celtic race from the more 'civilised' English.

The mineral aesthetics of granite landscapes

The specimens displayed at the Museum of Practical Geology were supposed to illustrate sections of the maps of the Geological Survey. In its discussion of the specimens of granite, for instance, Hunt's *Descriptive Guide to the Museum of Practical Geology* (1859) refers to the granite districts of western England, coloured pink on the map suspended on the wall of the museum (18). Granite is the first rock to be discussed in this guide, as in his other monographs such as *On Mines and Mining* (1878) and *British Mining* (1884), and its presence in Cornwall is considered at greatest length. The presence of granite is a key indicator, Hunt observes, of mineral veins, which maps can usefully help people to locate. Hunt also uses the map to highlight more general differences between the rocks of eastern England and those of more westerly areas, such as Cornwall, which contain the 'useful metals':

> To understand [...] the conditions under which lodes or veins are formed, it is necessary that the structure of our rock formations should be studied. If we examine with attention a geological map, made from a careful survey of the British Isles, we cannot but observe a marked distinction between the rocks which occur in the eastern counties, and those which distinguish the midland and western districts of England and the whole of Wales [...]. Throughout the whole of the eastern region there is almost an entire absence of those metalliferous minerals, other than iron, which are of commercial value [...]. To the south and south-west of these rocks, we reach the Old Red Sandstone, or Devonian series – and in Leicestershire [an anomaly here, as a midland region], Devonshire, and Cornwall, Granitic and Greenstone rocks occur, with Felspathic Traps and Basalt; all these rocks presenting, in the last-named counties, marked systems of lode formations rich in ores of the useful metals.
>
> (1884: 193)

Geographers have shown that maps can be used as tools for the consolidation of central government, by projecting an image of a cohesive nation for example (see Daniels 1998: 114), but at the same time we see here how maps can also make regional differences clearly visible, highlighting a 'marked distinction' in this case between the rocks of the eastern and western counties. As Rachel Hewitt puts it, 'maps assisted the process by which Britain's component regions were integrated into a unified nation' (2011: 4), but local geologists also resisted such integration, not least through the production of an independent, separate map of Cornwall (for discussion of the mapping of Cornwall see Naylor 2011). Hunt seems both to consider the nation as a whole and to emphasise, repeatedly, the distinctiveness of regions within it, most especially Cornwall. His mining publications operate within the framework of Britain (the title *British Mining* spells this out from the outset) and refer to the national map, but within this context he tends to begin with Cornwall and to discuss this region in particular depth, prioritising and highlighting its distinctiveness by drawing attention to its particular minerals and landscapes, which I will elaborate on shortly.

William Buckland, who became President of the Geological Society of London in 1824, similarly describes in his *Geology and Mineralogy* (1836) three very different geological regions within Britain, from the point of view of three travellers. The first begins in Cornwall, then travels through Devon to Wales, and then via the Isle of Man to Scotland, experiencing Britain as a 'thinly-peopled region of barren mountains' (1). The second crosses the 'Midland Counties' and finds a 'continued succession of fertile hills and valleys, thickly overspread with towns and cities', and a large 'manufacturing population, whose industry is maintained by the coal with which the strata of these districts are abundantly interspersed'. At this point Buckland includes a footnote referring to how 'any correct geological map of England' will show that the populous towns, including Bristol, Birmingham, Nottingham, Liverpool and Manchester, 'are placed upon strata belonging to the single geological formation of the new red sandstone' (1–2). The most convenient map to which he refers readers is a version of Greenough's map of England, published by the Geological Society of London. Buckland goes on to break down England into one further division: the third 'foreigner' travels from the coast of Dorset to Yorkshire over agricultural plains of sedimentary rocks such as chalk, 'without a single mountain, or mine, or coal-pit' (2). With the help of the geological map, then, Buckland, like Hunt, identifies 'great divisions' resulting from geological differences between rocks ranging from the primary series of the west and north to the limestone and chalk of the easterly regions. On the one hand the map seems to hold the nation together in one piece, but on the other it depends on exclusions and highlights differences within. Further, such geological divisions are said to determine populations: their numbers, their occupations, their physical condition, which depends 'on the more or less salubrious nature of their employments; and their moral condition, as far as it is connected with these employments' (3). Such distinctions between the rocks of eastern and western regions – and thus the industries, landscapes and people of these regions – are echoed through the rest of the nineteenth century, including in Hunt's work, as we shall see.

Hunt's focus in his museum guide is on differences in mineral wealth, but he also describes mineral wealth as inseparable from a landscape with particular aesthetic qualities. In describing such qualities in *British Mining* he again distinguishes Cornwall from the rest of England, this time in terms of the 'beautiful' and 'golden' plants that grow on its granite as well as the shapes of the granite itself, the hills and 'picturesque' valleys:

> In Cornwall, ranges of Granite hills covered with huge masses of 'moorstone' (Granite), heaped in fantastic forms, usually mark a mineral boundary. Gently undulating plains spread away from the bases of those hills, barren of vegetation, save the beautiful heath and the golden furze, which, when in full flower, give all the appearance of a garden to an otherwise waste country. These regions are commonly cut through by deep and often picturesque valleys, and within the shelter they afford, numerous plants, and especially shrubs, grow with a luxuriance not to be seen in any other part of England.
>
> (Hunt 1884: 398)

The 'golden furze', and uniquely rich 'luxuriance' of the plants in the Cornish valleys, then, seem to be a reflection of the wealth of minerals lying underneath the nearby surface, both of which apparently exist in more abundance in Cornwall than anywhere else in England. In a sense Cornwall is to England what England is to the rest of the world, according to the opening sentence of Hunt's *British Mining*: 'The mineral resources of the United Kingdom have been far in advance of those of any country in the world' (v). Hunt seems to express a sense of national pride in Cornwall that echoes that of the local geologists writing in early issues of the *Transactions of the Royal Geological Society of Cornwall*. In the second volume, published in 1822, John Hawkins observes that the German state of Saxony took the lead in the science of geology largely because of its mineral resources, and that Cornwall is even better situated to become a 'country' of geological importance. It exhibits its mineral deposits 'in a still more striking point of view', for instance, 'while the facilities for observation are, upon the whole, much greater than they can be in any inland country' (3–4). (Hawkins is presumably referring here to how the coastline surrounding most of Cornwall allows more rocks and strata formations to be visible to the naked eye than in a landlocked region like Saxony.)

Hawkins's use of the word 'country' here is interesting, as its meaning seems to slip between its different senses: between its earliest meaning (as Latin *contrata*) of 'a tract of land spread out before an observer' and its later meaning of 'native land' (from the thirteenth century onwards). In its general use as native land, 'country' includes the people who live in it, and became comparable to, and even interchangeable with 'nation', as Raymond Williams indicates. 'Nation' referred originally to a racial group and later to a politically-organised grouping, and although it began to be used in a clearly political sense from the sixteenth century onwards, 'country' remained more common in referring to the political unit of people until the eighteenth century

(Williams 1976: 71 and 178). What is striking about the frequent use of the word by geologists in the early nineteenth century is how it slips from the sense of a tract of land to a more political suggestion that Cornwall is a nation in its own right, distinct from England; a nation among nations. Hawkins goes on to propose that Cornwall's claims 'to be ranked among the primitive countries of the globe, as far as our patriotic feelings are concerned, will be readily admitted' (1822: 4). Hunt also adopts the term 'country', for the most part in its sense of a tract of land, but occasionally with more ambiguity, as where he refers to 'that important mining country, Cornwall' (1859: 91). Such usage points the way to the increasing use of geology to support the notion of Cornwall – geologically distinctive as it is – as a nation, as I will go on to discuss in this chapter.

In Hunt's *British Mining*, as in articles by members of Cornwall's geological society, the mineral qualities of Cornwall are of primary importance but are everywhere accompanied by accounts of its impressive landscapes. The wealth of its minerals seems reflected in the luxuriance of the plants in its picturesque valleys, which surpasses that which may be found anywhere else in England, as we have seen. In Hunt's other writings it is the sublimity of landscape that takes priority. An early poem, *The Mount's Bay* (1829), most explicitly refers to the sublimity of Cornwall's rocks, seen from the perspective of a traveller. Again and again this poem describes the 'wild and rugged rocks', designed to gratify 'the tourist's mood / To seek for a sublimer food'. For Hunt, the rocks of Cornwall can clearly provide more than mineral value; they can inspire their viewer with the thrill of sublimity:

> Or traveller – would you seek to see
> The beetling rocks immensity;
> Mount them and cast your eyes below;
> Thrilling the strong electric blow,
> Which all must feel, when from such height
> They gaze on depths majestic might. –
> On this sublime and favour'd spot
> Nature has wrought herself a grot; –
> And as it were in wantonness
> Robed Terror in Fantastic dress.

(Hunt 1829: 18–19)

Cornwall's landscapes are of course strikingly different from the rolling green fields of south-eastern and middle England. Geographers and other commentators frequently observe that such fertile, pastoral landscapes – threatened by industrialisation, ever-growing cities, and war – were crucial to the idea of England from the eighteenth century onwards, in literature, art and music.[2] William Blake provides an early canonical description of 'England's green and pleasant Land' in opposition to the 'dark Satanic mills' of new industry.[3] Romantic writers around the turn of the nineteenth century began to see new value in such orderly rural landscapes at the point when these seemed threatened by industrialisation and urbanisation. But Romantics also turned to the rockier landscapes of the north and west. Noah Heringman considers how the primitive landscapes of the Lake and Peak Districts functioned as representative national landscapes. The Peak District in particular combines a '"primitive" or disorderly karst topography' with 'increasing economic productivity', presenting a healthy, authentically natural, disorderly national landscape. The character of the nationally representative landscape thus depends 'on a relation between wildness and cultivation, on a productive disorder' (Heringman 2010: 241). Cornwall provides another location for such productive disorder, though at the same time as being representative of the nation's wealth of mineral resources it is depicted as unique, as different from the rest of England, possibly even a country in its own right. Rocks contribute to a sense of both national and regional importance and identity in their shaping of productive and distinctive landscapes, landscapes with mineral and aesthetic value, and, furthermore, in their association with the particular history and traditions of the natives or 'races' who live on them.

Primitive rocks and traditions

The most ancient rocks, to be found in such northern and westerly regions as the Peak District and Cornwall, tend to be associated with the oldest British traditions. Granite, in particular, was still widely thought to be the oldest, the most 'primitive' of all rocks, and to be highly resilient – it had survived since ancient times. (The Huttonian view that granite is an igneous rock and can thus intrude into previously formed sedimentary rocks won out in most circles by the mid-nineteenth century over Abraham Werner's theory, that granite was the first of all rocks to form in the primordial sea. Some formations of granite could be therefore be more recent, though James Hutton continued to use the term 'primitive' and granite often continued to be considered the oldest of rocks – see, for example, Wyatt 1995: 43–6.) Thus Hunt speculates in *The Poetry of Science* that the globe was once made out of one homogenous rock which may now exist in 'our granites' (1849: 312).[4] Much poetry of the time testified to the awesome power of the rocky cliffs to withstand the onslaught of the waves, to survive for millenia.[5] Hunt's poem again speaks of the sublime age of granite, which is associated here with the ancient traditions of the British race:

> 'Midst pensile rocks, in might sublime,
> Like some old registers of Time;
> Whose iron tablets have withstood
> The Lash of storms, and Ocean Flood,
> I view Boscawan's awful throne

Sacred to Druid rites alone,
Whose granite columns dare the blast,
But like Penumbras of the past
Tell not the present human race,
The secrets of this holy place.

(1829: 63)

Hunt alludes here to both the ancient past of the rocks and to an ancient race, associating the vast age of the rocks – those 'old registers of Time' – with the history of humankind. This becomes a savage history, as he goes on to imagine the ritual sacrifices of virgins whose blood dyed the granite crags. For the traveller, then, Cornwall offers more than wild, frightening landscapes; it is also a place of mystery and ancient traditions. The rocks seem to promise to put their beholder – in this case Hunt, and thereby his readers – in touch with the past. Musing upon them, he writes that 'Imagination takes me back / The course of ages, o'er the track' (1829: 63) to recall the 'mystic rites' through a kind of time travel which, as Ralph O'Connor observes, was a frequent imaginary device through the nineteenth century. O'Connor is one of a number of critics who explore the connections between geology and fiction, commenting that geology marketed itself as the key to facts more sensational than fiction, such as facts about prehistoric dinosaurs.

Although geologists at times aimed to banish literary narrative from their discipline – especially anything associated with that disreputable genre of romance – narrative was not always a problem; rather, for some geological writers, it presented great possibility in its potential to enable their work to reach wide audiences as itself a literary kind of sensation.[6] The Scottish literary geologist Hugh Miller was one of the most popular geological writers who presented his factual, geological work as sensational, claiming in *The Old Red Sandstone* that 'no man who enters the geological field in quest of the wonderful, need pass [...] from the true to the fictitious' (cited in O'Connor 2007: 3). Several times in his writings Miller employs a technique of gazing upon rocks – an exposed piece of cliff, a fossil – which then project him back to a prehistoric world of strange creatures. Hunt himself clearly wanted to get beyond the economic applications of geology, and of science in general, promoting the idea that the facts of science are poetic in *The Poetry of Science*. '[S]cientific facts', claimed Hunt, 'have a value superior to their mere economic applications.' The 'truths' generated by 'the labours of the chemist in his cell,' or by 'the multitudinous observations of the astronomer on his tower [...] give to the soul of the poet those realities to which he aspires in his high imaginings' (1849: vii and xvvii–xviii). For Hunt, as for Miller, the real world is as strange, if not stranger than an imagined world. 'Man', he continues, 'stands in the midst of a wonderful world, and an infinite variety of phenomena arise around him in strange form and magical disposition, like the phantasma of a restless night [...]. Truth is stranger than fiction' (xx).

'Primitive character'

Rocks, it seems, could unlock the secrets of an ancient, strange and wonderful past: not only the prehuman past of fish and trilobites but also aspects of human prehistory such as the sacrificial rites of druids. Many of the earlier geologists in Cornwall's Geological Society were similarly interested in ancient traditions and folklore: in myths of prehistoric stones, of the lost land of Lyonesse (see, for example, Boase 1822: 133; Barham 1827: 102). Geology and folklore were considered to be comparable occupations; the search for the ancient history of rocks runs parallel to the quest for ancient human traditions. Historians of science and literature have observed in particular how Hugh Miller's fascination with the deep time of geology blended together with his work as an antiquarian, as he saw geological and human history as existing on a continuum. For Miller, the antiquities and folktales of a 'Celtic race' were comparable to fossils, of which he was also a keen collector, and were in danger of suffering the fate of extinction like the now fossilised plant and animal species. As Simon Knell and Michael Taylor put it, 'Geology merged with local history and folklore – all "libraries" of the past. […] Like books and oral traditions, the fossils provided a means to extend the imagined past back through time' (2006: 85 and 94. See also Paradis 1996). By presenting their activities as comparable to that of geologists, folklorists and anthropologists increasingly attempted to claim for their own disciplines the professional scientific status that geology was managing for the most part to acquire by the mid-nineteenth century (see O'Connor 2007: 438–439; Bennett 1994: 25; Kuklick 1991: 43–4).

Miller's focus was mostly on fossils, whereas Hunt was most interested in 'primitive' rocks, which seem to reflect the 'primitive character' of inhabitants. As remains of a primordial past, both fossils and primitive rocks provide images for other kinds of survivals in the modern world, including ancient superstitions and races, but while fossils often seem to provide evidence of a progressive, evolutionary history, of old species and races giving way to new civilisations, 'primitive' rocks are a kind of anachronism, an eruption from the past, resistant to change or evolution, much like the 'lower races'. As John Haller observes, scientific theories about race tended to support the idea that evolution does not operate on the 'lower races', who are thus unfit for future development. The evolutionary progress of 'the Caucasian' is apparently far superior to 'the lower races' who 'broke into the modern world as mere "survivals" from the past' (Haller 1971: xiii). In 'The Giants', the opening chapter of his folklore collection *Popular Romances of the West of England*, Hunt locates the legendary race of giants inhabiting a distinctly primitive environment:

> Giants, and every form of giant-idea, belong to the wilds of nature. I have never discovered the slightest indication of the existence of a tradition of giants, of the true legendary type, in a fertile valley or in a well-cultivated plain. Wherever there yet linger the faint shadows of the legendary

giant, there the country still retains much of its native wildness, and the inhabitants have, to a great extent, preserved their primitive character.

(Hunt 1968: 36)

Again, here, Hunt is seeking to understand the Celtic character and its folklore much as he sought information about the primitive rocks underneath. The rocky land and its natives seem closely related, inseparable, even part of each other. Hunt frames the folktales from the outset with the aesthetics of the wild, rocky landscapes of the south-west region. He begins this opening chapter on giants by describing 'the uncultivated tracts which still maintain their wildness, austerely and sullenly, against the march of cultivation', where 'we are certain of finding rude masses of rock which have some relation to the giants'. Seated on 'the granite masses' on the hills of Cornwall he speculates about the character of those 'primitive' inhabitants who believe in giants (35). Giants 'can exist only in the memories of those races', Hunt goes on to claim, 'who are born and live amidst the sublime phenomena of nature' (37). While the inhabitants themselves seem primitive like the rocky landscape, they seem to share the widespread belief that giants have actively shaped such landscapes: Hunt refers to legends such as that giants built St Michael's Mount, and that their games with quoits and marbles explain the scattered presence of great boulders. 'There is scarcely a pile of rocks around our western shore upon which the giants have not left their impress', writes Hunt, and 'in nearly every part of the country where granite rocks prevail, the monuments of the giants may be found' (43).[7]

For Hunt, the primitive landscape of Cornwall is home to a distinct Celtic race whose origins can be traced back to the ancient race of giants. His 'Introduction' sets out his ideas that the Celtic race has certain characteristics, including 'minds wildly poetical, and great fertility of imagination, united with a deep feeling for the mysteries by which life is girdled' (Hunt 1968: 22). Like other 'primitive' races, then, the Cornish are characterised as irrational, superstitious and passionate, with 'deep feeling' rather than capacity to reason. They seem strongly resistant to progress or evolution. With a language of their own, the people of the south west, he says a little later, 'like all the Celts, cling with sincere affection to the memories of the past, and [...] even now regard with jealousy the introduction of any novelty and accept improvements slowly' (23). The Cornish character is also protected from change, or from evolution, it seems, by its 'singular isolation' as a peninsula, surrounded by the sea and almost cut off from (the rest of) England: 'England, with many persons, appeared to terminate on the shores of the river Tamar' (25). Thus the race of Celts seems again a reflection of the wild, uncultivated, primitive landscapes, of the most ancient, unchanging of rocks, stuck in the pre-evolutionary past with their ancient stories of giants. Hunt goes on to speculate that 'the Cornish giant is a true Celt', or maybe even belongs 'to an earlier race', which we then learn in the first chapter may be traced to a 'mighty race' of very large, strong men from whom the Celts originated (29–30 and 39).

By the mid-nineteenth century, biological understandings of race were becoming the dominant explanation of human difference, and 'primitive' races a subject of particular interest. As recent work in the history of anthropology has demonstrated, the growth of interest in 'primitive' races was motivated not so much by a 'humanitarian desire to understand the alterity of other "races" or "cultures" in far-flung corners of the Empire as by a desire to better regulate the savages within England itself', as James Vernon puts it (1998: 156. See also Kuklick 1991). Vernon goes on to observe the ambivalence with which the 'primitive' was treated: lost worlds and noble savages were on the one hand romanticised and mourned, while on the other their loss – like that of the animal species whose fossils were uncovered by geologists – was considered necessary for the progress of civilisation.[8] 'Like the colonial "primitive"', writes Vernon, '"the savage within" was a prisoner of nature and irrationality, a remnant from an earlier stage of civilisation against which the "civilised" could measure their own modernity.' Within this framework the Cornish, like the Scottish and Irish, and more 'far-flung races' such as the 'African Negro', were 'commonly assumed to occupy a lower point on the evolutionary scale' (1998: 156–7).

As Vernon notes, however, Cornwall occupied a somewhat unique position, being part of England while also considered a distinctive or even a separate nation. As we have seen, the various different forms of Hunt's work illustrate this position. *British Mining*, for instance, frames Cornwall within the wider nation while simultaneously emphasising its regional distinctiveness in terms of both its mineral wealth and its landscapes. *Popular Romances of the West of England* also emphasises the distinctiveness of Cornwall's landscapes, and, further, its supposedly 'primitive' race of Cornish Celts. Like many folklore collections, Hunt's contain numerous stories about rocks and the land, beginning with giants' games and also including stories about ancient monuments and stone circles, mines and caves. Most importantly, the preoccupation with geology frames the entire collection, albeit in a very different way to his works on mining. In various ways, rocks are used to underpin a sense of regional and racial differences, differences which are used to explain the existence of the tales in the first place: they are apparently those of a 'primitive race' which keeps 'many old legends […] alive' (1968: iv). We do not of course hear directly from the inhabitants of Cornwall themselves but only as their stories are related by folklorists. I have chosen here to focus on the more evident ground of the folklorist's views, in this case Hunt's, whose own stories about rocks help to position Cornwall as distinct from England, and to identify a distinct race of Cornish Celts.

Notes

1 For an example of the various studies of Davy as a poet-scientist see Heringman 2010: 6. For examples of references to Hunt's review see Hack 1999; Winyard and Furneaux 2010.

2 Daniels's foundational work considers how landscapes become national icons (1993). As well as other specific examples to follow in this paragraph, see Corbett, Holt and Russell 2002; Howkins 1986; Ebbatson 2005: especially 159–193; Parrinder 2006: 397. Williams points out that there has been an almost constant lament through the centuries for the apparently recent loss of a (mythical and idealised) 'Old England' located in rural communities (1993).

3 Blake, 'Jerusalem' (1804). Berberich's essay begins with Blake (2006).

4 Hunt later shifted his view in *On Mines and Mining* (1878) but granite continued to be associated with great age and sublimity.

5 See Davy, Harris, and other poems in the anthology by Kent (2000). Wordsworth also mentions the endurance of rocks in his travel writing (1974: 317), and to the eternity of hilly landscapes, of a 'naked summit', in his poetry (1936).

6 See O'Connor 2007. Buckland observes how 'narrative was as often a problem as a possibility for nineteenth-century geologists' (2010: 12).

7 Miller similarly reports tales of giants moving stones: a giantess is said to have flung the large stone in the parish of Edderton, for instance, while another even larger stone bears the imprint of a gigantic finger and thumb, and 'almost all the hills of Ross-shire' were formed by another 'great woman […] from a pannier filled with earth and stones, which she carried on her back' (1835: 44). In Greek mythology and in most of the Germanic and other folktales of giants in countries throughout Europe, giants are similarly credited with shaping or constructing rocky landscapes, from single stones to entire islands and mountains (see Motz 1982 for further examples, and for giants in England more specifically see Cohen 1999: 5).

8 For discussions of geology in the formation of ideas about race and extinction see Stepan 1982 and Brantlinger 2003.

Bibliography

Barham, T. F. (1827) 'Some arguments in support of the opinion that the Iktis of Diodorus Siculus is St. Michael's Mount', *Transactions of the Royal Geological Society of Cornall*, 3: 86–112.

Bennett, Gillian (1994) 'Geologists and Folklorists: Cultural Evolution and "The Science of Folklore"', *Folklore* 105: 25–37.

Berberich, Christine (2006) 'This Green and Pleasant Land: Cultural Constructions of Englishness', in Robert Burden and Stephan Kohl (eds) *Landscape and Englishness*, Amsterdam and New York: Rodopi, 207–224.

Boase, Henry (1822) 'Observations on the Submersion of part of Mount's Bay'. *Transactions of the Royal Geological Society of Cornwall*, 2: 129–144.

Brantlinger, Patrick (2003) *Dark Vanishings: Discourse on the Extinction of Primitive Races, 1800–1930*, Ithaca and London: Cornell University Press.

Buckland, Adelene (2010) 'Losing the Plot: the Geological Anti-narrative', *19: Interdisciplinary Studies in the Long Nineteenth Century*, 11: 1–16. Online. Available HTTP: <19.bbk.ac.uk/index.php/19/article/viewFile/578/603> (accessed 13 March 2012).

Buckland, William (1836) *Geology and Mineralogy*, 1 (4th edn), London: Bell and Daldy.

Cohen, Jeffrey Jerome (1999) *Of Giants: Sex, Monsters, and the Middle Ages*. Minnesota: Minnesota UP.

Corbett, David Peters, Ysanne Holt and Fiona Russell (2002) *The Geographies of Englishness: Landscape and the National Past 1880–1940*, New Haven and London: Yale UP.

Daniels, Stephen (1993) *Fields of Vision: Landscape Imagery and National Identity*, Princeton, NJ: Princeton UP.

—— (1998) 'Mapping National Identities: the Culture of Cartography, with Particular Reference to the Ordnance Survey', in Geoffrey Cubit (ed.) *Imagining Nations*, Manchester: Manchester Univeristy Press, 112–131.

Davy, Humphry (2000) 'Mount's Bay', in Alan Kent (ed.), *Voices from West Barbary – an Anthology of Anglo-Cornish Poetry 1549–1928*, London: Francis Boutle, 52–54.

Ebbatson, Roger (2005) *An Imaginary England: Nation, Landscape, and Literature, 1840–1920*, Aldershot: Ashgate.

Hack, Daniel (1999) '"Sublimation Strange": Allegory and Authority in *Bleak House'*. *English Literary History*, 66: 129–156.

Haller, John S. (1971) *Outcasts from Evolution: Scientific Attitudes of Racial Inferiority*, Carbondale and Edwardsville: Southern Illionis University Press.

Harris, John (2000) in Alan Kent (ed.) *Voices from West Barbary – an Anthology of Anglo-Cornish Poetry 1549–1928*, London: Francis Boutle: 134–137.

Hawkins, John (1822) 'On Some Advantages which Cornwall Possesses for the Study of Geology, and the Use which May be Made of Them', *Transactions of the Royal Geological Society of Cornwall*, 2: 1–13.

Heringman, Noah (2010) *Romantic Rocks, Aesthetic Geology*, Ithaca: Cornell University Press.

Hewitt, Rachel (2011) *Map of a Nation: A Biography of the Ordnance Survey*, London: Granta.

Howkins, Alan (1986) 'The Discovery of Rural England', in Robert Colls and Philip Dodd (eds) *Englishness: Politics and Culture 1880–1920*, London: Croom Helm, 62–88.

Hunt, Robert (1829) *The Mount's Bay*. Penzance: J. Downing and T. Matthews.

—— (1849) *The Poetry of Science, or Studies of the Physical Phenomena of Nature*, 2nd edn. London: Reeve, Benham and Reeve.

—— (1859) *A Descriptive Guide to the Museum of Practical Geology*, London.

—— (1878) *On Mines and Mining*, Volumes 3 and 4 of *Ure's Dictionary of Arts, Manufactures and Mines*. 1878 and 1879. London.

—— (1884) *British Mining*, London: Crosby Lockwood.

—— (1968) *Popular Romances of the West of England, or the Drolls, Traditions, and Superstitions of Old Cornwall*, New York and London: Benjamin Bloom.

Kent, Alan (2000) *Voices from West Barbary – an anthology of Anglo-Cornish Poetry 1549–1928*, London: Francis Boutle.

Knell, Simon and Michael Taylor (2006) 'Hugh Miller: fossils, landscape and literary geology', *Proceedings of the Geologists' Association*, 117: 85–98.

Kuklick, Henrika (1991) *The Savage Within: The Social History of British Anthropology, 1885–1945*, Cambridge: Cambridge University Press.

Miller, Hugh (1835) *Scenes and Legends of the North of Scotland, or the Traditional History of Cromarty*, Edinburgh: Adam and Charles Black.

Motz, Lotte (1982) 'Giants in Folklore and Mythology: A New Approach', *Folklore*, 93: 70–84.

Naylor, Simon (2011) 'Geological Mapping and the Geographies of Proprietorship in Nineteenth-Century Cornwall', in David Lingstone and Charles Withers (eds) *Geographies of Nineteenth-Century Science*, Chicago: University of Chicago Press: 345–370.

O'Connor, Ralph (2007) *The Earth on Show: Fossils and the Poetics of Popular Science, 1802–1856*, Chicago: University of Chicago Press.

Paradis, James G. (1996) 'The Natural Historian as Antiquary of the World: Hugh Miller and the Rise of Literary Natural History', in Michael Shortland (ed.) *Hugh Miller and the Controversies of Victorian Science*, Oxford: Oxford University Press: 122–149.

Parrinder, Patrick (2006) *Nation and Novel*. Oxford: Oxford UP.

Secord, James A. (1986) 'The Geological Survey of Great Britain as a Research School', *History of Science*, 26: 223–275.

Stepan, Nancy (1982) *The Idea of Race in Science*, London and Basingstoke: Macmillan.

Vernon, James (1998) 'Border Crossings: Cornwall and the English Imagi(nation)', in Geoffrey Cubit (ed.) *Imagining Nations*, Manchester: Manchester University Press: 153–172.

Williams, Raymond (1976) *Keywords: A Vocabulary of Culture and Society,* London: Croom Helm.

—— (1993) *The Country and the City*, London: Hogarth.

Winyard, Ben and Holly Furneaux (2010) 'Dickens, Science and the Victorian Literary Imagination', *19: Interdisciplinary Studies in the Long Nineteenth Century*, 10. Online. Available HTTP: <19.bbk.ac.uk/index.php/19/article/view/572/531> (accessed 13 March 2012).

Wordsworth, William (1936) 'The Prelude, XIII', in Ernest de Selincourt (ed.) London: Oxford UP: 147–152.

—— 'An Unpublished Tour' (1974) *The Prose Works of William Wordsworth*, vol. 2, in W. J. B. Owen and J. W. Smyser (eds) Oxford: Clarendon Press: 287–348.

Wyatt, John (1995) *Wordsworth and the Geologists*, Cambridge: Cambridge University Press.

9

CELTIC CULTURAL POLITICS

Monuments and mortality in nineteenth-century Brittany

Maura Coughlin

Over the course of the long nineteenth century, in French travel texts, in the collections of folklorists and in visual art and popular culture, the visible remains of Brittany's prehistoric and late medieval past were interpreted and framed as foundational to its Celtic culture. Represented in these various ways, Celtic coastal Brittany came to be seen as a peripheral place overlooked by modernity. Rather than valorise the Breton 'discoveries' of an individual, heroic writer or artist such as Paul Gauguin, this essay examines the reception and interpretation of a range of texts and visual culture (inclusive of painting) that re-works, constructs and underscores the identity of Brittany and Bretons as Celtic (Orton and Pollock 1980; Herbert 2002). Central to this argument is the useful concept of a 'place myth' as elaborated by art historian Nina Lübbren (2001). A 'place myth' is what develops as artists and writers engage with a rural place, its local culture of the past and its present; Lübbren notes that 'a small but growing number of art historians has begun to reconstruct the complex ways that geographic locations intersected with the production of cultural representations, particularly in late nineteenth-century France' (115). The notion of Brittany as an authentically Celtic place was discovered, reinforced and re-made in these various forms of representation, for as cultural geographer Allan Pred writes, place can be understood 'as a process whereby the reproduction of social and cultural forms, the formation of biographies, and the transformation of nature ceaselessly become one another' (1984, 292) and where place is not only what is observed but also what continuously takes place. Thus a landscape and its cultures are always intertwined in historically contingent processes of representation, performance and interpretation.

From the medieval period to the French Revolution, the Breton peninsula had shifting allegiances to the rest of France. With sea on three sides and marshland to the east, it was geographically isolated from the continent. From the 1790s onward, travelers often described the Bretons they encountered as remnants of a 'pure' Breton Celtic race independent of France or any other culture. Yet even the tales of intrepid Irish monks crossing the sea to Brittany in (impossible) stone boats, meant to establish Brittany's Celtic Christian origins, speak of the mobility along the coast and across the water typical of cultures that face the sea (Cunliffe, 565). Many Celtic cultures of the North Atlantic, networked by water travel, shared language, folklore and certain popular religious practices with Breton regional culture. Although Bretons may not be any more ethnically 'Celtic' than the rest of the French, the notion of an ancestral Celtic identity becomes central to regional cultural identity in the nineteenth century (Le Stum 1998, 27). From the Revolution onwards, many travel writers insist upon Brittany's insular culture and its racial 'purity'. Aboriginal isolation and authentic Celtic origins (that have been sent in retreat to the margins by modernity) as the defining aspect of Brittany's 'place myth' is especially evident in writings on the western Breton islands of Sein and Ouessant (Salomé 2003). For instance, many travel writers and folklorists describe the women of Ouessant as the last pure Celtic types of Brittany and likewise recount that the modern women of Sein are descended from malevolent, shipwrecking Druid priestesses (Corbin 1994, 225).

In literary and visual representations produced between the Revolution and the early twentieth century, Breton peasants are always spoken for and depicted by others (whether visitors or the educated Breton elite). Travelers repeatedly describe their fossilised backwardness and obstinate resistance to modernity (Corbin 1994, 210); others refer to the 'biblical' quality of everyday life in Brittany or read traditional ways of the province as survivals of Druidic culture that have been absorbed or replaced by fervent Catholicism (Puget 2006, 19). Modernity as a concept or social value is often constructed through such representations of cultural difference, according to folklore scholar Pertti Anttonen, who writes that:

> in folkloristic discourse, tradition has not meant indigenous practices to be continued, preserved or revitalised, but instead, the concept has stood for representations of national antiquity that were to be valorized and nostalgised but also to be left behind in order to have them speak for a national capacity for historical progress toward statehood and modernity.
>
> (2004, 177)

Thus, to use his general statements in this context, narratives of 'vanishing folk traditions' and Celtic culture in Brittany 'have served the production of modernity' (Anttonen 2004, 26). Clearly, the modernity of the imagined viewer or reader is often affirmed in comparison to such a 'backward' Brittany, but we may equally ask how the performance, recuperation or invention of Breton Celtic imagery also contributed to a modern identity for the province.

In spite of the global traffic in goods and slaves that passed through Brittany's ports in the eighteenth century, French writers of the nineteenth century focused upon coastal Brittany as a wasted, impoverished or exotic place that seemed even more provincial and remote than other French provinces (Salomé 2003, 127–163). After the Revolution, to unify the nation, French was imposed as the official tongue in Brittany, and several military campaigns were made to suppress further activity by the anti-revolutionary, royalist and deeply Catholic Chouan movement. Yet generations of French, British and American travel writers and visual artists contributed to a compounded 'barbarisation' of the province by depicting it as mired in an ancient, fossilized past (Postic and Laurent 2003, 381).

Interpreting the past

As an interest in Celtic culture grew with the foundation of the Celtic Academy in Paris in 1804, the ethnographic project began of collecting the 'vanishing' superstitions and folklore of Celtic Brittany (Gerson 1996). The Academy's founder, Jacques Cambry (1799) traveled in Brittany to produce an inventory of monuments that had survived the Revolution (Corbin 1994, 135). Cambry's itinerary or 'artistic topography'(Kauffmann 2004, 21) is the kind of story that 'transforms places into spaces or spaces into places' (Decerteau 1988, 118). This construction of Celtic Brittany was not only done by outsiders to the region: members of the Breton nobility enthusiastically joined the Celtic Academy in its early years. In the later nineteenth century, many elite Breton-born writers and artists took up the project of representing 'their own Brittany' to set the record straight. Yet even as they claim to write from personally-informed insight, more often than not, Cambry's vision of a sublime Brittany of haunted ruins and lingering myth is reiterated by artists, writers and photographers who view Bretons as folkloric reservoirs or guardians of Celtic and Druidic culture.

This repetition is especially evident in the visual conflation of Druids and Neolithic monuments. The opening plate of Cambry's travelogue, *Voyage dans la Finistère* ('Travel in Finistere'), first published in 1799, depicts a Druid standing atop a Neolithic table *menhir* or passage tomb. Like many Romantic era writers, Cambry ascribed these prehistoric monuments to the culture of the Druids, and read them as an alternative, native French tradition to Mediterranean classicism. The illustrations in the 1799 version, as well the images in the republished edition of 1835 (with additional critical commentary by Émile Souvestre), all animate Neolithic monuments with the placement of imaginary Druids or present day Bretons amid or on the stones. In a text of a few years later, *Celtic Monuments*, subtitled *Research on the Cult of Stones,* Cambry muses on the general French ignorance of this national legacy that 'if the monument of Carnac had existed near London, how many times it would have been engraved and celebrated by the poets in England! How other nations could have been made to respect this temple of the Celtic nation!' (1805, xxx). Like many antiquarians and historians of his day, he describes Brittany's many Neolithic monuments, known as *dolmen* and *menhirs*, as remnants of a great, lost Celtic Druidic culture (unaware that he was thousands of years off the mark). He reads the great alignments, such as Carnac, as sites of sacrifice and as funerary monuments; many later writers followed this lead with their own interpretations. Perhaps most importantly, Cambry set in motion a romantic, nationalist interpretation of Neolithic monuments as a native tradition of France that was resistant to the Roman Empire and unbeholden to Mediterranean classicism. The persistence of this mode of thought can be seen in the comments made in 1959 by minister of culture André Malraux when he declared the newly discovered Neolithic Breton cairn of Barnenez (c.4850 BC) a 'Megalithic Parthenon'.

Cambry inspired generations of Celtomaniac travelers to seek out the traces of a Celtic and feudal past in the romantic ruins of Brittany (Folgoas 1985, 226). In 1844, conflating Neolithic objects across Brittany, Scotland, Wales and Ireland with Druids, Celtic culture and Arthurian legend, republican historian Jules Michelet comments on his own tour of France that one cannot walk half an hour in some parts of Brittany 'without encountering some of those shapeless monuments called Druidical' (Michelet and Smith 1847, 271). It may never be known if Druids used these prehistoric stones as Cambry and his illustrators imagined, but the performance of a mythic history of place that he suggests is repeated in many forms of art and popular culture. In the early twentieth century, anecdotes of popular belief in the power of phallic standing stones to grant fertility to sterile women are seemingly supported by early twentieth-century (staged) postcards of women dancing around the stones at Pleumeur and Plonéour-Lanvern (Éveillard and Huchet 1999, 36–37). Throughout the nineteenth century and well into the twentieth, Neolithic monuments appear in painting and illustration as sites haunted (and even constructed) by Celtic spirits such as fairies (*fées*), imps (*lutins*), goblins (*korrigans*) and dwarves (*nains*) (Le Stum 2001).

Recycling the past

In reference to art and visual culture in Brittany, the elastic category of 'Celtic' culture is often used to signify difference from an undefined standard of classical Frenchness, as a catch-all to signify local difference, resistance to modern urban attitudes and to the forced imposition of the French culture and language. Mediterranean classical art made its greatest impact on French visual culture in the sixteenth century, as the School of Fontainebleau brought the Italian Renaissance to the French court. But this imported classicism had little immediate effect on Breton religious art and architecture which remained late medieval in style throughout and beyond the sixteenth century (Walker 2001, 252). In the early seventeenth century, Jesuit Counter-Reformation missions led by Julien Maunoir and Michel le Nobletz gradually introduced new dogmatic religious imagery. At the same time, they censored earlier forms of popular religious practices that put faith in omens, local healing saints and miraculous fountains. In order to bring the Breton church closer to Roman orthodoxy, such beliefs, labeled 'Celtic' were cast as mere superstition as new forms of doctrinal visual imagery were introduced to instruct the illiterate rural peasantry (Croix and Roudaut 1988, 13). Yet the Jesuit missions in Western Brittany did not so much stamp out folk belief in ghosts, death omens and miracle cures as harness these beliefs for their own purposes (Souvestre 1835, 21; Badone 1989, 179). Thus, the effective Christianisation of Brittany came from the fact that earlier forms of visual culture were appropriated, and the older beliefs were never entirely stamped out. For example, the famous Neolithic *menhir* of St Uzec, like many ancient stones, was appropriated as a Christian monument in the wake of these missions. Today the recut *menhir* still bears the engraving of the Arma Christi, although the crucifix once painted on it has faded away (Giraudon 2009).

The late medieval, plague-inspired image of the *Danse Macabre* appears in a religious context in Brittany in church wall paintings such as the well-preserved, medieval chapel of Kermaria-an-Isquit near the town of Plouha in the Côtes d'Armor. In the painted frieze (c. 1500) that runs across the upper walls, the skeletal, dancing figure of death repeatedly appears to warn the viewer of the random calling of death and the inevitability of his or her demise. This image of death is not particularly Celtic in origin; many versions of the *Danse Macabre* were painted, and later destroyed in England, France and Germany. Another well-known personification of death is Ankou, the Celtic grim reaper: a familiar figure in folklore of Ireland, Wales and Cornwall who has an exceptionally visual presence in Lower (Western) Brittany in the context of religious architecture. On ossuaries in Breton parish closes and in churches such as Ploumilliau, Ankou takes the form of a skeleton or corpse, bearing a scythe, an arrow or a spear. In Breton folklore, a visit from Ankou means the coming of death. His visit may be presaged by an omen or *intersign* that involves a perceptive reading of an unusual natural phenomenon (Badone 1989, 316).

Jesuit Missionaries did not use or recycle the *Danse Macabre* or the figure of Ankou directly in their teachings but they did call upon the well-established culture of death in Brittany and its emphasis on dying 'a good death' in order to frighten the illiterate rural viewer of the dangers of dying in a state of sin. *Taolennou* or portable altarpieces were first painted on sheepskins in the early seventeenth century. Their presentation of death differs from the fatalism of the *Danse Macabre* and the tales of Ankou because they focus upon the moral paths chosen by the living in order to avoid sin and damnation. The first *taolennou* were carried by priests into the countryside to re-Christianise the Breton rural population and to rectify religious devotion that had become an eclectic blend of Catholicism and earlier pagan-Celtic belief (Croix and Roudaut 1984, 123–132). They warned of the vices of idolatry, heresy, apostasy, stubbornness, sorcery and black magic (Croix and Roudaut 1988, 283). Well into the twentieth century, images from the *taolonneu* were reproduced as cheap popular prints that were purchased at religious events and tacked up in the home, becoming part of everyday life (Sauvy 1989, 199). In the later nineteenth century, modernist painters such as Emile Bernard, Paul Sérusier and Paul Gauguin in Pont Aven were inspired by what seemed to be local, Celtic primitivism in popular religious prints. These prints, first produced in Brittany, depicted locally significant Breton saints, sites and miracles and further addressed a local audience in a mixture of Breton and French texts (Beauducel 2009).

Like the competitive building of ever-taller Gothic cathedrals in the Ile-de-France region, and because of wealth derived from the international linen trade, particular Breton towns in Finistère competed in the building of their own elaborate parish closes or *enclos* in the sixteenth and seventeenth centuries. The *enclos* compounds were central to annual pardon rituals and included pilgrimage churches, multi-figured *calvaires* or sculpted stone calvary crosses, fountains, elaborate triumphal archways, ossuaries and even oratories (Walker 2001, 249). Both prior to and after the Counter Reformation, much of the sculpture of the *enclos* depicted the horrors of hell in frightening detail. On the *calvaires* and the sculpted porches are many visual reminders of saintly sacrifice and human mortality that reinforce the dogma of the Counter Reformation. Throughout the later nineteenth century, artists were fascinated by this sculptural tradition, often interpreting it as a primitive vestige of an isolated medieval past rather than understanding its earlier function as a programmatic demonstration of official doctrine.

As in the case of the prehistoric standing stones, the *calvaires* attracted the attention of travel writers who also described these as part of the (imagined) Celtic past kept alive by continuous devotion of the pious peasantry. In the later nineteenth century Paul Gauguin, like many artists before him, took liberties with the sites of these sculpted groups, moving them away from the heart of their towns, setting them dramatically by the wild Atlantic coast, and implying that the modern era peasant is fully in touch with (and continuous with) that past. In the case of the *Green Christ* (1889) Gauguin, like many who worked in artists' colonies, creates for his viewer a sense of authentic 'privileged access' or 'documentary romanticism' of ways of life on the wane (Lübbren, 40). Modernist accounts of avant-gardism in Brittany repeatedly credit Gauguin's use of the *calvaire* as a 'primitive' or anti-classical, local artistic tradition that could renew and invigorate modern painting (Perry 1993, 22).

In spite of this common misreading of the *calvaries* as a naïve form of popular art, there are many valid visual arguments to be made that connect the imagery of the *enclos* (other than the doctrinal) to Celtic traditions in northern European medieval art. On the margins of the *enclos* structures, especially on carved wooden beams and on roof edges, striking interlaced grotesques and animal imagery is common. Perhaps the most striking Celtic reference is that of a mermaid found on several of the older (pre-reformation) *enclos*. At Sizun and La Martyre in Northern Finistère a mermaid projects from the edge of the roof and, at the latter, a sinister caryatid on the church façade (who may be a stylized mermaid) is accompanied by a text in Breton that warns of the damp, cold (therefore Celtic, not Roman) hell that awaits the sinner (Badone 159).

Celtic identity and the cult of the dead

Most important to the collective embrace of Celtic identity in Brittany was the publication in 1839 of *Barzaz Breiz,* a collection of oral Breton traditional songs and bardic poetry, published by Hersant de la Villemarqué (Postic and Laurent 2003, 382). *Barzaz Breiz* was born of and embraced by the northern romantic nationalism of its moment, as already expressed in enthusiasm for texts like *Ossian* (1765) and the *Kalevala* (1830). Brittany's Celtic revival that follows this somewhat controversial marshaling of oral popular tradition by an educated Breton elite resulted in a widespread self-identification of Bretons with a Celtic past. Later folklorists such as Émile Souvestre, François-Marie Luzel, Paul Féval, Paul Sébillot, Anatole Le Braz and many others were fascinated by Brittany's linguistic affinity to other Celtic cultures as they gathered orally-transmitted folklore in the late nineteenth and early twentieth centuries. Many of their narratives relate ethnographic detail and everyday experiences of coastal Bretons to those of other Celtic cultures of the North Atlantic. Perhaps the most remarked upon of folk practices and beliefs, that seemed to most connect Breton popular culture with earlier Celtic ways, was the nineteenth-century Breton obsession with the cult of the dead.

In 1799, Cambry declared that 'the Breton nation is remarkable for its piety for the dead' (quoted in Badone, 1); many later travel writers remark on the almost obsessive reverence for the cult of the dead in Lower (Western) Brittany. He recounts the continuing practice of exhuming corpses from the graveyard several years after their burial, after which the skulls were preserved in painted wooden boxes that were then conserved in the church or in the ossuary (Cambry 1799, 146). Up until the First World War, it was still common practice for a body to occupy a grave in the parish close for only five years before being exhumed. At this point, the skull was transferred to an individual painted box that was displayed either in the church or the ossuary, and the other bones were placed with the other undifferentiated ones held in the ossuary. In Brittany, this practice of a secondary treatment of the remains continued long after it had died out elsewhere (Le Deunff 1999, 154). This seemingly medieval attitude toward the physical remains of the body was often branded Celtic when encountered in Brittany (Badone, 136).

As sociologist Ellen Badone notes, *Toussaint* (All Soul's Day and the Day of the Dead – November 1 and 2) coincides with the Celtic *Samhain,* or the beginning of winter, and like other popular holidays associated with the memory of the dead, it is most likely pre-Christian in origin (164). Breton women's cemetery visits to the dead on Toussaint appear with great frequency in the French press in the late nineteenth and early twentieth centuries. In a full-page image from the weekly illustrated supplement to the Parisian newspaper *Le Petit Journal* (31 October, 1897, n. 363) a young woman grieves on a grave, and behind her within the cemetery is an ossuary.[1] Depending upon the perspective of the viewer, this popular image may read two ways: a Breton viewer might identify two phases of the body after death – the recent burial in the ground and the later resting place of the bones. For an outside viewer (presumed to be more modern in attitude to death), the ossuary in the background might read as a juxtaposition of past and present: the macabre death practices of the past could be read in the ossuary, in contrast with the romantic cemetery burial in the foreground.

The retention of Celtic death practices and superstitions in coastal Brittany was given its fullest elaboration in the folklore, travelogues and fiction collected by Breton scholar Anatole Le Braz. His popular text *Legende de la Mort chez les Bretons Armoricains (Death Legends in Coastal Brittany*, 1893) details Bretons' persistent faith in death omens and superstitious demons such as night washing hags and Ankou, the skeletal Grim Reaper. Le Braz spoke Breton, but was born into the upper class and his texts always maintain a certain narrative distance from the superstitious legends reported. John Millington Synge attended Le Braz's lectures on Breton folklore in 1897 and read his works (1894) prior to his trips to the Aran Islands. Not surprisingly, Synge's collected Celtic myths and superstitions from the Aran (and Blasket) islands have many structural and narrative similarities to those recounted by Le Braz (Foster 1993, 100).

Before Le Braz collected his tales, self-taught Breton artist Yan Dargent painted a massive canvas *Night Washers (Les Lavandières de la Nuit,* Quimper Museum of Fine Arts,1861) that depicts spirits of the dead (*revenants*) who return to haunt the living (particularly on Toussaint) and, in this ghoulish case, wring them in their laundry.[2] In 1992, in St. Servais (the village of his birth and residence), in the small museum dedicated to Yan Dargent was an exhibition dedicated to this theme. This show enumerated the various iterations of this theme that is first depicted in the 1835 edition of Cambry (Berthou 1992). Many regional practices and superstitions characterize the Breton celebration of Toussaint (All Saints' Day on November 1 and All Souls' Day on November 2), which, more than any other time of the year, implies an interaction between the living and the dead.

Like Toussaint, the solstice bonfires of midsummer, Christianised and re-dedicated to St. John (*Les Feux de la Saint Jean* or, in Breton, *Le Tantad*) are frequently referred to as renamed Celtic practices that also relate to the cult of the dead (Badone 165). Le Braz tells that by the side of the fire a litany for the dead is recited for the *revenants* who may gather beside it, drawn to its warmth. He affirms the belief that because the Breton version of hell is cold, rather than hot, wandering souls are forever trying to get warm, and thus they gather by the bonfire's embers (Devlin 1987, 92; Le Braz and Gostling 1906, 133). In 1890, Scottish social anthropologist Sir James Frazer interpreted the midsummer bonfires as the residual remains of primitive magical practice (Frazer 1890: 284). Echoing Frazer, Le Braz notes on the bonfires in Finistère that 'perhaps in no other region of Brittany has the ancient Celtic nature-worship remained so unaltered' (Le Braz and Gostling 1906: 133).

In an illustration of the St. John's bonfires on the cover of *Le Petit Journal* published as a mid-summer issue of 1893 (1 July, n. 136), costumed Bretons dance around fires that emit great billowing clouds of smoke.[3] Their circular dance echoes the sculpted figures at the base of the stone *calvaires* behind them, where sculpted worshippers, surrounding multiple crosses, mark out the place as a site of ritual pilgrimage. In this image, visual traditions and rituals of the past and present are effectively collapsed, making the dancing Breton peasants seem continuous with this hybrid Celtic/Christian past in this place. At the turn of the century, painter Charles Cottet specialized in images of Breton rituals and everyday practices of loss and mourning. In the large painting, *St. John's Night Bonfire on Ouessant,* (1901, private collection, Brest) he depicts a gathering of locals at a midsummer fire on the island of Ouessant. In the moody darkness that was typical of this artist's work, a group of elder widows, cloaked in black, a few children and even fewer men, sit by a small ring of upright stones that contains a small fire of driftwood and seaweed. Following the account of Le Braz, we might imagine that they are pronouncing a litany for the dead. Beyond the fire's immediate glow, we can make out other simultaneous, distant fires that spread out along the shore of the island and illuminate the horizon like a false dawn, mapping points on the landscape like the bonfires described in Thomas Hardy's mythical villages of Wessex (Barrell 1982, 350). Cottet shows us that this midsummer practice, often thought of as Celtic in origin, is integral to the seasonal experience of place for residents of coastal Brittany.

Fin de siècle Celtomania

By the time that Cottet was working on the western islands of Sein and Ouessant, many decades of a fervent antiquarian Celtomania had their grip on Brittany (Salomé 219). In a range of nineteenth-century literary and visual sources, as studied extensively by sociologist Karine Salomé, the Breton islands are virtually fetishised as an imagined space of Celtic mystical activity – even when there is no archaeological record to support it (221). To cite one early and influential example, in René Chateaubriand's prose epic *Les Martyrs* (1809), the tragic, suicidal Druid priestess Velléda is the sole survivor of nine virgins who inhabited the isle (224). And Michelet's *History of France* discusses the ancient Celtic past of the island as:

> the abode of the sacred virgins who gave the Celts fine weather or shipwreck. There they celebrated their gloomy and murderous orgies; and the seamen heard with terror, far off at sea, the clash of barbaric cymbals. This island is the traditional birth-place of Myrddyn, the Merlin of the middle age.
>
> (Michelet and Smith 1847, 152)

Velléda is, not surprisingly, a quite popular theme for romantic and symbolist painters of treacherous *femmes-fatales;* one especially dramatic depiction of her story is by Jules-Eugène Lenepveu (1883) in the Museum of Fine Arts, Quimper.[4]

At the very close of the nineteenth century, as Phillipe Le Stum has extensively studied, the burgeoning French literary regionalist movement inspired the formation of the Union of Breton Regionalists (URB) in 1898, who identified with the earlier efforts of the Welsh Gorsedd to forge a pan-Celtic unity across the English Channel and the Irish Sea (Le Stum 1998). Performing a reinvented Celtic identity for Brittany, the newly-established Neo-Druid movement produced in the first decade of the twentieth century many festivals of bardic poetry, dance, song and costumed spectacles (27). Members of the URB, along with other Breton regionalists, folklorists, designers and artists, joined together to present Breton Celtic culture to a wider public as a modern and vibrant tradition rather than one forever mired in a distant past. Photographs of Neo-Druidic performances, many of which printed as postcards, represent these events as taking place in a landscape marked with a Celtic identity. As in Cambry's text, printed a century previously, the performing 'Druid' stands atop the Neolithic stone, appropriating the past monument to Celtic culture and re-territorialising or re-animating the landscape as a (modern) Celtic place.

Conclusion

By the early twentieth century, the Celtic nature of Brittany had become central to its place myth. By being discovered, interpreted, constructed and performed, this identity was as much a product of nineteenth-century romantic nationalism as of the province's cultural history. The reinterpretation and appropriation of a range of imagery, from ancient monuments of the Neolithic era to the dogma of the Counter Reformation consolidated this reputation. In turn, the ongoing traditional or folk practices of dealing with the dead, lighting Midsummer bonfires and according significance to prehistoric sites all maintained traditions that were easily appropriated to the idea of an authentic Celtic culture that thrived in the modern present.

Notes

1 The image can be seen on Gallica, the digital database of the Bibliothèque Nationale de France, <http://gallica.bnf.fr/ark:/12148/bpt6k716250n/f8>.
2 The image can be seen on the website of the Quimper Museum of Fine Arts <http://www.mbaq.fr/musee-collections/peinture-bretonne/oeuvre/o/les-lavandieres-de-la-nuit/>.
3 The image can be seen on Gallica, <http://gallica.bnf.fr/ark:/12148/bpt6k7160234>.
4 The painting can be seen on the website of the Quimper Fine Arts Museum, <http://www.mbaq.fr/fr/musee-collections/peinture-bretonne/oeuvre/o/velleda-effet-de-lune/>.

Bibliography

Anttonen, P. J. (2004). *Tradition Through Modernity: Postmodernism and Beyond in Folklore Scholarship*. Studia Fennica Folkloristica. Helsinki: Finnish Literature Society.

Badone, E. (1989) *The Appointed Hour: Death, Worldview and Social Change in Brittany.* Berkeley and Los Angeles: University of California Press.

Barrell, J. (1982) 'Geographies of Hardy's Wessex,' *Journal of Historical Geography* 8 (October), 347–61.

Beauducel, C. (2009) *L'Imagerie populaire en Bretagne aux XVIIIe et XIXe siècles.* Rennes: Presses universitaires de Rennes.

Berthou, J. (1992) *Les Lavandières de la nuit.* Saint-Servais: Musée Yan' Dargent.

Cambry, J. (1799). *Voyage dans le Finistère, ou état de ce département en 1794 et 1795.* Paris: impr. du Cercle social.

Cambry, J. (1805) *Monuments celtiques, ou recherches sur le culte des pierres.* Paris: Johanneau.

Cambry, J. and Souvestre, E. (1835). *Voyage dans le Finistère.* Brest: Come, fils ainé et Bonetbeau, fils.

Corbin, A. (1994) *Le Territoire du vide.* trans. Jocelyn Phelps, *The Lure of the Sea: the Discovery of the Seaside in the Western World, 1750–1840.* Berkeley: University of California Press.

Croix, A. and Fanch Roudaut, F. (1984) *Les Bretons, la mort et dieu de 1699 à nos jours.* Paris: Messidor / Temps actuels.

Croix, A. and Fanch Roudaut, F. et al, (1988) *Les Chemins du paradis.* Douarnenez: Le Chasse-Marée.

Cunliffe, B. (2001) *Facing the Ocean: The Atlantic and its Peoples 8000 BC–AD 1500.* Oxford and New York: Oxford University Press.

Decerteau, M. (1988) *The Practice of Everyday Life.* Berkeley: University of California Press.

Devlin, J. (1987) *The Superstitious Mind: French Peasants and the Supernatural in the Nineteenth Century.* New Haven: Yale University Press.

Éveillard, J. D. and Huchet, P. (1999) *Une Bretagne si étrange.* Rennes: Ouest-France.

Folgoas, M. O. (1985) 'L'Ankou dans la littérature bretonne d'expression française du XIXème siècle', unpublished thesis: Brest.

Foster, J.W. (1993) *Fictions of the Irish Literary Revival: a Changeling Art.* Syracuse, NY: Syracuse University Press.

Frazer, J. (1890) *The Golden Bough: A Study in Magic and Religion.* London: Macmillan.

Gerson, S. (1996) 'Parisian Litterateurs, Provincial Journeys and the Construction of National Unity in Post-Revolutionary France.' *Past and Present* 151(1): 141–173.

Giraudon, D. (2009) 'Patrimoine de Pleumer-Bodoù: le menhir de Saint Uzec' *Mythologie Française* 237: 11–23.

Herbert, R.L. (2002) 'City vs. Country: The Rural Image from Millet to Gauguin' in R. L. Herbert *From Millet to Léger: Essays in Social Art History.* New Haven: Yale University Press, 23–65.

Kauffman, T.D. (2004) *Toward a Geography of Art.* Chicago: University of Chicago Press.

Le Braz, A. and Gostling, F.M. (1906) *The Land of Pardons.* New York: Macmillan.

Le Deunff, R. (1999) *Les Ossuaries bretons.* Éditions de la Plomée: Guingamp.

Le Stum, P. (1998) Phillipe Le Stum, *Le Néo-Druidisme en Bretagne: origine, naissance et développement, 1890–1914.* Rennes: Ouest-France.

Le Stum, P. (2001) *Fées, Korrigans et autres créatures fantastiques de Bretagne.* Rennes: Ouest-France.

Lübbren, N. (2001) *Rural Artists' Colonies in Europe, 1870–1910.* Manchester: Manchester University Press.

Michelet, J. and Smith, G.H. (1847) *History of France.* New York: Appleton.

Orton, F. and Pollock, G. (1980) 'Les Données Bretonnantes: La prairie de représentation.' *Art History* 3: 314–44.

Ozouf, M. (1981) 'L'Invention de l'ethnographie française: le questionnaire de l'Académie celtique,' *Annales* 36: 210–231.

Perry, G. (1993) 'The Going Away—a Preparation for the "Modern"?' in C. Harrison, F. Frascina and G. Perry (eds) *Primitivism, Cubism, Abstraction: the Early Twentieth Century*. New Haven: Yale University Press, 2–45.

Postic F., and Laurent, D. (2003) 'Reconnaissance d'une culture régionale: La Bretagne depuis la révolution' *Ethnologie Française: revue de la société d'ethnologie Française* 33: 381–389. Pred, A. (1984) 'Place as Historically Contingent Process: Structuration and the Time- Geography of Becoming Places' *Annals of the Association of American Geographers* 74: 279–297.

Puget, C. (2006) *Peintres de la Bretagne et quête spirituelle*. Pont-Aven: Musée de Pont-Aven.

Salomé, K. (2003) *Les îles bretonnes: une image en construction (1750–1914)*. Rennes: Presses Universitaires de France.

Sauvy, A. (1989) *Le Miroir du coeur, quatre siècles d'images savantes et populaires*. Paris: Cerf.

Souvestre, E. (1835) *Voyage dans le Finistère*. Brest: Come and Bonetbeau.

Walker, S. (2001) 'Accommodating the Apocalypse: an examination of the relationships between the economics of salvation and the architecture of the Breton *enclos*', *The Journal of Architecture* 6: 249–277.

10

SPIRITED AWAY

Highland touring, 'Toctor Shonson' and the hauntings of Celtism

Peter Merchant

Three weeks after Smollett's plot for *The Expedition of Humphry Clinker* has him entering Scotland, Jery Melford – one of the novel's main letter-writers – is already acclimatised:

> DEAR PHILLIPS, If I stay much longer at Edinburgh, I shall be changed into a downright Caledonian ... The people here are so social and attentive in their civilities to strangers, that I am insensibly sucked into the channel of their manners and customs...
>
> (Smollett 1984: 221)

The only real obstruction is, aptly enough, at the mouth: 'I am not yet Scotchman enough to relish their singed sheep's-head and haggice' (Smollett 1984: 222).

The same month which saw the publication of *Humphry Clinker*, June 1771, found Samuel Johnson looking forward to a time when he too (accompanied and guided by James Boswell) might navigate that channel and 'climb the Highlands, or [be] tost among the Hebrides' (Boswell 1934, 2: 140). The plan was duly put into effect when in the autumn of 1773, after an interval of two years, Boswell persuaded Johnson to spend a hundred days with him in Scotland. Out of this came two books, with Johnson's *Journey to the Western Islands of Scotland* (first published 1775) ten years ahead of Boswell's *Journal of a Tour to the Hebrides* (first published 1785). It is the latter that more precisely plots and dates Johnson's hundred-day 'transit ... over the Caledonian Hemisphere' (Boswell 1950: 382), while the former enlarges more upon the reflections which the journey stirred.

Like Melford, Johnson was seeing Scotland a generation after moves had begun to legislate out of existence exactly those 'manners and customs' of which its people once seemed most proud. 'They have been not only disarmed by act of parliament', Smollett's character reports, 'but also deprived of their antient garb' (Smollett 1984: 239); 'the Highlanders have been obliged to change the form of their dress', agrees Johnson, as well as 'deprived of their arms' (Johnson 1971: 51–2, 90). In fact, 'so quick, so great, and so general' has the recent 'change of national manners' proved to be (Johnson 1971: 57) that a good deal else that used to stamp the Scots as downright Caledonians is also now 'wearing away' or 'passing fast away' (Johnson 1971: 108, 134–5) along with the sword and the plaid. For Johnson, this awareness of 'peculiarities' (Johnson 1971: 162) on the point of perishing turns the tour of 1773 into an attempt to deduce and describe the network of cultural practices to which those peculiarities belonged. It is with a disappearing culture as with a ruined building; so long as there are 'some parts yet standing' (Johnson 1971: 11), a speculative reconstruction of the entire system or structure remains possible. What Johnson 'came … too late to see' (Johnson 1971: 57) – at least, in its full-blown form – can therefore still be successfully surmised.

While Johnson's focus is on the difference that a generation has made to the manners and customs of a nation, Boswell's *Journal* concentrates more upon the changes which a hundred days of being sucked into the life of that nation appear to have wrought in the tastes and attitudes of Johnson himself. From the very beginning, on the day the pair first set out from Edinburgh, Boswell is orchestrating these changes as much as observing them:

> I bought some *speldings*, fish [generally whitings] salted and dried in a particular manner, being dipped in the sea and dried in the sun, and eaten by the Scots by way of a relish. He had never seen them, though they are sold in London. I insisted on *scottifying* his palate; but he was very reluctant. With difficulty I prevailed with him to let a bit of one of them lie in his mouth. He did not like it.
>
> (Boswell 1950: 55)

Four days later Johnson needs no prompting or persuading from his future biographer but, as his readiness to go where he has 'never been before' (Johnson 1971: 37) and see what he has 'never seen before' (Johnson 1971: 74) extends into an interest in tasting what he has never previously tasted, he simply sets about scottifying himself:

> At dinner, Dr. Johnson ate several plate-fulls of Scotch broth, with barley and peas in it, and seemed very fond of the dish. I said, 'You never ate it before.' – *Johnson*. 'No, sir; but I don't care how soon I eat it again.'
>
> (Boswell 1950: 87)

As Johnson approaches what he terms 'the savage parts of Scotland' (Johnson 1971: 127) – by which he means the Gaelic-speaking Highlands and islands, belonging historically to the Caledonian Celts, as opposed to the Lowland territories of the 'Sassenach' or Saxon Scots – the challenges become somewhat stiffer. On Thursday 26 August, a breakfast at which Johnson was 'disgusted by the sight' of some 'dried haddocks broiled' (Boswell 1950: 110) and a drive which saw him and Boswell forsaking 'fertility and culture' for 'nothing but heath' (Johnson 1971: 25), set the tone for the two months they were to spend exclusively among the people whom Johnson describes as Highlanders.[1] This wilderness was to prove a place of trials for him, both gastronomic and otherwise. Ten days out of Inverness he faced an ordeal by oatmeal bread, served in 'very thin cakes, coarse and hard, to which unaccustomed palates are not easily reconciled' (Johnson 1971: 55), but to which – however unfathomable it might appear both to him and to Jery Melford (Smollett 1984: 222) – he knew that there was a strong local and national attachment.

The oatcakes served at the Laird of Raasay's breakfast table – Boswell's *Journal* informs us (Boswell 1950: 167) – might easily therefore have become the last straws or shibboleths which showed that Johnson, like Melford, was not Scotchman enough. In the hope of averting any such conclusion, Boswell intensified his efforts to demonstrate the contrary. Virtually from the moment when what he would term their 'wild Tour' (Boswell 1950: 84) started to head out towards the western coast, he had encouraged Johnson to keep taking his scottifying medicine and to continue imagining himself a Scotchman:

> At Auchnasheal, we sat down on a green turf-seat at the end of a house; they brought us out two wooden dishes of milk, which we tasted. One of them was frothed like a syllabub.... Dr. Johnson was much refreshed by this repast. He was pleased when I told him he would make a good Chief.
> (Boswell 1950: 142–3)

This reinventing of the man who was 'the great English Moralist' (Boswell 1950: 335) is carried a stage further on Skye:

> He was quite social and easy ... and, though he drank no fermented liquor, toasted Highland beauties with great readiness. His conviviality engaged them so much, that they seemed eager to shew their attention to him, and vied with each other in crying out, with a strong Celtick pronunciation, 'Toctor Shonson, Toctor Shonson, your health!'
> (Boswell 1950: 261)

The new name bibulously bestowed on Johnson matches the fresh identity into which he is unbending. By the time the two travellers reach the isle of Coll he has unbent so far that, when Boswell 'took the liberty to put a large blue bonnet on his head', Johnson 'seemed much pleased to assume the appearance of an ancient Caledonian' (Boswell 1950: 324–5). The *Journey*'s inquiry into the primitive manners of the savage parts of Scotland has here come close to falling on its inventor's head in a fashion all the more felicitous for being so unexpected. Instead of reconstructing those manners and customs, the previously unreconstructed embodiment of all that goes to make 'a *John Bull* ... a blunt *true-born Englishman*' (Boswell 1950: 20) appears engaged in reconstructing himself.

At the stage of his first setting out, any aspirations in this direction – or any hopes of the kind with which in the twentieth century Louis MacNeice went to the Hebrides, 'that the Celt in me would be drawn to the surface' (MacNeice 1990: 23) – would have been quite incongruous for Johnson. The prospect held out to him by the 'wild Tour' of 1773 was altogether more philosophical: recuperation of the Celt in us all, rather than reconnection with the Celt in him personally. To locate and to seize the ancient Caledonian might be to understand everybody's beginnings. Just as in his 1755 *Dictionary of the English Language* Johnson had turned to the '*Roman* and *Teutonick*' languages in order to find the ancestors of many English words, so when he toured the savage parts of Scotland – and was able to explore the evolutionary vacuum chamber that those regions so conveniently constituted – he would surely stand a chance of finding our prototype and common fountainhead. This conviction came in large part from the leading civil historians of the day – among them Adam Ferguson, who in Edinburgh joined Johnson for dinner (Boswell 1950: 45). Their 'four-stages theory', as it is generally termed, 'characterized the most savage societies as those engaged in hunting, fishing, or shepherding activities and the most polished societies as the ones that pursued agriculture and commerce' (Wheeler 2000: 182). On the far side of Inverness, where such polish was lacking, a lost world of arrested development therefore lay waiting to be discovered, with a wealth of material for anybody interested in plotting and pondering the origins of civil society. The Anoch innkeeper whom Johnson meets on his second day out of Inverness, just as he approaches 'the bosom of the Highlands', is immediately seen in exactly this light: 'His life seemed to be merely pastoral, except that he differed from some of the ancient Nomades in having a settled dwelling' (Johnson 1971: 37). Such evolutionary throwbacks are all the more to be prized because their days seem numbered: 'The state of life, which has hitherto been purely pastoral, begins now to be a little variegated with commerce' (Johnson 1971: 89). The gap between the Highland 'mountaineer' and Adam Smith's Commercial Man is growing ever narrower, as the previously ring-fenced world of the Highlander ('their rocks secluded them from the rest of mankind, and kept them an unaltered and discriminated race') admits more modern influence, with the result that the Highlanders 'are now losing their distinction, and hastening to mingle with the general community' (Johnson 1971: 47). In this sense much had changed since the battle fought in 1746 on Culloden Moor. Some ghosts from that era – such as Flora Macdonald (Johnson 1971: 67) – still peopled the Scotland that Johnson and Boswell were seeing; but Culloden and the legislation enacted after it unavoidably represented a sharp break with the Gaelic past. Already in 1773 it was possible to pronounce Romantic Scotland dead and gone.

Whether this qualified as a consummation devoutly to be wished was an important matter for debate. In so far as Johnson treats the Highlands and islands of Scotland as a classic wilderness, placing under intense scrutiny the social arrangements of the world he left to enter it, pressing philosophical questions are bound to arise as he traverses it: 'whether a great nation ought to be totally commercial?' (Johnson 1971: 91); 'whether the Savage or the London Shopkeeper had the best existence' (Boswell 1950: 81). Johnson is as busy comparing different modes of life as he had been in his *History of Rasselas, Prince of Abissinia* (2009/1759). Common sense, however, continues to tell him what it told him four years previously: that there could be 'nothing more false' than to uphold 'the superior happiness of the savage life' (Boswell 1934, 2: 73). Although the life of Commercial Man may sometimes have many pains, that of the ancient Caledonian or Highland 'mountaineer' has no pleasures amenable to reason. It is not the London shopkeeper who stands in need of scottifying, but the savage who needs to have the shopkeeper's store of civility and useful knowledge imparted to him. The west coast of Skye brings out all of Johnson's pride in English trade, money and elegance:

> As we sailed along, Dr. Johnson got into one of his fits of railing at the Scots. He owned that they had been a very learned nation for a hundred years, from about 1550 to about 1650; but that ... they had not any of those conveniencies and embellishments which are the fruit of industry, till they came in contact with a civilized people.
>
> (Boswell 1950: 248).

There follows an inflammatory comparison with 'the Cherokees' which, in his *Journey,* Johnson might have been expected to reconsider. As it turns out, he is entirely unrepentant, and no less inclined in print than he had been in Alexander MacLeod's boat to proclaim what the Scots have gained by the 1707 Act of Union: 'Till the Union made them acquainted with English manners, the culture of their lands was unskillful, and their domestick life unformed; their tables were coarse as the feasts of Esquimeaux, and their houses filthy as the cottages of Hottentots' (Johnson 1971: 28). In Johnson's mind that battle with the 'coarse' and the 'filthy' plainly continues in the 1770s. It has merely moved out to the likes of Iona, with its 'remarkably gross, and remarkably neglected' inhabitants: 'The island, which was once the metropolis of learning and piety, has now no school for education, nor temple for worship, only two inhabitants that can speak English, and not one that can write or read' (Johnson 1971: 152). Iona has suffered a sad declension but, according to Johnson's 1749 poem *The Vanity of Human Wishes*, such is the 'transit' of all except the steadiest of luminaries: 'They mount, they shine, evaporate, and fall' (Johnson 1964: 95). The consolation for Johnson is that after the fall comes an opportunity for redemption. What Mr Braidwood is achieving at his Edinburgh 'college of the deaf and dumb' confirms that an enlightened humanitarianism can help the Scots to realise their potential, and secure the improvements of which their condition is capable. As Katie Trumpener observes, it is not for nothing that Johnson's *Journey* ends here:

Johnson envisions Scotland as a deaf-and-dumb school whose scholars ...
move from the backwardness of Erse to the cosmopolitanism of English,
their seemingly insurmountable handicaps proving capable of 'so much
help' from a teacher who is patient and wise.

(Trumpener 1997: 94–5)

Through the Act of Union, therefore, Scotland has an invaluable opportunity
to extricate itself from the Celtic peripheries and join the rest of Britain in the
prosperous mainstream of modern life.

At the same time, Johnson notes that the Scots themselves are torn between
commitment to the cosmopolitan and adherence to the ancient. The young
Laird of Coll is praised both as a moderniser – 'so desirous of improving
his inheritance, that he spent a considerable time among the farmers of
Hertfordshire, and Hampshire, to learn their practice' (Johnson 1971: 76) – and
as a man 'desirous to continue the customs of his house' (Johnson 1971: 128).
A balance is struck which acknowledges that the customs of the house warrant
conservation as much as the surrounding estate requires improvement. Johnson
too is at times attached to the ancient; at Auchinleck, for instance, he finds
himself 'less delighted with the elegance of the modern mansion, than with
the sullen dignity of the old castle' (Johnson 1971: 161). Lord Monboddo, who
called Johnson 'a *Jacobite fellow*' (Boswell 1950: 376), felt that his hankering after
the old as against the modern went further still. Several of Johnson's critics in
the later twentieth century felt the same. Jeffrey Hart, in 1960, represented the
Journey as a work suffused with nostalgia for the old order, and turning its notes
to tragic when it witnessed the collapse of traditional Highland society as well
as when it contemplated 'the destruction of pre-Reformation Christian culture'
(Hart 1960: 45). Thomas Curley argued in 1976 that '[t]hrough successive
encounters with Highlanders' Johnson 'learned to revise his previous feelings
about the culture: pity and condescension evolved into a manifest admiration
for pastoral simplicity' (Curley 1976: 200). In 1995 Pat Rogers saw in Johnson's
Journey a paradox which 'has never been fully explored': namely, that despite
its author's well-documented hostility to the Scots the text 'is plainly deeply
sympathetic to many of the people and social mores encountered' (Rogers
1995: 192). Such analysis suggests that Johnson's intellectual recoiling from the
ancient Highlander as unacquainted with English manners is by no means the
whole picture. Rather, he perhaps becomes imperceptibly fascinated by what
he is ideologically constrained to rail at, the primitive and customary aspect
of Scottish life, and warms to it more and more. If so, instinct and logic – or
perception and ideology – are no less at war within Johnson over his view of
Highland culture and 'pastoral simplicity' than over his attitude to the existence
of ghosts. Boswell speaks of Johnson's imagination inclining him 'to a belief
of the marvellous, and the mysterious' even as 'his vigorous reason examined
the evidence with jealousy' (Boswell 1950: 18). Johnson himself recognised
a difference between what he might publicly maintain, with regard to the

existence of ghosts, and what he – and others – could not help privately feeling: 'All argument is against it; but all belief is for it' (Boswell 1934, 3: 230).

The rhetoric which in Johnson's *Journey* serves to effect that same cancelling of the 'against' by the 'for' has been traced through the text by Freya Johnston. The recourse to litotes is crucial, she finds, as reflecting a form of 'double vision' – or 'a dubiously antithetical cast of mind that fluctuates between the romantic and the empirical, the straight path and the devious excursion, between elegant progress and barbaric rudeness' – and as 'permitting the author to display two competing moods and forms of evaluation at one and the same time' (Johnston 2005: 169, 171, 179). When Johnson reports that he and Boswell were 'not without some mournful emotion' as they 'contemplated the ruins of religious structures, and the monuments of the dead' (Johnson 1971: 144), or deplores 'such frigid philosophy as may conduct us indifferent and unmoved over any ground which has been dignified by wisdom, bravery, or virtue' (Johnson 1971: 148), the words he writes give their actual sentiments but also – since these sentiments are reached through the negation of their opposites – paint that more reserved response which his grammar is denying. Boswell and Johnson are two travellers suitably transported and yet, like the audiences which the latter felt that Shakespeare's plays should have (Johnson 1968, 1: 77), 'always in their senses'. Hovering as he therefore does between two quite different reactions, Johnson exhibits what he himself might have termed 'vacillancy' (of which his dictionary definition is 'a state of wavering; fluctuation; inconstancy') or even 'oscillation' ('the act of moving backward and forward like a pendulum'). Certainly with respect to Scotland and the Scots Johnson had exhibited that tendency before; his defiant insistence that 'the noblest prospect which a Scotchman ever sees, is the high road that leads him to England!' (Boswell 1934, 1: 425) emphatically reversed the rueful reflection of twenty-five years earlier, 'who would … change the rocks of Scotland for the Strand?' (Johnson 1964: 48) Once he set foot on Scottish soil, however, he exhibited it more than ever; for the savage parts of Scotland provoked in him both the sceptical and even scornful response of the true-born Englishman and – when he was wearing his other hat (or bonnet) – the sympathetic and even sentimental response of the cordial and expansive 'Toctor Shonson'. The 'wild Tour' indeed becomes a means for him to shift his ground, or (as Curley puts it) 'to revise his previous feelings', even as its successive stages unfold.

Thus it is that Johnson's *Journey*, a generation on from Culloden, gives us a surprisingly scottified English tourist, and also models what would soon become the familiar vacillations of that figure when in the bosom of the Highlands. In the next generation the type took on a compelling fictional life at the hands of Walter Scott, whose birth in Edinburgh in 1771 curiously coincided with Jery Melford's prospective rebirth – as 'a downright Caledonian' – in that same city. Scott's novel *Waverley* (1814) opposes 'belief' in Romantic Scotland to that sober rationality which must assemble the 'argument' against it. Edward Waverley – whose 'wavering and unsettled habit of mind' (Scott 2007: 34) means that his nature matches his name – is drawn in by a glamour to which he submits against his better judgement. Flora Mac-Ivor not only speaks to Waverley about 'the Celtic Muse' (Scott 2007: 114) but fulfils that role for him, becoming an agent of his enthralling exposure to Scottish Gaelic culture: clans and chiefs and songs in Erse, and romantic Jacobitism. Like any 'waverer' (defined in Johnson's *Dictionary* as 'one unsettled and irresolute'), he is impressionable and easily intoxicated. The intoxication inevitably produces an equal and opposite disenchantment, when the romance of Waverley's life ends and its 'real history' commences (Scott 2007: 301). This division in the hero's life reflects the dividedness of the author's sympathies, as explained in a letter of 1813. Here Scott remarks that, if he found himself back in the tumult of 1745, a side of him would certainly support the Rebellion, even though his 'better reason' would demur, and that he remains torn between allegiance to the new order and a sentimental attachment to the old: 'I am not the least afraid nowadays of making my feelings walk hand in hand with my judgement, though the former are Jacobitical the latter inclined for public weal to the present succession' (Grierson, *et al.*, 1932–7, 3: 302–3).

Scott's writing set the terms for a long-running historical controversy over what is gained – or lost – when Hanover succeeds to Stuart, English replaces Erse, the Lowlands assert themselves over the Highlands. More broadly still, Scott encouraged his readers to ask whether when the pendulum swings from Celt to Saxon the change is for the better or not. That question remained on the literary agenda a century later, when George Meredith's novel *Celt and Saxon* was published. Appearing posthumously in 1910, the year of *Howards End*, this nearly qualifies as a second exercise in 'only connect'. Not only is it the case that 'Celt and Saxon are much inmixed with us', but '[a]n ideal of country, of Great Britain, is conceivable that will be to the taste of Celt and Saxon in common, to wave as a standard over their fraternal marching' (Meredith 1910: 179, 182). In order to make it conceivable, however, John Bull – so firmly entrenched in the life of the nation – will have to disappear or mend his ways. Not all Victorian writers would have agreed. Some of Meredith's contemporaries had either had quite different ideas about what might make for a harmonious mixing or rejected his premiss altogether. Juliet Shields (Shields 2007) has very tellingly juxtaposed two works of 1850 which put sharply contrasting positions. One of them, Dinah Craik's novel *Olive*, imagines an amalgamation of Saxon with Celt; but the stance of the other, Robert Knox's *The Races of Men*, is completely uncompromising on this matter. According to Knox, 'no minds are more distinct than the Saxon and the Celtic'; and the lesson we learn not just from history close to home ('There has been no amalgamation of the Celtic and Saxon races in Ireland. They abhor each other cordially') but from the experience of other nations besides is that the two races 'never will mix – never commingle and unite' (Knox 1850: 229, 54, 177).

Knox's vision of the Celt as racially distinct and profoundly 'other' was challenged in the 1860s by Matthew Arnold. Arnold's book of 1867 *On the Study of Celtic Literature* argued that the co-presence in English people of 'the steady-going Saxon temperament and the sentimental Celtic temperament' (and of other elements which are 'Latinised') is an accomplished fact (Arnold 1976: 88) and, moreover, is salutary. Awkward though 'the commixture of elements in us' might seem, 'this mixed constitution of our nature' can be made to work to the advantage of 'us English ourselves':

> Then we may have the good of our German part, the good of our Latin part, the good of our Celtic part; and instead of one part clashing with the other, we may bring it in to continue and perfect the other, when the other has given us all the good it can yield, and by being pressed further, could only give us its faulty excess.
>
> (Arnold 1976: 130–3)

This is a foretaste of Arnold's pleading in *Culture and Anarchy* for 'flexibility', so that we can preserve a balanced blend of Hellenism with Hebraism, and for 'indulgence', so that in everything we can accept an interplay of elements (Arnold 1869: lviii, 105):

> an English Barbarian who examines himself, will, in general, find himself to be not so entirely a Barbarian but that he has in him, also, something of the Philistine, and even something of the Populace as well. And the same with Englishmen of the other two classes.
>
> (Arnold 1869: 106)

What Arnold avoids assuming, either here or in his earlier discussion of Saxon and Celtic characteristics, is that the separate elements in the mix are equally weighted or can be considered equally valuable. The English 'commixture' envisaged in the *Study* is not a union of equals but, as both Vincent Pecora and Gerry Smyth have demonstrated, a 'quite asymmetrical' arrangement in which the Celt is recessive and under the 'benign domination' of the Saxon (Pecora 1998: 368; Smyth 1996: 42). However, even if in a minority, the Celts are still 'a part of ourselves' (Arnold 1976: 134); and Arnold's project is to find out that Celtic part in us, refuting 'the round assertion that it is vain to search for Celtic elements in any modern Englishman' (Arnold 1976: 77).

The battlelines are therefore firmly drawn: there are those who set out with 'the determination to find everything in Celtism and its remains', and also those who are driven by 'the determination to find nothing in them' (Arnold 1976: 33–4). To Arnold, the round assertions of both sides are suspect. Whatever his view had been when he took his Highland tour in 1864 and admitted to 'a great *penchant* for the Celtic races' (quoted in Buckler 1989: 65), the subsequent lectures on Celtic literature (1865–66) and then the published *Study* itself show him inclining to a more dubiously antithetical position. Qualification abounds, and the litotes of 'not without some mournful emotion' becomes in Arnold's *Study* the mid-air state of being not without some hauntings of Celtism: 'The Englishman ... is mainly German ... The Germanic part, indeed, triumphs in us, we are a Germanic people; but not so wholly as to exclude hauntings of Celtism' (Arnold 1976: 103). Arnold's careful formulation precisely expresses what his most palpable predecessor, both as a Highland tourist and as 'the great English Moralist' (Boswell 1950: 335), had felt in the savage parts of Scotland nearly a hundred years earlier. Samuel Johnson, on that occasion, went ghost-hunting among 'the remains of pastoral life' (Johnson 1971: 99) – '[i]nquiring after the reliques of former manners' (Johnson 1971: 142), seeking to pin down what by then was only 'very faintly and uncertainly remembered' (Johnson 1971: 112) – but ended up finding a kind of Celtic ghost in his own mixed constitution. Although the John Bull in him might be benignly dominant, and what 'at bottom' had always defined the man (Boswell 1950: 20), *A Journey to the Western Islands of Scotland* is a text, and a tour, in which we can sense the phantom presence of 'Toctor Shonson' keeping John Bull company.

Note

1 'Under the denomination of "Highlander" are comprehended in Scotland all that now speak the Erse language, or retain the primitive manners, whether they live among the mountains or in the islands; and in that sense I use the name...' (Johnson 1971: 50).

Bibliography

Arnold, Matthew (1869) *Culture and Anarchy: an essay in political and social criticism*, London: Smith and Elder.
—— (1976) *On the Study of Celtic Literature*, in M. Arnold *On the Study of Celtic Literature and Other Essays*, introduction by Ernest Rhys, London: Dent. (Originally published in 1867.)
Boswell, James (1934) *The Life of Samuel Johnson, LL.D.*, vols. 1–4 in G. B. Hill and L. F. Powell (eds) (1934–50) *Boswell's Life of Johnson*, 6 vols, Oxford: Clarendon Press. (Originally published in 1791.)
—— (1950) *The Journal of a Tour to the Hebrides*, vol. 5 in G. B. Hill and L. F. Powell (eds) (1934–50) *Boswell's Life of Johnson*, 6 vols, Oxford: Clarendon Press. (Originally published in 1785.)
Buckler, William E. (1989) '*On the Study of Celtic Literature*: a critical reconsideration', *Victorian Poetry*, 27: 61–76.
Curley, Thomas M. (1976) *Samuel Johnson and the Age of Travel*, Athens, GA: University of Georgia Press.
Grierson, H. J. C. *et al.* (eds) (1932–7) *The Letters of Sir Walter Scott*, 12 vols, London: Constable.
Hart, Jeffrey (1960) 'Johnson's *A Journey to the Western Islands*: history as art', *Essays in Criticism*, 10: 44–59.
Johnson, Samuel (1964) *Poems*, ed. E. L. McAdam, Jr., with George Milne, New Haven, CT and London: Yale University Press.
—— (1968) *Preface to the Plays of Shakespeare*, in A. Sherbo (ed.), *Johnson on Shakespeare*, 2 vols, with an introduction by Bertrand H. Bronson, New Haven, CT and London: Yale University Press. (Originally published in 1765.)

—— (1971) *A Journey to the Western Islands of Scotland*, ed. Mary Lascelles, New Haven, CT and London: Yale University Press. (Originally published in 1775.)

—— (1979) *A Dictionary of the English Language*, unpaginated facsimile edition, London: Times Books. (Originally published in 1755.)

—— (2009) *The History of Rasselas, Prince of Abissinia*, ed. Thomas Keymer, Oxford and New York: Oxford University Press. (Originally published in 1759.)

Johnston, Freya (2005) *Samuel Johnson and the Art of Sinking 1709–1791*, Oxford: Oxford University Press.

Knox, Robert (1850) *The Races of Men: a fragment*, Philadelphia, PA: Lea and Blanchard.

MacNeice, Louis (1990) 'The Hebrides: a tripper's commentary', in A. Heuser (ed.) *Selected Prose of Louis MacNeice*, Oxford: Clarendon, pp. 23–8. (Originally published in 1937.)

Meredith, George (1910) *Celt and Saxon: a novel*, London: Constable.

Pecora, Vincent P. (1998) 'Arnoldian Ethnology', *Victorian Studies*, 41: 355–79.

Rogers, Pat (1995) *Johnson and Boswell: the transit of Caledonia*, Oxford: Clarendon Press.

Scott, Walter (2007) *Waverley*, ed. P. D. Garside, Edinburgh: Edinburgh University Press. (Originally published in 1814.)

Shields, Juliet (2007) 'The races of women: gender, hybridity, and identity in Dinah Craik's *Olive*', *Studies in the Novel*, 39: 284–300.

Smollett, Tobias (1984) *The Expedition of Humphry Clinker*, ed. L. M. Knapp and P.-G. Boucé, Oxford and New York: Oxford University Press. (Originally published in 1771.)

Smyth, Gerry (1996) '"The natural course of things": Matthew Arnold, Celticism and the English poetic tradition', *Journal of Victorian Culture*, 1: 35–53.

Trumpener, Katie (1997) *Bardic Nationalism: the romantic novel and the British empire*, Princeton, NJ: Princeton University Press.

Wheeler, Roxann (2000) *The Complexion of Race: categories of difference in eighteenth-century British culture*, Philadelphia, PA: University of Pennsylvania Press.

PART III

Memory, myth and politics

11

CORNISH CRUSADERS AND BARBARY CAPTIVES

Returns and transformations

Jo Esra

Throughout the seventeenth century, many Cornish seafarers were amongst those taken by Barbary corsairs, and held captive in Islamic North Africa. Captives were taken in coastal raids, from vessels along the coast of Devon and Cornwall and other parts of Britain, as well as from the Mediterranean, which hosted a notoriously mutable and ambivalent mercantile network frequently punctuated by mutual piracy and captive-taking. Whilst some accounts are dubious, what is apparent is that captives were taken in numbers which had a profound economic and emotional impact on West Country communities. Cornwall, with a high level of dependence on seafaring, and a vulnerable geography, was particularly badly affected (Gray 1990; Matar 1998, 1999, 2005; Vitkus 2001, 2003).

Held for ransom, exchanged for Muslim captives, sold or kept as slaves, many died in captivity. Occasionally, captives did manage to return home, some producing captivity narratives recounting their experiences. However, a returning captive – or those claiming to have been held captive – could generate anxieties and suspicions regarding their 'true nature' and whether they had 'turned Turk' (Schen 2008; Matar 1998, 2005). Barbary captives were not merely considered unfortunate individuals in foreign climes. Domestic anxieties converged upon the body of the returned captive, as a potential site of unstable identity and social disruption. Islamic conversion was commonplace, and communities were instructed to examine returned captives for circumcision: renegades could be interrogated and executed if considered unrepentant, possibly through impalement. Three such executions were recorded in 1620 (Matar 1998: 72). Furthermore, climatic influence on the humours was thought to instigate deeper bodily changes: Britons, with their cold, moist disposition, were thought particularly vulnerable to foreign influence, including Islamic conversion (Floyd-Wilson 2003; Paster 2004). The returned captive was therefore a source and a site of cultural apprehension: the returning insider as disruptive outsider, a foreign stranger, 'unnatural' and 'outlandish', with the potential to initiate disorder.[1]

However, whilst there is a wealth of seventeenth-century archival document-ation, reading Barbary captivity within *popular* representations of Cornwall frequently involves engaging with a textual haunting: an unsettling presence which is often marginal, off the page, or under erasure (Wigley 1995). The origins of 'to haunt' is to return, or to bring home, and this chapter will discern such a spectre of Barbary captivity as it haunts three Cornish folktales from the collections of Robert Hunt (1865, 2 volumes) and William Bottrell (1870, 1873), which all contain narratives of returning home to Cornwall from Islamic territories.[2]

Hunt and Bottrell participated in the developing nineteenth-century discipline of 'Folk-Lore', the study of 'traditional' or 'popular' art, narratives, knowledges and practices which were primarily disseminated through oral communication and behaviours (Dorson 1972: 1). Within this discipline stories, customs, ballads and proverbs were viewed as 'fragments' to be collected, arranged and studied, in order to 'obtain a shadowy image' of a culture under erasure (Hunt 1865a: 32).[3] Located within a discourse incorporating earlier topographical writings, Romanticism and the Celtic Revival – which gave primacy to an older, pre-industrial, more romantic Cornwall – these collections have contributed to the emergence of a particular construction of Cornwall. Mapped across an imagined landscape of magic, supernatural beings, ancient traditions and hauntings, the meaning and significance of this 'older' Cornwall is thus constituted not only through experience, but deeply embedded narratives and the emotional responses and *subsequent* experiences they create (Ryden 1993; Walter 1988; Tuan 1977). This chapter will situate Hunt and Bottrell's narratives of returns from Islam within wider textualities and contexts, highlighting a series of returns to home and imagined origins in order to identify how Barbary captivity, as an ambiguous but undoubtedly traumatic episode in Muslim-Christian relations, has shaped the imagined and perhaps competing landscapes of Cornwall.

The first narrative concerns the Pengersick family, consisting of several tales told in both Bottrell and Hunt.[4] Whilst fighting in 'outlandish countries, far away to the east', inhabited by the 'heathen worshippers of Termagaunt', Lord Pengersick falls in love with a Saracen princess. He vows not to wed another. However, he returns to Cornwall and, breaking his promise, marries. Travelling once again to fight in the east – although it is not clear on whose side – he renews his relationship with his love, who is now Queen. Abandoning her during battle, he once again returns to Cornwall, discovering his wife has had a son whilst he has been away. Enraged when his Saracen lover and their son arrive at Pengersick Castle, he casts them into the sea. The child is rescued by his mother's ship, which sails back to the east, but the Queen returns to haunt Pengersick's lands as a white hare, the shape heartbroken Cornish maidens transform into to torment their deceiver.[5] Years pass, his first wife dies, and the old Lord remarries. The new Lady Pengersick has desire for her stepson, young Pengersick. She is rejected, despite her magical interventions, and persuades her husband to sell his son into Barbary captivity. He approaches a ship from:

a city where the people mostly lived by piracy; the crew of this ship – which sailed under any colour that suited their ends – made it their business to land in lonely places, carry off young people, and sell them in Barbary for slaves

(Bottrell 1873: 260).

Contextually, this last passage would seem to allude to the fortified North African city of Algiers, considered the primary base of the corsairs, dependent not only upon trade, but slave labour and the ransom money for European Christian captives. Predatory pirate ships would drag empty casks and fly false colours to convince prize ships they were fellow slow merchant vessels: by the time the victim was close enough to realise, it was too late.[6] However, this plot is foiled by the old Lord's other long-lost son, Arluth, who has returned to Cornwall, and the two brothers sail to the Saracen Queen's homeland. Young Pengersick's long absence leads the people of Pengersick to assume he has been taken as a Barbary captive, and they endeavour to raise a ransom. Meanwhile, he has married a Saracen princess and acquired magical arts before returning to wreak his revenge. Young Pengersick's newly-acquired skills – he returns to Cornwall '[a]fter procuring many magical books and other things, necessary for the practice of the occult sciences' (Bottrell 1873: 263) – can also be read as predicated upon translation and transformation, as part of the sophisticated knowledge systems of the medieval Muslim worlds, which were so vital to the development of science, medicine and philosophy in the west (Toomer 1996; Tolan 2000; Metlitzki 1977).

The second tale, 'The Haunted Mill-Pool of Trove; and the Crusaders' is set in St Buryan, West of Penzance (Bottrell 1870: 277–87). Levelis is apprenticed to a knight and spends many years in the east, whilst his uncle has taken over the lands at Trove to which he is heir. Levelis returns from crusade unexpectedly, as a knight, with an English wife and children: she had secretly followed Levelis to the wars in disguise before marrying him. Unable to settle, however, he goes back to crusading. His corrupt uncle manages to persuade his isolated wife she is a widow and should marry him, but the wedding is halted when the two older children go missing, rumoured sold to 'Turks and Pagans' (Bottrell 1870: 284). An apparition of Levelis appears to the uncle and he flees: upon Levelis's return, he relates a battlefield vision of his children occurring at that very time. Sadly, the children are found drowned in the now haunted mill-pool.

Discerning Barbary captivity within both these tales involves 'tracing the trace of a trace' (Wigley 1995: 165). The brief, haunting presence of Barbary captivity at key narrative points supposedly accounts for the absences of characters, but is itself placed under erasure – as no captives were taken; and displaced – as the visits to Muslim territories are undertaken voluntarily. Both these folktales do, however, conflate Barbary captivity with, what was for Europe, the major historical period informing all subsequent Muslim–Christian interactions: the medieval Crusades, which spanned primarily the eleventh to the thirteenth centuries, although crusading activity continued into the fifteenth century.[7] In doing so, they return to other textualities, including revisiting the 'Popular Romances' of Hunt's subtitle.[8] The Romance genre, emerging during the Crusades and influenced by Arabic storytelling, responded to an expansion of geographic and intellectual boundaries, and attempted to negotiate and narrate the ambiguities of Islamic–Christian contact through a fluid genre marked by textual returns and transformations: translation, rewriting and reinvention (Metlitzki 1977; Robinson 2007; Heng 2003; Whetter 2008). Motifs of medieval Romance are scattered throughout these folktales. Saracen princesses fall in love with Christian knights, characters return transformed through supernatural or magical means, and the appearance of 'Termagaunt', a fictitious Muslim deity who appeared in medieval morality plays and Romances, forms a Saracen trinity with Appolyn and Mahound.[9]

The nineteenth-century European cultural movements of nationalism, Romanticism and colonialism returned to the Crusades, transforming them from Enlightenment vilification as the bloodthirsty fanaticism of the 'Dark Ages' into a morally just precursor of European colonialism. Romanticism's return to the Crusades formed part of a wider, idealised, engagement with medievalism which disregarded historical contexts whilst privileging nostalgia.[10] Although the status of Cornwall within the medieval Romance cycle itself is an area of debate, revivalist constructions emerging after the 1860s sought inspiration from medieval Arthurian Romance, returning to an image of Britain before the arrival of the English, reinventing a Celtic Cornwall (Deacon: 2010: 7–8).[11] King Arthur himself is said to live on in the form of the Cornish *chough*, a belief reflected in the image of the bird used by the Old Cornish Societies, alongside the motto 'King Arthur is not dead' in Cornish (Hunt 1865b: 66–8).

Cross-cultural encounters with Islam provoke ambiguity, and I would argue that these tales demonstrate a tension between a diverse, outward-looking Cornwall, and a simpler, more insular Cornwall constructed through a series of returns. Muslim geographies are textually elsewhere, out of sight, 'outlandish' and 'eastern': the narratives focus on the impact *within Cornwall* of these returns. Returning attempts to resolve divergence and difference: however, whilst Saracen queens and princesses are assimilated into the Cornish landscape, the returning insider resembles the outsider.[12] Levelis is initially unrecognised, 'brown as a berry and bearded like a Turk' (Bottrell 1870: 279), whilst young Pengersick returns with mysterious and magical skills. Even linguistic divergence is collapsed: 'The [outlandish] lady thought our ancient language sounded much like her eastern tongue', relates Bottrell in his Pengersick narrative, 'and that made her feel all the more at home', whereas young Pengersick returns in possession of an 'unknown tongue', in addition to mysterious 'eastern' knowledge and magical powers (1873: 264). Differentiated from the dangerous 'dark-eyed maids of Palestine', Madam Levelis is English: 'a native of some place east of Cornwall, [and] was regarded as a foreigner by the people of the west, whom she could not understand' (Bottrell 1870: 279, 282).

The Levelis narrative observes that the Cornish demonstrate more hostility to the English than to 'people from distant countries' (Bottrell 1870: 280). Here, Cornish difference, particularly in the far west, is represented as originating in the insular, primitive and unworldly, and paradoxically reinforced through *non-encounters* with Islam. In a narrative interlude, crammed with Cornish place-names and revivalist motifs of unique and ancient traditions, Levelis encourages hundreds to join him on Crusade. However, these men and women 'had never been out of the smoke of their own chimneys before'; their understanding of Islam was from miracle plays, resulting in the belief that Muslims spoke Cornish; and once east of Penzance the followers ask whether they have arrived in the Holy Land, stopping at every stream to eat their 'fuggans, hoggans and pasties', before returning home (Bottrell 1870: 281). The remainder leave long before reaching the Tamar, where they spend 'long and weary wanderings from one side of the county to the other' in their attempt to find a short cut back to St Buryan. Bottrell concludes that '[o]ur Cornish warriors were right to come back safe and sound, and let Levelis and St George slay the dragons and the Turkish knights whilst they stayed at home to raise the tin, and tell their drolls'(Bottrell 1870: 282).

This tale prompts a return to other textualities which produce fragments of narrative origins linking both St Buryan – an important pre-Reformation ecclesiastical centre – with Crusade, and western parishioners with failing to honour their pledge (Orme 2000: 78–9). For example, elsewhere, Bottrell refers to a Harley manuscript 'A grete myracle of a knyghte, callyde Syr Roger Wallysborrow', who returns from Crusade protected by a fragment of 'the true cross' embedded in his thigh (Anon.; Bottrell 1873: 270). He names the parish where the relic emerges from his flesh – possibly Grade on the Lizard peninsula, known as St Cross in 1261, the only church along the coast dedicated to the Holy Cross – before also returning to his parish of St Buryan with the remainder of the relic: the themes of bodily returns and transformations become literally intertwined with a sense of place (Henderson 1964: 75–6).

Furthermore, those who signed up for the Third Crusade, called in 1188 as a response to the recapturing of Jerusalem by the Muslim King Saladin, were not only given plenary indulgence – a complete remittance of the penalties for sins already forgiven – but were also excused paying debts whilst on crusade.[13] However, it became apparent that not everyone had fulfilled their vow, despite being threatened with excommunication (Tyerman 1996: 170–1). Two documents survive representing enquires into the matter: one concerns Lincolnshire, the other, Cornwall. Catalogued in 1876 as *cruce signati*, Nicholas Orme and Oliver James Padel's (2005) subsequent examination of the manuscript has revealed it signifies an investigation into those who failed to fulfil their pledge. It lists forty-three or forty-four names from seven of the eight medieval Cornish parishes – the missing parish is in East Cornwall. In addition, these people were neither higher clergy or from the knightly class who had volunteered for the crusade, but failed to go: they included a tailor, a smith, a gamekeeper (*Gualterus de foresta*), a miller, a merchant, two tanners, a shoemaker and two women.[14]

The contexts and textualities of the final narrative, Hunt's 'The Penryn Tragedy', form a more complex set of relations than the other two tales. Hunt tells of a son whose piratical activities result in his captivity in Algiers. He escapes, and earns his fortune apprenticed to a surgeon on an East Indies merchant ship. Returning to Cornwall after fifteen years' absence, he discovers his parents are living in poverty on the outskirts of Penryn, and his sister has married beneath her status. Posing as a poor stranger, he stays the night with his parents, revealing his fortune to his mother before they retire. The mother persuades the father to murder the stranger for his wealth. When the sister arrives in the morning, and the son's true identity is revealed, the father kills himself, closely followed by the mother. The daughter then dies through 'being overcome with horror and amaze of this deluge of destruction' (Hunt 1865b: 255).

From the outset there is a declaration of authentic origins for the tale, which reside within a supposedly lost historical pamphlet. This defines 'The Penryn Tragedy' as a 'legend': a highly localised, mono-episodic and historicised narrative related as believable and unique to the area (Tangherlini 1994: 22; Bhattacharjee 2006: 105; Dégh 2001: 23–47).[15] Hunt's framing text also cites six versions of this narrative, including the 'lost' pamphlet he calls *News from Penryn in Cornwall, of a most bloody and unexampled Murder*.[16] The account he reproduces is from Davies Gilbert's 1838 *Parochial History of Cornwall*, itself a text founded upon the manuscript histories of William Hals and Thomas Tonkins, Cornish historians working in the late seventeenth and early eighteenth centuries. Gilbert's version is from William Sanderson's *A Compleat History of the Lives and Reigns of Mary, Queen of Scotland, and of Her Son and Successor, James the Sixth, King of Scotland her son James*, first published in 1656, and this is assumed to be an accurate version of the original document, although, for example, he does add a treacherous Jewish character (Sanderson 1656: 463–465).[17] Sanderson gives a cautionary moral framework to the tale, using reports of '*Theft, Rapine,* [plunder] *Murthers,* and such like' to 'mind us hourely to beg of God… least we fall into Temptations of sin and Satan' (Sanderson 1656: 465).

Hunt also refers to George Lillo's 1736 play, *Fatal Curiosity: A True Tragedy*, set in Penryn and based on the events of the pamphlet narrative, which emphasizes a return to an original, true source. The play appeared in numerous printed editions, with the sixth edition, *A Fatal Curiosity An Affecting Narrative, Founded on Facts*, published in Liverpool in 1767, providing an additional text, a letter from Sir Walter to Lady Ralegh, composed at Winchester while he was awaiting his execution. Other editions included a German translation and subsequent German plays supposedly inspired by *Fatal Curiosity* (Sandbach 1923). However, Lillo erases the protagonist's involvement in piracy and his time as a Barbary captive, merely mentioning his being robbed by 'lawless pyrates; by the *Arabs* thrice' (Lillo 1736: 35).

This narrative is repeated frequently within historical, folkloric, topographical and travel writings concerned with Cornwall and Cornish identity throughout the nineteenth century which, whilst shifting in emphasis and detail, all undergo a series of returns back to either Lillo or Sanderson, not the pamphlet which Hunt identifies as *News from Penryn*. These include, for example, Samuel and Daniel Lysons (1814), Joseph Polsue (1868) and Charles Dickens (1869). Some accounts, such as that by Samuel Drew and Fortescue Hitchens in their 1824 'Dreadful Effects of the Love of Gold, in a Horrid Murder Committed near Penryn', and Sabine Baring-Gould's brief account in 1899, merely provide a synopsis of *Fatal Curiosity*, without piracy, North Africa or Barbary captivity.

These complex, excessive, and unstable intertextual relations are produced by a ghostly document which consistently remained out of view. Sanderson also left the possibility of residual knowledge of the family's identity, originating with his closing comments: 'the imprinted relation conceals their Names in favour to some Neighbour of Repute and Kin to that Family. The same sense makes me therein silent also' (Sanderson 1656: 465). As the geographer Yi-Fu Tuan points out, '[m]yths flourish in the absence of precise knowledge' (1977: 85), and such a statement, combined with lost origins and gaps in the historical record, has instigated a textual layering, embedding this legend within the landscape.[18] This layering has included locating the murder as occurring in a barn at Bohelland Farm, on St Gluvias church land, which was introduced to the narrative from the early nineteenth century.[19] More recent transformations of 'The Penryn Tragedy' have increased this sense of localised Cornish identity, particularly the 1997 and 2003 productions of Justin Chubb's *Bohelland* by The Cornish Theatre Collective. The play references the pamphlet, one of which is extant, through the woodcut imagery on their publicity material, although transformed once again, being referred to as 'The Bohelland Tragedy'. Performed partially in Cornish, against a background of smuggling and witchcraft, *Bohelland* follows the tradition of Hunt, rather than the seventeenth century pamphlet itself.

The pamphlet was published in 1618 anonymously, with the full title *Newes from Perin* [not 'Penrin'] *in Cornwall: Of A Most Bloody and vn-exampled Murther very lately committed by a Father on his owne Sonne (who was lately returned from the Indyes) at the Instigation of a mercilesse Step-mother, Together with their Severall most wretched endes, being all performed in the Month of September last* – a murder performed as well as committed, suggestive of its dramatic content. This was a black-letter news or murder pamphlet, which was unlikely to be reprinted, and, as with Sanderson's text, unconcerned with Cornish identity. Such pamphlets were ephemeral, reporting on 'unusual', 'monstrous' or 'unnatural' events within a moralising framework, warning of sinful living and illustrating God's providential control of human affairs, which legitimised the publishing of gratuitously horrifying stories (Lake and Questier 2002: 146; Clark 1983: 186). Whilst *Newes from Perin* has been included in scholarship on seventeenth-century pamphlets in this context, the practices of Barbary captivity, and the protagonist's identity as an ex-captive, has not been explored (Lake and Questier 2002: 176–8; Clark 1983: 107).

The pamphlet does depict the common theme of a domestic crime, and, through their concentrating on an unstable and inverted social order, such representations could demonstrate the tragic consequences of undermining authority from within. The threat of social disorder was located in the familiar and the intimate, mapped onto family breakdown and articulated through a struggle between the devil and human sin on one side, and divine providence, justice and mercy on the other (Lake and Questier 2002: 147–8; Dolan 1994: 4). Unlike subsequent versions, *Newes from Perin* contains a virtuous mother who has died from grief due to her son's errant ways, and whose husband remarries. Internal authority is thus undermined not only through the problematic figure of the unruly son and returning captive, but also a stepmother who was 'more respecting her owne future estate, then his [the father's] present welfare: And [...] preferred the good of [her] owne Children before them, to whom they are but mothers in Law' (f.8).

An outward focus in women was viewed as making her particularly inclined towards sin, which gave the devil agency, and multiple sins formed a chain which could lead to murder (Flather 2007: 18–19; Martin 2008: 18–19). Whilst it is the father in the narrative who actually commits the act of prolicide, the stepmother's sins of covetousness and greed allow the devil a foothold. As is common in morality tales, the devil makes an appearance in *Newes from Perin*: not physically, but as a spectral being, although sometimes woodcuts would show a devilish figure:

> the Devill, that is alwayes ready to take holde of the least advantage [...] to increase his kingdome, whispered this comfort in her eare, shewing her the golden temptation: saying, all this will I give thee, if though wilt but make away a poore stranger that sleepes under thy mercy.
>
> (f)

Newes from Perin also makes a series of textual returns to reinforce the moral theme. The appearance of a screech owl at the window originates in medieval texts, with the owl's shrieks foretelling disaster and symbolising the wailing of the sinner in hell (Miyazaki 1999: 28); whilst the Biblical story of the prodigal son, a common source of sixteenth- and seventeenth-century theological debates regarding forgiveness of sin and the process of redemption, also informs the narrative in an inverted form. Sin was initiated by the son, responsible for his mother's death and his father's poverty, as well as other 'bloody and un-repented sinnes [...] Theft, Piracy, Murther, Drunkennes, Swearing, Lust, blasphemy and the like' (f3). These form a chain of sins which lead to the tragic conclusion, rather than the joyful reunion of the Biblical tale (Haeger 1986: 128–138).

Providential happenings were also characteristic of Barbary captivity narratives, as well as moral pamphlets, demonstrating evidence of being God's elect. This also enabled tales of remarkable escapes in spectacular circumstances. Providence and mutability punctuate *Newes from Perin,* and the pamphlet also provides an account of the son's time as a galley slave, detailing the harsh conditions and treatment, giving the narrative generic tropes of a captivity narrative (Snader 2000: 91; Matar 2001: 32–8; Walsham 2001). Whilst many believed that conversion meant automatic release from captivity, the Qur'an recommended, rather than commanded, Muslims to release co-religionists. However, only a Christian could be a galley slave (Matar 1998: 25–7, 32). Many captives did convert to Islam: William Davies observed in his account published in 1614 that there were more renegades in Barbary than 'natural Turkes' (B3v). Narratives of forced conversions became commonplace, despite the observations of others to the contrary (Matar 1998: 31). The galley slave therefore became an important motif to reinforce religious fidelity through adversity, especially if a captive returned wealthy; or in order to claim charity if they returned destitute. However, the survival and return of a Barbary captive in itself would be enough to provoke suspicion, and 'secret renegades' were thought to be commonplace within the seafaring communities (Matar 1998: 63–71).

In addition, contemporary texts tended to articulate moral and social decay through the vulnerability of the inhabitants of the British Isles to foreign contamination, as well as through a domestic framework. John Deacon, in his *Tobacco Tortured* wrote how,

> We leaue our ancient simplicitie [...] in a forreine ayre and [...] do too greedily sucke vp from foreigners, not their vertues, but vices, and monstrous corruptions, as well in religion and manners [...] so many of our English-men's minds are terribly *Turkished* with *Mahometan* trumperies.
> (1616: 10).

Similarly, Barnaby Rich, also in 1616, stated that '[w]e haue stol[en] the *Turke* and *Infidel* of his infidelity and vnbeliefe' (10). The mobile body of the returning Barbary captive – in *Newes from Perin,* a literal site of unstable identity and social disruption – could absorb, return and communicate this contamination, which instigated unnatural vices and barbaric impulses. The barbaric practices of the Turks were frequently recorded, including parricide and prolicide, echoed in *Newes from Perin*. Richard Knolles in his *The Generall Historie of the Turkes*, published in 1603, wrote of a recent incident, concluding, 'what can be thereunto more contrarie, than for the father most vnnaturally to embrue his hands in the bloud of his own children? [...] A common matter among the *Othoman* [Ottoman] Emperours' (3).

However, historically, Islamic society was tolerant and highly absorbent. Conversion itself was relatively simple and offered superior living conditions and economic opportunities than those available back home, regardless of social or ethnic origins: indeed, converts to Islam from the British Isles did tend to be of lower social status (Matar 1998: 41–4). The attractions of Islam were necessarily and inevitably transferred, with the motivation for conversion explained through religious and medical discourses of sin and humoural predisposition – tropes made available within *Newes from Perin* – which could result in murder and damnation if not resisted.

I would suggest, therefore, that the return of Hunt's nineteenth-century narrative to an *absent* originating text has enabled and reinforced a sense of localised Cornish identity. However, the material *presence* of the pamphlet uncovers the illusion of a fixed starting point, as narrative emphasis and details shift. Situating the pamphlet within wider contexts reveals the extent to which Barbary captivity and the moral impulse of the pamphlet have been consistently placed under erasure; and how the narrative is transformed within folkloric cartographies which attempt to map a textual return to an 'older', pre-industrial Cornwall. Furthermore, it would seem a virtually identical German murder was reported in 1618, and in 1649 in Bohemia (Westwood and Simpson 2005: 105). The story of a son, believed dead but returning home wealthy to find his parents in poverty, then being murdered for his money whilst posing as a stranger, provides a highly adaptable narrative which is not geographically specific. Ironically, a pamphlet produced primarily for a London readership, set far enough away to prevent verification, has been assimilated within that specific 'isolated' location. In addition, recovery of *Newes from Perin* reveals both a narrative of Barbary captivity, and its subsequent marginalisation: an erasure of the element which delivers the possibility of authenticity to the narrative's geographical setting.

Within all three of Hunt and Bottrell's narratives discussed in this chapter, Barbary captivity has been marginalised or erased, or conflated with Crusade and the related literary genre of Romance, as transformed through the nineteenth-century cultural movement of Romanticism. The folkloric work of Hunt and Bottrell, as part of the Celtic Revival within which it is situated, has contributed to one of the dominant discursive constructions of Cornwall and Cornish identity which still has resonance in the present day. However, I would argue that returning to Barbary captivity within these collections transforms these imaginings of the Cornish landscape.

Captivity narratives are generically multiple, partly constituted through modern discourses of trauma, and the impulse to 'tell and transform'. The struggle to articulate trauma beyond the body therefore produces narratives which attempt to navigate and resolve traumatic episodes within the available early-modern discourses of divine providence and humoral medicine. Similarly, it has been argued that medieval Romance emerged due to the inability of historical narratives to relate the failure, and negotiate the trauma, of crusade, including crusade cannibalism on the bodies of Saracens in Syria (Heng 1998: 98 – 174). The conflation of history and fantasy produced a genre where historical trauma could be reinterpreted and transformed. In this reading, therefore, the marginal and repressed presence of Barbary captivity within Hunt and Bottrell's folktales becomes interpreted as a product of cultural trauma. Another, alternative, Cornwall emerges: a landscape haunted by those who could not, or would not, return.

Notes

1 Whilst Cornwall was 'accustomed' to mobility at this time, for example through their involvement with settling colonies and the Newfoundland fisheries, cultural understandings of mobility were highly ambivalent during this period. Long periods of absence also had an inevitable emotional impact on those at home. For a history of Cornish mobility see Payton (2005) *The Cornish Overseas: A History of Cornwall's 'Great Emigration'*, Fowey: Cornish Editions Ltd., especially pp. 30–53; for early-modern mobility and the working poor, see Fumerton (2006) *Unsettled: The Culture of Mobility and the Working Poor in Early Modern England*, Chicago and London: The University of Chicago Press.

2 Bottrell (1870, 1873) *Traditions and Hearthside Stories of West Cornwall* vols 1 and 2, Penzance: W. Cornish; Hunt (1865) *The Drolls, Traditions and Superstitions of Old Cornwall (Popular Romances of the West of England)* 1st and 2nd Series, London: John Camden Hotten. These were the first collections of Cornish folktales published: Hunt's two-series collection, whilst published first, included much folklore collected by Bottrell, also known as 'An Old Celt', earlier on in the century. Barbary corsairs also feature in two other narratives in Bottrell (1870) set at sea. 'The White Witch or Charmer of Zennor', pp. 69–114, includes an account told by an 'aged seaman' who had served on a privateer ship of a heroic sea battle involving Spanish privateers and Barbary corsairs, pp. 108–10; and in 'Nancy Trenoweth, the Fair Daughter of the Miller of Alsia', pp. 189–209, some Cornish sea 'rovers' outwit a ship of Muslim pirates by getting them drunk, pp. 205–9.

3 Hunt describes these items as having 'floated down to us as wreck upon the ocean. We gather a fragment here and a fragment there, and at length, it may be we learn something of the name and character of the vessel when it was freighted with life and obtain a shadowy image of the people who have perished'. This is echoed in the Cornish language motto of the Federation of Old Cornwall Societies, formed in the early 1920s: 'Kyntelleugh an brewyon es gesys na vo kellys travyth': 'Gather ye the fragments that are left, that nothing be lost'. Berresford Ellis (1974) *The Cornish Language and Its Literature*, London: Routledge and Kegan Paul, p. 158.

4 Bottrell, 'A Legend of Pengersec', op. cit., 1873, pp. 251–67; Hunt, 'How Pengerswick became a Sorcerer', 'The Lord of Pengerswick an Enchanter', 'The Witch of Fraddam and Pengerswick', op. cit., 1865b, pp. 322–7.

5 Usually only the deceiver can see the white hare, and whilst sometimes it saves him from danger, it tends to cause the death of the betrayer. Amongst fishermen the white hare appears to warn of tempests. Hunt, op. cit., 1865b, pp. 162–4, 481.

6 Another decoy method used was for Islamic converts on the corsair vessel to call out in the language of the prize ship. An ex-captive from Exeter, Joseph Pitts, describes how a corsair ship hung out the King's colours which tricked the victim into lowering their sails: they plundered and sank the ship. Pitts (1704) *A True and Faithful Account of the Religion and Manners of the Mohammetans*, Exeter.

7 Crusade was viewed as a kind of penance, along with pilgrimage, and a crusade to Jerusalem itself was a form of pilgrimage, although traditional pilgrims did not fight. 'To take the cross' was to take a vow to go, and those who did sewed a cross onto their clothing as a symbol of that vow – referred to as *se croisier* in medieval French, and *crucizo* in medieval Latin, where the terms crusade and crusader developed – but up until the fifteenth century the expeditions were usually just referred to as pilgrimages. Nicholson (2004) *The Crusades*, Westport, CT: Greenwood Press, pp. xxxix, xli–xlii.

8 'Romance' referred to the linguistic and literary endeavours of transforming and translating Latin texts into vernacular French, or romance language, the practice described in Old French as 'mettre en romanz'. B. Fuchs (2004) *Romance*, Oxford and New York: Routledge, p. 37.

9 By *c*.1500, the word 'Termagaunt' had come to refer to violent, overbearing people, particularly women. Schaus (2006) *Women and Gender in Medieval Europe: An Encyclopedia*, New York and London: Routledge, p. 594; Metlitzki (1977) *The Matter of Araby in Medieval England*, New Haven and London: Yale University Press, pp. 136–87.

10 However, there is palpable ambiguity within the genre due to tensions between the supposed civilising agenda of crusading, and the Protestant conviction that crusading was a product of Catholic intolerance and barbarism. Krueger (2000) 'Introduction' in Krueger (ed.) *The Cambridge Companion to Medieval Romance*, Cambridge: Cambridge University Press, pp. 1–9, p. 1; Riley-Smith (2005) *The Crusades: A History*, London: Continuum, p. 300; Madden (2005) *The New Concise History of the Crusades*, Lanham, MD: Rowman and Littlefield, p. 214.

11 The status of Cornwall in relation to Englishness within medieval Romance has not been fully explored. For example, within the cycle 'The Matter of England', the non-Arthurian romances, scholars have stated that there is an English ideology constructed through the discourses of history and chorography which situates Ireland and Scotland as little more than outlying regions of England. See: Fulton (2010) 'A Single Nation?' in E. Treharne and G. Walker (eds) *The Oxford Handbook of Medieval Literature in English*, Oxford: Oxford University Press, pp. 515–40. Rouse (2005, *The Idea of Anglo-Saxon England in Middle English Romance*, Cambridge: D. S. Brewer) usefully discusses whether the Englishness constructed in the Matter of England romances is a homogenous whole, or contains regional tensions.

12 This 'same-ing' of Muslim women, removing any agency which they may have, is a trope of medieval romance. Kahf (1999) *Western Representations of the Muslim woman: from termagant to odalisque*, Austin: University of Texas Press, p. 53.

13 Plenary indulgence could also be obtained by those who were too old, ill, or unfit to crusade. The vow would be taken and, if enough money was paid towards funding the crusade, a plenary indulgence could be obtained. This was attractive to the dying wealthy, who would receive full forgiveness of their sins at a time when they were unlikely to commit many new ones. This group, known as *crucesignati/crucesignatae*, were targeted by crusade propagandists. Maier (2000) *Crusade Propaganda and Ideology: Model Sermons for the Preaching of the Cross*, Cambridge: Cambridge University Press, p. 63.

14 The Cornish document is in the Canterbury Cathedral Archives, DCc MSSB/A/7, and briefly described in the 1876 *Historical Manuscripts Commission, Fifth Report*, London: George Edward Eyre and William Spottiswoode, Appendix, p. 462: 'Hec sunt nomina cruce signatorum in Archidiaconatu Cornubie'. See Orme and Padel (2005) 'Cornwall and the Third Crusade', *Journal of the Royal Institution of Cornwall*. 71–7.

15 'Legend', from 'legenda', or 'things to be read', has been transformed from being used in Catholic hagiography for the stories of the Saints, into signifying the idea of dubious origins as part of a Protestant project to contrast with the 'real' saints and martyrs of the Reformation, used to imply 'inauthentic'. Folklore studies shifted this meaning once again. Collinson (2003) *Elizabethans*, London: Continuum International Publishing Group, pp. 151–77.

16 These are: Gilbert; Lysons; Lillo; Sanderson; and 'The celebrated Mr. Harris of Salisbury' in his *Philological Inquiries* (1781), who repeats Lillo's dramatic plot. Hunt, op. cit., 1865b, pp. 255, 253.

17 Sanderson was writing within an apocalyptical culture leading up to 1666, of which 1656 was also an important year: the year supposed to bring the downfall of Rome. Prophecies of doom included those of Turkish invasion, with mass conversions to Christianity by Muslims and Jews in 1699. B. S. Capp (1979) *Astrology and the Popular Press: English Almanacs 1500–1800*, London: Faber, pp. 170–7.

18 St Gluvias church records for the relevant years are either missing or water damaged; there are no Bohelland land deeds for those years; and a contemporary map does not show land beyond the church.

19 Lysons and Lysons (1814) mentions the site of the house at 'an estate called
    Bohelland' (119) is still pointed out as the scene, whilst Drew and Hitchens (1824)
    state that '[a]bout half a mile on the northern side of Gluvias church, is still a barn
    which nearly occupies the site of a house, in which was committed a singular
    murder […] it furnished Lillo with a plot for one of his dramas entitled 'The Penryn
    Tragedy'[…] This place is now called Behelland Barn' (294).There is now a modern
    housing estate at Bohelland.

Bibliography

Anon., 'A grete myracle of a knyghte, callyde Syr Roger Wallysborrow', BL Harl. Mss
    2252 (temp. Hen. VIII).
Anon., *Newes from Perin in Cornwall: Of A Most Bloody and vn-exampled Murther very lately
    committed by a Father on his owne Sonne (who was lately returned from the Indyes) at the
    Instigation of a mercilesse Step-mother, Together with their Severall most wretched endes, being all
    performed in the Month of September last,* London: 1618.
Baring–Gould, S., *A Book of the West II: Cornwall*, London: Methuen, 1899.
Bhattacharjee, K., 'The Legend, Popular Discourse and Local Community: The Case
    of Assamese Legends', in M. D. Muthukumaraswamy (ed.) *Folklore as Discourse*,
    Chennai, India: National Folklore Support Centre, 2006, pp. 105–117.
Berresford Ellis, P., *The Cornish Language and its Literature*, London: Routledge and Kegan
    Paul, 1974.
Bottrell, W., *Traditions and Hearthside Stories of West Cornwall* vol. 1, Penzance: W. Cornish,
    1870.
—— *Traditions and Hearthside Stories of West Cornwall* vol. 2, Penzance: W. Cornish, 1873.
Capp, B. S., *Astrology and the Popular Press: English Almanacs 1500–1800*, London: Faber,
    1979.
Chubb, J., *Bohelland*, The Cornish Theatre Collective. Online. Available at www.cornish-
    theatre-collective.co.uk/bohelland1997.html (accessed 4 May 2010).
Clark, S., *The Elizabethan Pamphleteers: Popular Moralistic Pamphlets 1580–1640*, London:
    The Athlone Press, 1983.
Collinson, P., *Elizabethans*, London: Continuum International Publishing Group, 2003.
Davies, W., *True Relation of the Travailes and most miserable Captivitie of William Davies, Barber-
    Surgion of London, under the Duke of Florence*, London: 1614.
Deacon, B., *Cornwall and the Cornish*, Penzance: Alison Hodge, 2010.
Deacon, J., *Tobacco Tortured, Or the Filthie Fume of Tobacco Refined*, London: 1616.
Dégh, L., *Legend and Belief*, Bloomington: Indiana University Press, 2001.
Dickens, C., 'As The Crow Flies. Due West. Penryn to the Land's End', *All the Year Round*
    N.S. vol. 1 (22) Saturday 1 May, 1869, p. 514.
Dolan, F., *Dangerous Familiars: Representations of Domestic Crime in England 1550–1700*,
    Ithaca and New York: Cornell University Press, 1994.
Dorson, R. M., 'Concepts of Folklore and Folklife Studies' in R. M. Dorson (ed.) *Folklore
    and Folklife: An Introduction*, London: The University of Chicago Press, 1972, pp. 1–50.
Drew S. and Hitchens, F., 'Dreadful Effects of the Love of Gold, in a Horrid Murder
    Committed near Penryn', in S. Drew and F. Hitchens, *The History of Cornwall, From
    the Earliest Records and Traditions, to the Present Time*, vol. 2, Helston: William Penaluna,
    1824, pp. 294–295.
Flather, A., *Gender and Space in Early Modern England*, Suffolk: The Boydell Press, 2007.
Floyd-Wilson, M. *English Ethnicity and Race in Early Modern Drama*, Cambridge: Cambridge
    University Press, 2003.

Fuchs, B., *Romance,* Oxford and New York: Routledge, 2004.

Fulton, H., 'A Single Nation?' in E. Treharne and G. Walker (eds) *The Oxford Handbook of Medieval Literature in English,* Oxford: Oxford University Press, 2010, pp. 515–40.

Fumerton, P., *Unsettled: The Culture of Mobility and the Working Poor in Early Modern England,* Chicago and London: The University of Chicago Press: 2006.

Gilbert, D., *The Parochial History of Cornwall, Founded on the Manuscript Histories of Mr. Hals and Mr. Tonkin,* 4 vols, London: J. B. Nichols and Son, 1838.

Gray, T., 'Turks, Moors and the Cornish Fishermen: Piracy in the Early Seventeenth Century', *Journal of the Royal Institution of Cornwall,* 1990: 457–475.

Haeger, B., 'The Prodigal Son in Sixteenth- and Seventeenth-Century Netherlandish Art: Depictions of the Parable and the Evolution of a Catholic Image', *Simiolus Netherlands Quarterly for the History of Art,* 16 (2/3), 1986: 128–138.

'Hec sunt nomina cruce signatorum in Archidiaconatu Cornubie', *Canterbury Cathedral Archives,* DCc MSSB/A/7.

Henderson, C., *The Cornish Church Guide and Parochial History of Cornwall,* Truro: Barton, 1964.

Heng, G., 'Cannibalism, the First Crusade, and the Genesis of Medieval Romance', *Differences,* 10 (1) 1998: 98–174.

—— *Empire of Magic: Medieval Romance and the Politics of Cultural Fantasy,* New York and Chichester: Columbia University Press, 2003.

Historical Manuscripts Commission, Fifth Report, London: George Edward Eyre and William Spottiswoode, 1876.

Hunt, R., *The Drolls, Traditions and Superstitions of Old Cornwall (Popular Romances of the West of England),* 1st series, London: John Camden Hotten, 1865a.

—— *The Drolls, Traditions and Superstitions of Old Cornwall (Popular Romances of the West of England),* 2nd series, London: John Camden Hotten, 1865b.

Kahf, M., *Western Representations of the Muslim woman: from termagant to odalisque,* University of Texas Press, 1999.

Knolles, R., *The generall historie of the Turkes,* London: 1603.

Krueger, R. L., 'Introduction' in R. L. Krueger (ed.) *The Cambridge Companion to Medieval Romance,* Cambridge: Cambridge University Press, 2000, pp. 1–9.

Lake P. and Questier, M., *The Anti-Christ's Lewd Hat. Protestants, Papists and Players in Post-Reformation England,* New Haven and London: Yale University Press, 2002.

Lillo, G., *Fatal Curiosity: A True Tragedy,* London: 1736.

—— *A Fatal Curiosity An Affecting Narrative, Founded on Facts,* Liverpool: 1767.

Lysons, S. and Lysons, D., *Magna Britannia, Being a Concise Topographical Account of the Several Counties of Great Britain: Cornwall,* London: Thomas Cadell, 1814.

Madden, T. F., *The New Concise History of the Crusades,* Lanham, MD: Rowman and Littlefield, 2005.

Maier, C. T., *Crusade Propaganda and Ideology: Model Sermons for the Preaching of the Cross,* Cambridge: Cambridge University Press, 2000.

Martin, R., *Women, Murder, and Equity in Early Modern England,* New York and Oxford: Routledge, 2008.

Matar, N., *Islam in Britain 1558–1685* Cambridge: Cambridge University Press, 1998.

—— *Turks, Moors, and Englishmen in the Age of Discovery,* Chichester: Columbia University Press, 1999.

—— 'Introduction: England and Mediterranean Captivity, 1577 – 1704', in D. J. Vitkus (ed.) *Piracy, Slavery, and Redemption: Barbary Captivity Narratives from Early Modern England,* New York and Chichester: Columbia University Press, 2001, pp. 1–52.

—— *Britain and Barbary, 1589–1689,* Gainesville, FL: University Press of Florida, 2005.

Metlitzki, D., *The Matter of Araby in Medieval England*, New Haven and London: Yale University Press, 1977.

Miyazaki, M., 'Misericord Owls and Medieval Anti-semitism', in Debra Hassig (ed.) *The Mark of the Beast: The Medieval Bestiary in Art, Life, and Literature*, New York: Garland, 1999, pp. 23–47.

Nicholson, H., *The Crusades*, Westport, CT: Greenwood Press, 2004.

Orme, N., *The Saints of Cornwall*, Oxford: Oxford University Press, 2000.

Orme, N. and Padel, O. J., 'Cornwall and the Third Crusade', *Journal of the Royal Institution of Cornwall*, 2005: 71–7.

Paster, G. K., *Humoring the Body: Emotions and the Shakespearean Stage*, London: The University of Chicago Press, 2004.

Payton, P., *The Cornish Overseas: A History of Cornwall's 'Great Emigration'*, Fowey: Cornish Editions Ltd, 2005.

Pitts, J., *A True and Faithful Account of the Religion and Manners of the Mohammetans. In which is a particular Relation of their Pilgrimage to Mecca, The Place of Mohammet's birth; And a description of Medina, and of his Tomb there. As likewise of Algier, and the Country adjacent: And of Alexandria, Grand-Cairo, &c. With an Account of the Author's being taken Captive, the Turks Cruelty to him, and of his Escape. In which are many things never Publish'd by any Historian before*, Exeter: 1704.

Polsue, J., *A Complete Parochial History of the County of Cornwall, Compiled from the Best Authorities and Corrected and Improved from Actual Survey* vol. 2, Truro: William Lake, London: John Camden Hotten, 1868.

Rich, B., *My Ladies Looking Glasse. Wherein may be discerned a wise man from a foole, a good woman from a bad, and the true resemblance of vice masked under the vizard of virtue*, London: 1616.

Riley-Smith, J., *The Crusades: A History*, London: Continuum, 2005.

Robinson, B., *Islam and Early Modern English Literature: The Politics of Romance from Spenser to Milton*, Hants: Palgrave, 2007.

Rouse, R. A., *The Idea of Anglo-Saxon England in Middle English Romance*, Cambridge: D. S. Brewer, 2005.

Ryden, K. C., *Mapping the Invisible Landscape: Folklore, writing and the sense of place*, Iowa City: University of Iowa Press, 1993.

Sandbach, F. E., 'Karl Philipp Moritz's "Blunt" and Lillo's "Fatal Curiosity"', *The Modern Language Review*, 18 (4) 1923: 449–457.

Sanderson, W., *A Compleat History of the Lives and Reigns of Mary, Queen of Scotland, And of Her Son and Successor, James the Sixth, King of Scotland her son James*, London: 1656.

Schaus, M., *Women and Gender in Medieval Europe: An Encyclopedia*, New York and London: Routledge, 2006.

Schen, C. S., 'Breaching "Community" in Britain: Captives, Renegades, and the Redeemed', in M. J. Halvorson and K. E. Spierling (eds) *Defining Community in Early Modern Europe* Hants: Ashgate, 2008, pp. 229–246.

Snader, J., *Caught Between Worlds: British Captivity Narratives in Fact and Fiction*, Lexington: The University Press of Kentucky, 2000.

Tangherlini, T. R., *Interpreting Legend: Danish Storytellers and Their Repertoires*, New York: Garland, 1994.

Tolan, J., 'Introduction', in J. Tolan (ed.) *Medieval Christian Perceptions of Islam* New York and London: Routledge, 2000, pp. xi–xxi.

Toomer, G. J., *Eastern Wisedome and Learning: The Study of Arabic in Seventeenth-Century England*, Oxford: Oxford University Press, 1996.

Tuan, Y-F., *Space and Place: The Perspective of Experience*, Minneapolis: University of Minnesota Press, 1977.

Tyerman, C., *England and the Crusades 1095–1588*, Chicago: University of Chicago Press, 1996.

Vitkus, D. J. (ed.), *Piracy, Slavery, and Redemption: Barbary Captivity Narratives from Early Modern England*, New York: Columbia University Press, 2001.

—— *Turning Turk: English Theater and the Multicultural Mediterranean 1570–1630*, Basingstoke: Palgrave Macmillan, 2003.

Walsham, A., *Providence in Early Modern England*, Oxford: Oxford University Press, 2001.

Walter, E. V., *Placeways: A Theory of the Human Environment*, USA: UNC Press, 1988.

Westwood, J. and Simpson J., *The Lore of the Land. A Guide to England's Legends, from Spring-Heeled Jack to the Witches of Warboys*, London: Penguin, 2005.

Whetter, K. S., *Understanding Genre and Medieval Romance*, Aldershot: Ashgate, 2008.

Wigley, M., *The Architecture of Deconstruction: Derrida's Haunt*, Cambridge, MA: MIT Press, 1995.

12

RE-ENACTING SCOTTISH HISTORY IN EUROPE

David Hesse

In the past two decades, 'Scotland' has become an established genre in historical re-enactment. In Europe, North America and Australasia, many dozens of hobbyist groups regularly come together to recreate scenes and characters from the Scottish past. This chapter discusses *European* re-enactments of Scottish history.[1] It first examines the cultural practice that is historical re-enactment and its development since the 1960s. It then explores the Scottish genre, the moments in Scottish history which hobbyists find usable for their performances. It addresses the issue of authenticity, the activists' attempts to separate myth from fact and to stage the past, by their reckoning, 'as it really was'. It discusses the role of female players in the predominantly male community of Scottish re-enactment. Lastly, the chapter analyzes the players' relationship to Scotland, the place on the map. The hobbyists' insistence that a re-enactor requires skills and knowledge rather than blood and residency in order to become a proper Scot of the past may enrich our understanding of 'ethnic' performances. Historical re-enactors and 'roots re-enactors' have much in common.

To re-enact the past

In everyday usage, 'historical re-enactment' stands for the theatrical recreation of past events and periods for the purpose of entertainment and/or education. This is how the term will be used here.[2] In academic discourse, 're-enactment' may also denote an historical method. The British philosopher and historian R.G. Collingwood (1889–1943) popularised the term in the 1940s, recommending that every historian should temporarily 'become' the people he or she studied. To comprehend the lives of the past, Collingwood argued, 'the historian must re-enact the past in his own mind' (Collingwood 1946: 282).

Notably, such re-enactment remained a cognitive effort; Collingwood never suggested the historian should get up and wield a broad-sword.

Physical re-enactments may be encountered at the museum. At least since the 1926 opening of Colonial Williamsburg in the U.S., staff at 'living history' museums try to bring history alive by wearing costume and re-playing past events. The idea is that history will be better understood when recreated in the flesh.[3] This idea is increasingly found in the academic domain as well. Since the 1970s, many historians of science and experimental archaeologists argue that, in order to really understand researchers and craftsmen of the past, one has to recreate their workshops by employing period equipment and techniques.[4]

History has been replayed in ceremonies and on the theatre stage for many centuries.[5] However, as a participative hobby for the masses, historical re-enactment originated in the late 1960s, when thousands of amateurs began to physically reproduce the past in social clubs. The battle shows at the U.S. Civil War centennials between 1961 and 1964, and the early role-playing events of the *Society for Creative Anachronism*, founded in Berkeley, California, in 1966, are alternatively seen as the beginning of hobbyist re-enactment.[6] The spread of historical re-enactment must be understood as a symptom of what Jay Winter calls the memory boom, an increasing public preoccupation with the past and its commemoration.[7] Spreading affluence among the baby boomer generation of the West inspired new forms and markets of mass leisure, while a growing sense of nostalgia and anti-modernism made the past increasingly attractive as an exciting counter-world on these markets.[8] In the 1960s, historical re-enactment was recognised as an entrance into this counter-world, a way of experiencing history, both as an active performer and a passive spectator. Unsurprisingly, scholars of tourism and marketing have approached re-enactment and its economic potential with particular enthusiasm.[9]

Hobbyist re-enactors are amateurs. Their performances are examples of what has come to be known as 'public history'.[10] History is increasingly interpreted and written in the public domain – a development which some have welcomed as a democratisation of knowledge and others rejected as an age of dilettantes. Re-enactors are part of this development. They perform in their spare time, on weekends and at evenings, and return to their 'normal' lives when the battle is over. They rarely get paid for their performances; on the contrary, they invest significant sums in their hobby. Re-enactment requires a degree of affluence for full participation.

To those who perform it, re-enactment provides a *sensuous* experience. The weight of armour, the mud of the trenches, the tiring effect of a Jacobite night march – historical re-enactment is all about 'feeling' the past with one's own body. Vanessa Agnew argues that the popularity of historical re-enactment is indicative of an 'affective turn' in Western approaches to the past (Agnew 2007, 301). Notably, re-enactment may be strenuous; not unlike extreme sports, the playing of the past provides its proponents with raw, unfiltered and sometimes painful sensations. There is a strong narrative of self-hardening and stamina in re-enactment culture, and some genres like 'full-contact medieval jousting' verge on costumed martial arts.[11]

The profound public interest in such *sensuous history* is indicative of both a widespread longing for physical experience in a largely sedentary modernity – and of a latently anti-intellectual sentiment among some history enthusiasts. Physical experience is open to anyone. The 'authenticity' sought is not one of fact but one of direct experience. Such affective interest in the past can take on an anti-intellectual air; distrust of bookish historians and scholarly theory are widespread among the agents of the memory boom.

By the end of the twentieth century, re-enactment became an extraordinarily popular discipline of global entertainment. Many thousands of re-enactment clubs worldwide research and perform the past. While seldom noted by Anglophone scholars, re-enactment is popular far beyond the English-speaking West. A whole industry of weavers, blacksmiths, and sandal-makers produces the material culture so important to recreators of the past. Several magazines, such as *Skirmish* in Britain and *Karfunkel* in Germany, cater to the interests of the community. The internet has much to do with re-enactment's surge, connecting even the most arcane interests into vital subcultures.

Before turning to the Scottish subculture, one should note that re-enactment, like any other form of historical interpretation, may cause controversy and dissent. If re-enactors select contested histories, their performances become political. This may be fruitful. Randal Allred understands re-enactments of the U.S. Civil War as a form of revision and catharsis (Allred 1996). In such reading, re-enactment becomes a method of reconciliation, of coming to terms with a difficult, traumatic past, of *Vergangenheitsbewältigung*.[12] But re-enactors may also interpret the past in unforgiving, irredentist ways. In the Baltic countries, for example, re-enactors of World War II often reduce the local collaborations with Nazi Germany to patriotic acts of anti-Soviet resistance. Veterans and re-enactors of the Latvian Legion Waffen-SS take to the streets of Riga together every year in March to spread their view of the past – much to the dismay of anti-fascists and the Russian minority.[13]

Sometimes it is not interpretation but the topic itself that provokes. Impersonators of Nazi and slave trade history have to face serious questions about their moral motivations.[14] Are they really just harmless collectors of boots and buttons, or potentially political, eager to resume the wars of the past? In October 2010, a Republican Candidate for U.S. congress was criticised by the media for being a member of the 5th SS Panzer Division Wiking re-enactment group.[15] While he insisted that his masquerade was harmless and non-political, the press and the voters did not believe him and accused him of supporting Nazi ideology.

The Scottish genre

In the 1970s, most hobbyist re-enactors performed the schoolboy favourites of heroic history – Roman legions, medieval knights, Vikings, pirates, the Wild

West, the Napoleonic era and, in the U.S., the Civil War. But as re-enactment gained popularity in the 1980s and 1990s, 'battlefields' became crowded and enthusiasts began to diversify. A 2010 observer at a large multi-period event in Europe may, for example, encounter Norman invaders at Hastings (from Germany), early American fur traders (from Britain), the Prussian King's eighteenth-century guard of giant soldiers, or 'Lange Kerls' (from Germany), Confederate soldiers (from Slovakia), Republican volunteers in the Spanish Civil War (from Britain), Swiss anti-aircraft troops during World War II (from Britain), SS-Gebirgsjäger during the Winter War (from Finland), even U.S. soldiers in Vietnam (from Poland).[16] It is perhaps only a question of time before re-enactors of the First Gulf War will enter the arena.

Our observer is also likely to come across the Scots, wearing tartan and flying a St Andrew's flag. While certainly no mainstream department, Scottish history became a proper re-enactment genre in the 1990s. When the leading German re-enactment magazine *Karfunkel* published a series of special editions on the most important re-enactment periods, it focused on Vikings, Celts, the Staufer (Hohenstaufen) dynasty, Romans, Germanic tribes, the Gothic period, Templers – and on Scotland (Karfunkel Codex 5: 2007). In 2010, at least 35 re-enactment clubs on the European continent specialised in Scottish history. They were active in Germany, the Netherlands, Belgium, France and the Czech Republic. Scottish re-enactment remained largely confined to North-Western Europe; no such recreations took place in South-Eastern Europe and in Scandinavia. Scottish history appears to strike a special chord in Germany, Flanders, and the Netherlands.

Together, the continental re-enactors cover roughly two millennia of Scottish history. They portray 'Scottish' Celts and Picts, throwing rocks at the Romans at Hadrian's wall. They perform as medieval warriors, fighting the English alongside Wallace and Bruce in Scotland's War of Independence (c. 1296–1328). They are Highland mercenaries in the Thirty Years War (1618–1648), Jacobite rebels on their way to defeat at Culloden (1745–1746), British Highland regiments fighting the French in America (1760s) and at Waterloo (c. 1790–1815). In Germany, one group performs as a Scottish Confederate militia, combining kilts and battle flags and echoing the long-standing mythology of the 'Scottish' South.[17] Finally, there are Scottish soldiers of both World Wars, enduring hardship in Flanders and France but ultimately beating the Hun, liberating Europe, parading victoriously.

These many 'Scottish' groups differ greatly in equipment, historical accuracy and visual effect. However, they all share two essential qualities; they portray Scottish Highlanders, and they are at war. No Europeans re-enact Scotland's urban or civilian history – Clydeside shipyard workers, for instance, philosophers of the Scottish enlightenment or Scottish wool merchants in the early modern Low Countries. Not every moment in the Scottish past appears to be usable for re-enactment. European hobbyists focus on martial Highland history. A closer examination of five re-enactment groups may substantiate this point.

Terra Crom are a troupe of historical re-enactors from Paris. They specialise in late medieval Scotland, the 'Braveheart period', as they happily concede (Interview Terra Crom, 11 July 2009). They set up their tents at Celtic and medieval festivals throughout France and provide a range of 'Scottish' entertainment; Highland Games, military parades, fire spectacles and Celtic music. Children get to fight real Scotsmen with fake swords while their parents may sample Malt Whisky from a 'Celtic' ceremonial cup. Their warriors wear tartan chequered belted plaids and paint their faces with blue woad. Clearly, much of the history they re-enact never happened.[18]

Mackay's Regiment of Foote portray the Scottish Highand mercenaries who fought in Germany during the Thirty Years War. Their inspiration is an historical regiment raised by Sir Donald MacKay of Far (1591–1649) in 1626. MacKay's men fought with the anti-Habsburg forces, first for Danish King Christian IV and later, from 1630 to 1635, for Gustavus Adolphus and his successors. The German re-enactors reject 'Braveheart-Scots' and fantasy Highlanders. By their own reckoning, they seek to re-enact the past 'more authentically', *as it really was*, and they hope to educate their audiences: '... we provide knowledge not only about the Thirty Years War, but also about the role of the Scots in that time' (Website Mackay's Regiment 2010).[19] Their Captain is an advocate by profession.

Clan MacBran are a band of Jacobite rebels from Flanders and the Netherlands. They depict anti-Hanoverian Highlanders in the turbulent years of 1745/46 and are equally concerned with getting the facts right. The Clan's 25 members spend much time and money on the acquisition and production of what they consider 'authentic' costumes and weapons. 'Sometimes we make concessions. But only if it's really necessary. We try to keep it close to the real thing', says William MacBran, a chemistry teacher in real life (Interview Clan MacBran, 23 May 2009).[20]

In the Czech Republic, the Montgomerie's Highlanders [sic] have accepted Jacobite defeat and enlisted in the British colonial Army. The Czech re-enactors portray the 77th Highland Regiment of Foot which was raised in 1757 by the 11th Earl of Eglinton, Archibald Montgomerie (1726–1796) and took part in most campaigns of the French and Indian War between 1757 and 1763. The Montgomeries hold their own Woodland Battle at Stará Libavá in rural Moravia, and they regularly join the Czech Republic's only Highland Games (established in 2000) at Sychrov Castle, in Bohemia (Personal Communication, Montgomerie's Highlanders, 4 October 2010).

The 48th Highlanders of Holland finally re-enact a postcolonial Highland regiment. The group was founded in the Dutch town of Apeldoorn in 1991 to commemorate the centenary of the 48th Highland Regiment of the Canadian Army (established in 1891) which helped to liberate the Netherlands from Nazi occupation in World War II. The 48th Highlanders of Holland are technically a pipe and drum band, but see themselves as a 'living monument to the liberators of our town' (Personal communication, 48th Highlanders, 1 March 2010).[21] In their attempt for an exact reproduction of uniforms and style, the Dutch

TABLE 12.1 Re-enacting Scottish history in Europe (2009/2010)

Group Name	Country	Period	Web
Woads	Netherlands	Iron Age/Celtic	http://www.woads.nl/
Sassenachs War Pipes and Drums	Netherlands	Iron Age/Celtic	http://www.sassenachs.nl/
Alauni	Germany/Austria	Iron Age/Celtic	http://www.alauni.at/
Clan Morgainn	Germany	Medieval	http://www.clann-morgainn.de/
Terra Crom	France	Medieval	http://www.terra-crom.org/
Scottish Marauders	France	Medieval	http://scottish-marauders.1talk.net/
Lechfeld Highlanders	Germany	Medieval	http://www.lechfeldhighlander.de/
Die Schwotten	Germany	Medieval	http://www.schwotten.de/
Clan Sith	Germany	Medieval	http://traumreich.eu/anamcara/index.html/
Warriors of Kintail	Germany	Medieval	http://thewarriorsofkintail.jimdo.com/
Rotthal or Red Valley Highlanders	Germany	Medieval	http://www.rtm-roterbaron.de/
Neckar Highlanders	Germany	Medieval	[-]
Clan MacCarrock	Germany	Medieval	http://www.clan-maccarrock.com
Clan McDohl	Germany	Medieval	http://www.mcdohl.de/
Clan MacKean	Germany	Medieval	http://www.clan-mac-kean.de/
Black Watch Vienna	Austria	Seventeenth century	http://blackwatch-vienna.at/
Mackay's Regiment of Foote	Germany	Thirty Years War	http://regiment-mackay.de/
Clans of Caledonia	Germany	Jacobites and Renaissance	http://www.clans-of-caledonia.de
Clan MacConn of Drumfinnan	Germany	Jacobites	[-]
Clan MacBran	Netherlands/ Belgium	Jacobites	http://www.clanmacbran.nl/

Name	Period/War	Country	Website
Clan Chattan	Jacobites	Germany	http://www.jacobite-history.de/
Les Régiments du Passé	Jacobites/ Royal-Ecossais	France	http://regimentsdupasse.net/
Montgomerie's Highlanders	French and Indian War	Czech Republic	http://scottish.livinghistory.cz/
87th/88th Regiment of Foote	Seven Years War	Germany	http://www.87th88thfoot.de.tl/
92nd Gordon Highlanders	Napoleonics	Netherlands	http://www.gordonslivinghistory.nl/
92nd Gordon Highlanders	Napoleonics	Germany	http://www.92ndgordonhighlanders.de/
42nd Black Watch	Napoleonics	Germany	http://blackwatch.interfree.it/english/index.html
42nd Black Watch	Napoleonics	Italy	http://www.napoleonische-gesellschaft.de/
Charleston Highlanders	Scottish immigrants in ninteenth-century Charleston/ U.S. Civil War	Germany	http://www.santee-artillery.de/
Passchendaele 1917 Pipes and Drums	WWI	Belgium	http://www.fleming-pipeband.be/
Somme Battlefield Pipe Band	WWI	France	http://sommebattlefieldpipeband.fr
1st Gordon Highlanders	WWI and WWII	Netherlands	http://www.livinghistory.nl/
5th Bn Black Watch	WWII	Germany	[-]
48th Highlanders of Holland	WWII	Netherlands	http://www.48th-highlanders.nl/
XII Manitoba Dragoner Memorial Pipes and Drums	WWII	Netherlands	http://www.12md.nl/
Normandy Highlanders	WWII	France	http://www.nh-pipeband.org
Royal Scots Fusiliers/ Argyll and Sutherland Highlanders	WWII	Czech Republic	[-]

Highlanders contacted the original regiment, stationed in Toronto. A retired pipe major of the Canadian regimental band, Mr Ross Stewart, who died in 2001, came to the Netherlands several times during the 1990s to drill his Dutch imitators. Canadian veterans have met with the band when visiting the Canadian War Cemetery in nearby Holten, and the Dutch re-enactors' website is linked on the Canadian regimental pages. The copy found the original's approval.

The quest for authentic Scottish history

European re-enactors of Scottish history focus on warfare and the Highlands. This hardly comes as a surprise. Heroic warfare is the key attraction in *all* genres of historical re-enactment. The hobby originates in battle commemorations and mock tournaments, and it still revolves around guns, swords, and uniforms. Re-enactment is about 'the glitter of the buttons and the wave of the flags', the glamour of warfare (Allred 1996, 5). It is true that there has been a shift towards more civilian re-enactments in the past decade, a shift which many re-enactors believe results from the growing number of women joining the hobby (see below). William MacBran of the Dutch-Flemish Clan MacBran remarks: 'the more female members you have, the more civilian your re-enactment group becomes' (Interview Clan MacBran, 23 May 2009). But recreations of civilian history usually still serve as a mere backdrop to military action.

As outlined above, some histories may be controversial to re-enact. Scottish history is not one of them. The Scots are re-enacted as the 'good guys', fighting on the right side. To re-enact a Scottish soldier seems a morally safe enterprise. As medieval and Jacobite rebels, the Scots are construed as defenders of local identity, underdogs who oppose a (mythical) English oppression, even 'internal colonialism' – good guys. As British or even Canadian soldiers of the twentieth century, the Scots are liberators of Western Europe, fighting the Germans in two World Wars. Even the Czech Montgomeries who portray a British colonial regiment in the French and Indian War consider their Highlanders noble people, not conquerors. Like the Native Americans, they argue, Highlanders are victims of imperial politics, tribal people, forced to fight. Such a victim mythology ignores the very active roles Scots played in the British Empire's colonial enterprise.[22]

The re-enactors' focus on the *Highlands* comes as no surprise either. Scotland has been associated with Highland images for more than 200 years. The reason for this is the Scottish embrace of Highland culture in the late eighteenth and nineteenth century, a process best known as 'Highlandism' (after Edward Said's Orientalism). Scottish military men, but also poets and politicians, celebrated and adopted Highland folklore and aesthetics at a time of rapid industrialisation and social change. Scotland styled herself a Highland nation, and the Highland soldier became 'a proud symbol of Scotland's ancient nationhood', as T.M. Devine points out (Devine 2004, 356). The kilted soldier is at the heart of what has been called Scotland's 'invented tradition' or 'tartan monster' (Trevor-Roper 1983; Nairn 1977).

Importantly, the image of Scotland as a Highland warrior nation was exported via the global channels of popular culture and the British military. The poems of Ossian (1760s), Walter Scott's novels (1810s–1820s), Queen Victoria's Highland diaries (1865/1884), Harry Lauder's stage shows (1910s–1920s), and, more recently, films such as *Rob Roy* (1953), *Highlander* (1986) and *Braveheart* (1995) disseminated and rewrote the myth of the Highlander. At the same time real kilted soldiers, embodiments of the Highland myth, fought and paraded for Britain in Waterloo, Crimea, India, Flanders and Hong Kong. Unlike other national mythologies, the Scottish Highland myth came to be exceptionally well-known throughout the world. By today, these images have arguably produced a Scottish dreamscape which serves as a global playground for a variety of tribal and ancestral fantasies. For example, the film *Braveheart* was a U.S. production, directed by an Australian, and largely filmed in Ireland.

It is this Scottish dreamscape which inspires most re-enactors. Many dedicated hobbyists begin with a Hollywood film or a novel. William MacBran of Clan MacBran states that he watched *Braveheart* about '50 or 60 times, I stopped counting' (Interview Clan MacBran, 23 May 2009). Clan McConn of Drumfinnan, a Jacobite group from Germany, recall that their passion for Scotland began in 1978 with a German television series based on R.L. Stevenson's *Kidnapped*. (Interview Clan McConn, 12 September 2009). The Czech Montgomeries explain:

> None of us have provable Scottish ancestry and different people have different reasons for joining our ranks. Some may have got inspired by the *Rob Roy*, *Braveheart* or *Highlander* movie, some have read the *Northwest Passage* and the *Last of the Mohicans* too many times, others joined in as they liked history, culture or music of Gaidhealtachd.
>
> (Personal communication, Montgomerie's Highlanders, 4 October 2010)

The Czech re-enactors searched for a past that would allow them to combine their favourite films and novels. By selecting the French and Indian War, they have found a way of playing both Indians and Highlanders – without violating re-enactment culture's authenticity rule. As re-enactors, they cannot invent their own Scottish-Indian history, that would be fantasy. They need to find a genuine historical moment to re-enact.

Historical re-enactors seek to recreate the past *as it really was*. A German re-enactment group portraying the Grenadier Company of the 42nd Royal Highland Regiment in the years 1808 to 1815 states: 'We reconstruct the appearance of the unit, its uniform and equipment as detailed and historically correct as possible' (Website Napoleonische Gesellschaft, 15 October 2010). The Dutch-Flemish Jacobites of Clan MacBran stress that their goal is to be 'a hundred per cent' true to the past. Someimes they have to make concessions, but only to avoid major damage. Their leader, William MacBran, explains:

> We try to get everything as accurate as possible. But you won't reach 100 percent. You would have to starve yourself in certain periods [in order to be authentic]. But when you have children you can't say: we don't eat today.
>
> (Interview Clan MacBran, 23 May 2009)

Some hobbyists may get quite obsessed with accuracy and call themselves 'authenticity fascists' (Gapps 2009, 396). They seek to *become* the past, to resemble the chosen period so much that full mimicry is possible. They insist that if you do it right you may achieve a 'period rush' or 'authenticity high', a moment when the present fades and the re-enacted history becomes the main reality (Horwitz 1999, 7). If you do it wrong, on the other hand, you will be called a fake, a 'farb' or a 'tablecloth Scot', after your grandmother's tablecloth which you allegedly wear as a kilt.[23]

The Scottish dreamscape is a problematic topic for re-enactment. It conflicts with the hobbyist culture's authenticity injunction. Hollywood films and Walter Scott's novels may inspire people to re-enact the past but they only rarely provide useful historical facts. 'Scottish' re-enactors begin their hobby by deconstructing the Scottish myths in their heads. Some will give up fairly quickly when they realise that the Scottish history of their favourite movies and novels is not congruent with what they find in scholarly books or on the more authoritative websites – that, for example, William Wallace never wore a modern kilt or blue face paint. They will experience what Daria Radtchenko called the 'trauma of knowing', deconstructing their beloved myths until there is nothing left to play with (Radtchenko 2006).

The dedicated, however, will try to move beyond the Highlander stereotypes and discover the grain of historical truth in the myth. They will, in the words of anthropologist Paul Basu, try to 'refine' their Highlandism and carefully assemble historical information without ruining the beauty of the mythical image which first attracted them (Basu 2007, 67, 93). Historical re-enactment may become a journey into the dreamscape's foundations.

The German Mackays were successful. They came across a German translation of an eyewitness report on the original Mackay mercenaries and a series of period woodcuts which depict their regiment at Szczecin in c. 1631, wearing tartan chequered belted plaids.[24] From these sources they are able to distil enough Scottishness to satisfy both their re-enactors' commitment to accuracy and their love for the Highland myth. The Mackays found what Hugh Trevor-Roper always denied there was; the invented tradition's historical core, the bits and pieces out of which it was made.

Women dressing up men

Discussions of 'authentic' Scotsmen must raise the issue of Scotswomen. Where are the women in this world of swinging kilts and martial display? Historical re-enactment is a world of profoundly conservative gender roles; the men fight and the women cook. This is true for almost all re-enactment genres. This division of labour is usually made in the name of historical accuracy. Most commanding officers stress that women are welcome to join the group – if they are willing to portray 'authentic' female lives of the re-enacted period. The German 92nd Gordon Highlanders state:

> Yes, we have women with us, and they are very welcome, because we are not only interested in the military aspects of our period [the Napoleonic Wars], but in the whole way of life; how people lived back then, what did they eat and drink, what were the worries, fears, and joys, the sentiments of the different social classes.
>
> (Personal communication, 92nd Rgt, 1 October 2010)[25]

Apparently, women are expected to portray all this. And indeed, there seems to be no shortage of women willing to recreate the civilian backdrop for their warrior husbands and sons at Scottish re-enactment events. What do they gain from it?

It is not difficult to spot that male re-enactors of Scottish history have a strong interest in re-enacting manly soldiers. They use the Scottish Highlander as a template of manhood, an ideal type of man. To re-enact a kilted warrior is to become a man again. Interestingly, this practice of enhancing masculinity by dressing up as a Highlander has historical precedent. In Victorian times, as industrialisation and mechanisation challenged traditional manhood and 'transformed' men into office clerks, tourists from the Lowlands, England and Europe tried to reconnect with their manhood while stalking deer in the North, 're-enacting' their lost masculinity dressed up as Highlanders.[26]

What do women gain from performing as Scottish housewives of the past? Interestingly, one recurring female explanation is that the sight of 'men in skirts' is enjoyable. Female re-enactors state again and again in interviews that they like to dress up their men as 'real men'. They explain that 'if you see a man in a kilt, that's manly, and strong, and warlike' (Interview Mirjam, Sassenachs War Pipes and Drums, 23 May 2009). Many men on the other hand say that their interest in Scotland was first aroused by their wives or girlfriends who bought them a kilt. The erotics of the kilted Scotsman – which fascinated Queen Victoria and Anaïs Nin and which still rule Diana Gabaldon's fantasy novels – seem to be of some importance at re-enactment events.

There are, of course, exceptions, women who will not be content with dressing up men. A German-born female academic serves as a 'regimental agitant' in Earl of Loudoun's Regiment of Foote, based in Scotland. As a soldier, she wears a uniform and fires muskets. 'I thought that this was more interesting than sewing in a tent', she says. She cannot see anything inauthentic about her performance and stresses that there are 'tons of documents which prove that women fought at the battle frontline in the English Civil War and the 30 Years War' (Interview Earl of Loudoun's Regiment, 11 March 2010). The re-enactor rebels by doing her own research.

If the search for a usable past proves unsuccessful, one may always switch to re-enacting what never happened. This will mean to enter the realms of live action role play, where alternative histories are being brought to life in truly hyperreal performances. The warriors of Clan MacMahoon (from Germany) have written their own Clan lore after which they hail from a town at the foot of Ben Tee in Scotland but were brutally evicted in the seventeenth century – not by the evil landlords or the English, but by Orcks, mixing in here Tolkien's Lord of the Rings (Website Clan MacMahoon, 9 December 2009). Women may choose their roles freely in this fantasy Clan, unlimited by history.

Roots re-enactment?

To some, the re-enactment of Scottish history is a rediscovery of local history. The Mackays of Germany portray early modern Highland mercenaries who fought on German soil and who recruited among Germans. 'To re-enact the Scots means to re-enact a piece of our own past', explains their Captain. Historical re-enactment thus may speak of a growing public awareness of the historical Scottish migrations to mainland Europe.[27] Much more often, however, the issue of place is surprisingly irrelevant in historical re-enactment. There is nothing unusual about the portrayal of Vikings in Brazil or of the Vietnam War in France. Similarly, Scottish history may be re-enacted anywhere in the world, and re-enactors will often not bother to explain their choice but ask back: 'Why not?' The overwhelming majority of 'Scottish' re-enactors do not claim historical links to Scotland.

Re-enactors will not be coy about their appropriation of Scottish history. In a way, they are Collingwoodians in the true sense. To them, the imitation of the past is an issue of technique and open to anyone who has the skills. An ethnic link will make no one a better re-enactor or Scotsman of the past. A contemporary Glaswegian is just no competition for a Belgian Jacobite, according to Wee Jock MacMelville of Clan MacBran:

> In our group there's probably a few people who know more about Scottish history than some Scots themselves. We were near Fort William, where they stuck that little tower, in Glenfinnan. And in that visitor centre there was that Scottish family and we heard them commenting: Oh and they had a battle there, and a battle there, and then they went all the way down there to London and had a battle there! And we thought: I'm sorry, but you're talking shite. But then I'm too polite to say: I'm sorry that's not correct. I mean, correcting a Scotsman about their history while you're not a Scotsman, I don't know how they would take it. So okay, I know more about your history than you do yourself, but they might know more about Belgian history than I do myself [laughs].
>
> (Interview Clan MacBran, 23 May 2009)

To the re-enactor, authority comes with knowledge, not with blood or place. The Belgian re-enactor is prepared to defend his Scottish performance against Scottish amateurism, but he is also ready to give away 'his' Belgian history to anyone who knows more about it than he does. It is performance that makes the Scot and the Belgian of the past.

Re-enactors then may be not all that different from roots enthusiasts in North America and Australasia, at least not from those who regularly and colourfully celebrate their Scottish ancestry at Highland Games and Clan Gatherings.[28] They, too, pick their usable moments of Scottish history. They will not celebrate modern Scotland (the Royal Bank of Scotland? The deep fried Mars bar?), but choose to be Highlanders at war. Their Scottish performances are entirely voluntary. Genes will force no one to wear a kilt. There is nothing coercive about blood. Most Americans and Australians could choose other 'ethnic options', to use Mary Waters' expression.[29] If they wear the kilt and express their Scottish heritage, they make a decision, however conscious, both to live out the Scot and to favour the Scot.

Importantly, anyone who has the skills can join them in their roots re-enactment. As Celeste Ray has shown, the root-seeking community is an open system, an opt-in scene that welcomes friends and spouses and anyone who feels a Scot at heart (Ray 2001, 99–126). It is *skill and knowledge* which make the Scot; wearing the kilt, quoting Burns, playing the pipes, knowing the history, tossing the caber, dancing the Highland fling, etc. The performance of Scottish folklore does not express a deep and unalterable 'ethnicity', but affinity for the Scottish past and myths thereof. Without affinity, there will be no ethnic celebration.

Acknowledgements

The author is grateful to David McCrone, Tom Devine and Vanessa Agnew for their valuable comments on an earlier draft of this chapter.

Notes

1 North American and Australasian re-enactors of Scottish history yet await scholarly treatment. Celeste Ray registered the importance of re-enactment, see C. Ray (2001) *Highland Heritage. Scottish Americans in the American South*, Chapel Hill, NC: University of North Carolina Press, pp. 169–72.

2 The world of hobbyist re-enactment is refreshingly under-researched. Quasi-ethnographic case studies include T. Horwitz (1999) *Confederates in the Attic. Dispatches from the Unfinished Civil War*, New York: Vintage, orig. 1998. J. Thompson (2004) *Wargames. Inside the World of 20th Century Reenactors*, Washington, DC: Smithsonian Books. See also I. McCalman and P. A. Pickering (eds) (2010) *Historical Re-Enactment. From Realism to the Affective Turn*, Houndmills: Palgrave MacMillan.

3 See J. Schlebecker (1968) *Living Historical Farms. A Walk to the Past*, Washington, DC: Smithsonian. J. Anderson (1982) 'Living History. Simulating Everyday Life in Living Museums', *American Quarterly* 34:3, pp. 290–306. J. Carstensen *et al.*, eds (2008) *Living History im Museum*, Münster: Waxmann Verlag.

4 See, e.g. P. Heering (2008) 'The Enlightened Microscope. Re-enactment and Analysis of Projections with Eighteenth-Century Solar Microscopes', *British Journal for the History of Science* 41:3, Sept, pp. 345–67.

5 S. During (2007) 'Mimic Toil. Eighteenth-century Preconditions for the Modern Historical Reenactment', Rethinking History 11:3 (Sept 2007): 313–333. R. Schneider (2011) *Performing Remains: Art and War in Times of Theatrical Reenactment*, New York: Routledge.

6 T. Horwitz, *Confederates in the Attic*, p. 136. J. Thompson, *Wargames*, 33–7. R. Turner (1990) 'Bloodless Battles. The Civil War Reenacted', *The Drama Review* 34:4. D. Hall (1994) 'Civil War Reenactors and the Postmodern Sense of History', *Journal of American Culture* 17:3, pp. 7–11. R. Allred (1996) 'Catharsis, Revision, and Re-enactment. Negotiating the Meaning of the American Civil War', *Journal of American Culture* 19:4, pp. 1–13.

7 J. Winter (2006) *Remembering War. The Great War between Memory and History in the 20th Century*, New Haven, CT: Yale University Press.

8 D. MacCannell (1999) *The Tourist. A New Theory of the Leisure Class,* Berkeley: University of California Press, orig. 1976. J. M. Fladmark (ed.) (1994) *Cultural Tourism*, London: Donhead. D. Lowenthal (1996) *The Heritage Crusade and the Spoils of History*, New York: Free Press.

9 G. M. Moscardo and P. L. Pearce (1986) 'Historic Theme Parks: An Australian Experience in Authenticity', *Annals of Tourism Research* 13:3, pp. 467–479. C. Halewood and K. Hannam (2001) 'Viking Heritage Tourism. Authenticity and Commodification', *Annals of Tourism Research* 28:3, pp. 565–80.

10 F. Bösch et al. (eds) (2009) *Public History. Öffentliche Darstellungen des Nationalsozialismus jenseits der Geschichtswissenschaft*, Frankfurt/Main: Campus. P. Ashton and H. Kean (eds) (2009) *People and their Pasts. Public History Today*, New York: Palgrave MacMillan.

11 D. Slater (2010) 'Is Jousting the Next Extreme Sport?' *New York Times,* 8 July. Randal Allred asks: 'Is there some relish for a test of one's mettle and stamina in this love of hardship? Allred, 'Catharsis, Revision, Re-enactment', p. 6.

12 The phrase 'trauma re-enactment' has been used by psychologists since the 1940s to denote the involuntary re-playing of traumatic experience. See, e.g. J. Wisdom (1949) 'A Hypothesis to explain Trauma Re-enactment Dreams', *International Journal of Psychoanalysis* XXX, pp. 13–20.

13 The march takes place on 16 March, or 'Latvian Legion Day' (Latviešu legiona atceres diena).

14 On slavery re-enacted, see M.-C. Philip (1994) 'To Reenact or not to Reenact?', *Black Issues in Higher Education* 11:18, pp. 24–8. J. Walvin, 'What should we do about Slavery? Slavery, Abolition and Public History', in I. McCalman and P. A. Pickering (eds) *Historical Reenactment. From Realism to the Affective Turn*, pp. 63–78.

15 J. Green (2010) 'Why is this GOP House Candidate dressed as a Nazi?' *The Atlantic*, 8 Oct.

16 Normans: [http://www.furor-normannicus.de/]. Fur traders: [http://mountainmanuk. yuku.com/]. Lange Kerls: [http://www.lange-kerls.de/]. Confederates: [http://www. gelo.sk/samov/indexsk.htm]. Spanish Republicans: [http://www.lacolumna.org.uk/]. Swiss WWII: [http://reduitimluftbernerkompagnie.com/]. SS-Gebirgsjäger: [http:// www.gaissmair.net/]. Vietnam: [http://www.militarni.pl/?lang=1&cat=133] (15 Oct 2010).

17 On the bizarre but persistent idea that the mentality of the U.S. South is a result of Scottish immigration, see R. Berthoff (1986) 'Celtic Mist over the South', *The Journal of Southern History* 52:4, pp. 523–46.

18 See [http://www.terra-crom.org/] (30 March 2010).

19 '... und vermitteln Wissen nicht nur über die Zeit des Dreißigjährigen Krieges, sondern auch über die Rolle der Schotten in dieser Zeit, ihr Leben, ihre Bekleidung und Bewaffnung.' [http://www.regiment-mackay.de/] (12 March 2010)

20 See also [http://www.clanmacbran.nl/] (12 March 2010).

21 See also [http://www.48th-highlanders.nl/] (1 March 2010).
22 See T. M. Devine (2004) *Scotland's Empire, 1600–1815*, London: Penguin, orig. 2003.
23 Re-enactors claim that the derogatory 'farb' is either short for 'far be it from me to tell him that he's wrong', or that it had first been used to denote clumsy German re-enactors who had come to the U.S. to play native Americans with their faces painted red. 'Farbe' is the German word for paint. See Allred, 'Catharsis, Revision, and Reenactment', pp. 11–12 (n.2).
24 R. Monroe (1995) *Kriegserlebnisse eines schottischen Söldnerführers in Deutschland 1626–1633*, ed. and trans. H. Mahr, Neustadt a.d. Aisch: Schmidt, Philipp.
25 'Und ja, es sind auch Frauen bei uns, sehr erwünscht, denn nicht nur der militärische Aspekt der Zeit interessiert uns, sondern das ganze Spektrum oder Lebensbereich: wie lebte man damals, was wurden gegessen und getrunken, was waren die Sorgen, Ängste und Freuden, die Empfindungen der verschiedenen Stände oder sozialen Klassen.' Personal communication, 92nd Regiment, Germany (1 Oct 2010).
26 See M. M. Martin (2009) *The Mighty Scot. Nation, Gender, and the Nineteenth Century Mystique of Scottish Masculinity*, New York: SUNY Press.
27 See D. Worthington (2004) *Scots in Habsburg service, 1618–1648*, Leiden: Brill. S. Conway (2009) 'Scots, Britons, and Europeans. Scottish Military Service, 1739–1783', *Historical Research* 82:215, Feb., pp. 114–30. T.M. Devine and D. Hesse (eds) (2011) *Scotland and Poland. Historical Encounters, 1500–2010*, Edinburgh: John Donald.
28 See E. Hague (2002) 'The Scottish Diaspora. Tartan Day and the Appropriation of Scottish Identities in the United States', in D.C. Harvey et al. (eds) *Celtic Geographies. Old Cultures, New Times*, London: Routledge, pp. 139–156. See also M.F. Jacobson (2006) *Roots, too. White Ethnic Revival in Post-Civil-Rights America*, Cambridge: Harvard University Press.
29 M. Waters (1990) *Ethnic Options. Choosing Identities in America*, Berkeley: University of California Press.

Bibliography

Agnew, V. (2007) 'History's Affective Turn. Historical Reenactment and its Work in the Present', *Rethinking History* 11:3: 299–312.

Allred, R. (1996) 'Catharsis, Revision, and Re-enactment. Negotiating the Meaning of the American Civil War', *Journal of American Culture* 19:4: 1–13.

Basu, P. (2007) *Highland Homecomings. Genealogy and Heritage Tourism in the Scottish Diaspora*, London: Routledge.

Collingwood, R. G. (1946) 'History as Re-enactment of Past Experience', in R G. Collingwood, *The Idea of History*, Oxford: Oxford UP, 1–334.

Devine, T. M. (2004) *Scotland's Empire, 1600–1815*, London: Penguin.

Gapps, S. (2009) 'Mobile Monuments. A View of Historical Reenactment and Authenticity from inside the Costume Cupboard of History', *Rethinking History* 13: 3: 395–409.

Horwitz, T. (1999) *Confederates in the Attic. Dispatches from the Unfinished Civil War*, New York: Vintage.

Interview, Clan MacBran (23 May 2009).

Interview, Clan MacConn of Drumfinnan (12 Sept 2009).

Interview, Earl of Loudoun's Regiment (11 March 2010).

Interview, Sassenachs War Pipes and Drums (23 May 2009).

Interview, Terra Crom (11 July 2009).

Karfunkel Codex, 5: 2007 [http://www.karfunkel.de/] (accessed 15 Oct 2010).

Nairn, T. (1977) *The Break-Up of Britain*, London: NLB.

Personal communication, 92nd Regiment, Germany (1 Oct 2010).

Personal communication, Montgomerie's Highlanders (4 Oct 2010).

Personal communication, The 48th Highlanders of Holland (1 March 2010).

Radtchenko, D. (2006) 'Simulating the Past: Reenactment and the Quest for Truth in Russia', *Rethinking History* 10:1: 127–148.

Ray, C. (2001) *Highland Heritage. Scottish Americans in the American South*, Chapel Hill, NC: University of North Carolina Press.

Trevor-Roper, H. (1983) 'The Invention of Tradition: The Highland Tradition of Scotland', in E. Hobsbawm and T. Ranger (eds) *The Invention of Tradition*, Cambridge: Cambridge UP, 1983, 15–42.

Website, Clan MacMahoon [http://www.macmahoon.de] (9 Dec 2009).

Website, Mackay's Regiment of Foote [http://www.regiment-mackay.de/] (accessed 12 March 2010).

Website, Napoleonische Gesellschaft [http://www.napoleonische-gesellschaft.de/html/42nd_royal_highland_regiment.htm] (15 Oct 2010).

13

RECONSTRUCTING WEST WALES

Welsh representations and cultural memories of Cornwall

Garry Tregidga

In 2005 the political magazine *Cornish Nation* published an obituary dedicated to the memory of the Welsh nationalist Gwynfor Evans. At one level this might be interpreted as a simple act of solidarity with a fellow Celtic nation after the death of an iconic figure described as the 'greatest Welsh politician of the twentieth century' (*Cornish Nation* 2005: 3). Yet the fact that the obituary was actually the longest article in the magazine, combined with the author's use of such familiar headings as 'Remembering Gwynfor' and 'Cornwall pays tribute', suggests the existence of a deeper desire to adopt Evans as a 'spiritual leader' for the sister cause of Cornish nationalism. This contemporary example raises wider issues in regard to the precise nature of the relationship between Cornish and Welsh identities both in the past and present. Part of the appeal of a critical Celtic Studies approach is that it offers an opportunity for comparative analysis, thereby enabling scholars from the humanities and social sciences to usefully compare and contrast the experiences of one particular territory within a broader spatial context. In this chapter, however, the focus is placed on the way in which memories of a common Brythonic past have been articulated and interpreted at a popular level in Cornwall. There is a particular emphasis on the early decades of the twentieth century when the Welsh model was an attractive route for those individuals who wished to link the so-called Celtic Revival to the Liberal-Nonconformist agenda. Yet the chapter also points to the practical and ideological problems with such a project in the context of competing narratives from the official Cornish Revivalist movement.

The ermine or the dragon? Constructing a Celtic past

The creation of Cowethas Kelto-Kernuak (Celtic-Cornish Society) in 1901 is regarded by Amy Hale as a 'pivotal' event in the Celtic Revival in Cornwall

(1997: 101). Although there had been a growing interest in the Duchy's ancient language and heritage in previous decades, it appears that this was the first organisation to consciously articulate a cultural agenda based on perceptions of Cornwall's 'difference' when compared to England. Louis Duncombe Jewell, the society's secretary and founder, explained in the following year that its four key aims were: the preservation of Cornwall's pre-historic relics; the promotion of Cornish sports and customs; the revival of the Cornish language and the creation (or 're-establishing') of the Cornish Gorsedd (Hale 1997: 100). Yet central to the rationale of Cowethas Kelto-Kernuak was the belief that Cornwall's cultural renaissance should take place in a Celtic context. Duncombe-Jewell's immediate objective in the early 1900s was for Cornwall to be fully accepted as a Celtic nation by the Pan-Celtic Congress and this task was to be finally realised under Henry Jenner's leadership in 1904. Subsequent developments included the formation of Gorseth Kernow in 1928, which was consciously based upon Breton and Welsh institutions, and finally a political movement in 1951 entitled Mebyon Kernow (Sons of Cornwall). Philip Payton (1997a) points out that this construction of 'Celtic Cornwall' involved 'a calculated co-option of elements of a wider "Celtic Revival" that had already by the late nineteenth century made a significant impact in Scotland, Ireland, Wales and Brittany' (28). By comparing Cornwall with other Celtic areas this enabled the Revivalists to appear more credible since they could be seen as part of a wider '"Regionalist" movement which [was] striving in various parts of Western Europe to revive local patriotism' (*Cornish Guardian*, 6 September 1912). An early example can be seen in the successful propaganda campaign for a separate Anglican diocese for Cornwall. In 1869 the Rev. Wladislaw Somerville Lach-Szyrma, Anglican vicar of Newlyn and a leading Revivalist, deployed Celtic identity as a way of justifying Cornwall's ecclesiastical independence from Exeter when he argued that the Cornish had 'far more connection' with the people of Wales and Brittany than with their Anglo-Saxon 'neighbours in Devon' (Morris 1983: 247).

Yet underneath these general references to Celtic connections were often complex cultural, political or spiritual differences. Lach-Szyrma's comparison in 1869 is a good example since in terms of religious identity nonconformist Wales stood in stark contrast with Catholic Brittany. For Lach-Szyrma (1889) himself this does not appear to have been a problem since he saw the new diocese of Truro, created in 1877, as an opportunity to bring together contrasting religious traditions so that a united Church of Cornwall based on Anglicanism could 'regain the position she once held under the Brito-Celtic saints' (132). But there was also a more sectarian approach. In the late nineteenth and early twentieth centuries the Celtic Revivalists appeared to publicly distance themselves from the dominant Methodists who accounted for over 60 per cent of those who attended a place of worship in Cornwall in 1851. Payton concluded that this was no coincidence since the leading figures associated with the Cornish movement at the time, such as Jenner, Duncombe-Jewell and Canon Gilbert Doble, were either Roman Catholics or 'High Anglicans' in the Church of England. Their romantic objective was to 'rebuild a pre-industrial Celtic-Catholic culture in Cornwall' that existed before Methodism. From this perspective the Cornish Revival was a conscious 'project' that took inspiration from the medieval period (Payton 1992: 132; Payton 1996: 267–69). Bernard Deacon (1985) points out that this attitude reflected an assumption that the rise of Methodism in the eighteenth century had actually 'shattered the older traditions [and] established a crucial historical break between modern Cornish and "Celtic" pre-industrial Cornwall' (44). It is certainly easy to portray the followers of John Wesley, with their utilitarian instincts and temperance beliefs, as the Protestant force that swept aside the remnants of Cornwall's ancient folk culture of feast days and festivals because of a perceived association with alcohol and immorality. But Payton adds that this contrasted with the success of the Welsh Revivalists 'who managed to address their aspirations to the Methodist majority'. Cowethas Kelto-Kernuak failed to promote the Revival to a wider audience because it was unable to engage with the 'mass of Cornish people' (Payton 1992: 132; Payton 1996: 267–69).

In these circumstances the model of nonconformist Wales was not the automatic choice for many Revivalists. Indeed, Jenner (c.1929) concluded that Brittany was still the Celtic 'country which beyond all others most resembles Cornwall in the characteristics and mentality of its people' (33). This was despite 'the greater size' of continental Brittany,

> the more primitive condition of the people, the modern influence of France rather than of England, the centuries-old difference of political jurisdiction and the very marked difference in the religion of what is now probably the most intensely Catholic district under the French republic.

It was the latter fact that probably most influenced the early Revivalists. Given the religious tendencies of the leading figures in the movement in the late nineteenth and early twentieth centuries it was not surprising that they should look for a Roman Catholic model. In 1924 Doble, who was a leading Cornish scholar of the early Celtic saints, revealed his High Anglican beliefs when he declared that 'in Methodist Cornwall, the standard of morality was very low'. The only hope, he believed, was to copy the 'discipline' of the Celto-Catholic nations of Brittany and Ireland (*Royal Cornwall Gazette*, 20 August 1924). For Jenner the connection with Ireland had to be publicly avoided since it was 'tainted with controversial politics' especially in the aftermath of the 1916 Easter Rising (44). Yet Brittany offered a more attractive option based on perceptions of a common Brythonic past, centred on geographic, linguistic and religious similarities. A good example of this emphasis on the historic bonds between Cornwall and Brittany can be seen in the second Gorseth Kernow at Carn Brea in 1929. A poem entitled 'Welcome to the Bretons' was included in the souvenir programme that marked the visit of a contingent of 'cousin bards' who had travelled over to Cornwall to participate in the ceremony. As the opening lines suggest, the Gorseth was seen in romantic terms as a catalyst that was bringing together two nations that had been separated by force in the distant past:

> On thy soil, Old Cornwall, see at last,
> Now a thousand years are past,
> As thy children, lost so long before,
> Britons coming back once more:
> This be the cry that back thy echoes give,
> 'Brittany and Cornwall for ever live!'
> One from another nothing shall us rend,
> Briton will love Briton till world shall end!
> > (*Programme of the Gorseth at Carn Brea* 1929: 7)

Geological connections meant that the two peninsulas could be described as 'two granite masses thrust out into the Atlantic [that] were alike before they were inhabited by the ancient peoples who raised in them similar stone monuments' (8). Bonds of kinship dating back to the mythical creation of a 'new Britain' in Armorica by those Britons 'who crossed the sea rather than remain as subjects to Saxon usurpers' were maintained until the late Middle Ages. Yet central to this narrative of Cornu-Breton unity was the impact of the Reformation. The unknown person who wrote the Gorseth's 1929 programme emphasised that the underlying ties of 'land and blood' were severed by the religious changes that took place in the English state in the sixteenth century. While Brittany was able to preserve its cultural heritage through the medium of the Roman Catholic Church, the process of Anglicisation that accompanied the rise of Protestantism and the Church of England meant that Cornwall 'gradually ceased to use its own language, and so forgot its own ballads, music and traditions' (8). Brittany was therefore a reassuring model for those conservative Revivalists who wanted to reconstruct the Celto-Catholic world of Medieval times since it did not just show 'what Cornwall was, or might have been, but of what Cornwall still may be if, with the same spirit, it will keep what is left to itself of Cornishness' (8).

The view that Roman Catholicism was the critical factor in preserving Breton cultural distinctiveness was well established. Even in the 1860s it was claimed by Tom Taylor (1865) that 'the upholding of national usages, faiths, ceremonies, traditions, and glories, has been ever a religion in Brittany' in contrast to Cornwall or Wales. A good example could be seen in relation to ballads and poetry, which 'wells out of the Celtic nature wherever it is left to itself, [and] has not had its course checked or crossed in Brittany by such influences as the Protestant Methodism of Wales' (xv). When the Rev Thomas Taylor (1916), vicar of St Just-in-Penwith, wrote a history of Celtic Christianity in Cornwall it was significant that he included an entire chapter devoted to Brittany, with little specific reference to Wales. While the book as a whole went no further than the Medieval period, reference was made once again to the events of the sixteenth century and to the recent success of the Bretons in reviving their ancient mystery plays. The author concluded that this Breton example provided a model for those 'who are zealous for the traditions of their Cornish forefathers' (49). Similarly, when Leonard Eliott Eliott-Binns (1955), a former canon of Truro

Cathedral, wrote his study of Medieval Cornwall there was still an emphasis on the way in which its historic Celtic identity had been preserved by Catholicism:

> Both the Bretons and the Cornish love their land and all that concerns it, with a love as tenacious and enduring as the grim cliffs which they have in common. But in Brittany the drawling tones of the ancient tongue can still be heard; and almost within living memory some of the Breton towns retained their medieval aspects ... But what has done most in Brittany to preserve the atmosphere of by-gone days is the continuity of religion. There the outlook and habits of the past have been retained; the taper still burns at immemorial shrines, and grave nunlike women are to be found on their knees at the foot of wayside calvaries, whilst the peasants, in their homely garb, still throng the festivals and pardons.
>
> (6–7)

'They were all Welshmen': Cornu-Welsh politics in the early twentieth century

It is intriguing that an alternative model associated with Wales was being put forward by other individuals and groups at this time. Even in the Medieval and Early Modern periods there had been a tendency to link the Cornish to the Welsh on ethnic grounds. For example, Richard Carew in his *Survey of Cornwall* (1602) remarked that the Cornish 'together with the Welsh, their ancient countrymen', still had bitter memories 'of their expulsion long ago by the English' (67). Historical writings in the eighteenth and nineteenth centuries developed this theme with frequent references to a common past. For example, William Borlase (1769), the prominent antiquarian, wrote of the 'Cornish Britons' who, faced with Saxon incursion, had 'retired into Wales and Cornwall' (40–44). In 1814 Daniel and Samuel Lysons described Cornwall as 'one of the last retreats of the Britons' and added that 'their country was thus called ... Cornish-Wales' (Borlase 1769: iii). The related term of 'West Wales' had often been used to distinguish Cornwall from 'North Wales' (i.e. contemporary Wales) and this reference was well understand amongst intellectuals and antiquarians in the early twentieth century (*The Times*, 5 February 1912 and 7 January 1913). This meant, that for some Cornish Revivalists, they had the option of looking towards Wales rather than Brittany for their immediate inspiration. A good example was George Pawley White, a founder member of Mebyon Kernow and a Methodist preacher who had family connections to Wales. Growing up in the years before the First World War, he recalled that his family had a strong sense of both Cornish and Celtic ancestry and in an oral history interview he used a humorous story from his childhood to recall his annual visits to his maternal grandparents in Wales:

> We used to be taken to South Wales once or twice every year and I can always remember my father saying to me when we were going over the

railway bridge at Saltash, 'Be careful here', he said, 'you are going into England now and you must behave yourself!' And when we got half way through the Severn Tunnel going into Wales he said 'it's all right, you can relax now. We are in Wales'. So I always knew that I wasn't English.

(Pawley White interview, 25 January 2000)

Moreover, Pawley White's personal experiences are symbolic of cultural and economic connections between Cornwall and Wales in the recent past. Even on a superficial level one can point to similarities in popular culture with rugby, for example, emerging as a common signifier of cultural distinctiveness in relation to sport (Seward 1997: 176; Jenkins 2007: 232). Religious nonconformity was the dominant spiritual force with the Anglicans, accounting for less than 30 per cent of church worshippers in Cornwall and Wales in 1851 (Lake, Cox and Berry 2001: 1–2). In both places, a chapel-based culture led to the popularity of male voice choirs and brass bands reflecting the existence of a mining-based economy. There is also a need for an in-depth study of economic connections during the nineteenth and early twentieth centuries since there is evidence of close kinship and business links between South Wales and parts of Cornwall. A good example is Arthur Pendarves Vivian, Liberal MP for West Cornwall from 1868–1885. Although Vivian's family had originated in Cornwall, their economic interests had diversified to cover copper works, smelting and collieries. With the decline of mining in Cornwall the family started to employ 'many Cornishmen' in South Wales. Significantly, Vivian's establishment status meant that he also served both communities as Sheriff of Cornwall, Deputy Lieutenant for Glamorgan, President of the Royal Institution of Cornwall and a Lieutenant Colonel in the 2nd Battalion of the Welsh Regiment (Jaggard 1999: xviii). He was not alone in this respect since John Williams, the dominant 'powerbroker' in regional Liberal politics and possibly the wealthiest businessman in Cornwall in the mid-nineteenth century, also had Welsh ancestry and extensive business interests in South Wales (Jaggard 1999: xvi).

But a significant difference was the way in which Welsh politics had been able to embrace both a distinctive agenda and a nationalist rhetoric based on notions of Celtic identity at a relatively early stage. In 1868 the Liberals became for the first time the dominant political force in Wales, with a platform that embraced greater democracy, land reform and religious nonconformity. The election was interpreted in a nationalist context with claims that it 'will not only serve to raise the prestige of the ancient Cymric race among the other nations, but it will have a still more important result for ourselves – it will serve to create confidence in us toward one another' (Edwards 1913: 232). By the 1880s a political movement entitled Cymru Fydd had emerged in association with Welsh Liberalism under the leadership of Tom Ellis and then David Lloyd George. It provided an opportunity to campaign for a range of issues including Home Rule and the disestablishment of the Anglican Church in Wales. Although Cymru Fydd appeared to lose its sense of direction in the 1890s, the years leading up to the First World War saw a renewed interest in Welsh nationalism. A Welsh devolution bill was discussed by the House of Commons on the eve of war in 1914 and Anglican Disestablishment finally implemented in 1920. Moreover, the Welsh movement had obtained a leading champion at Westminster. David Lloyd George's popularity as a reforming Chancellor of the Exchequer enhanced his reputation back home in Wales. In 1913 J. Hugh Edwards published a major biography in which the first volume traced the history of Cymru up to the birth of the Welsh politician before even discussing his achievements. References to 'The Coming of David Lloyd George' and 'predictions' of his future greatness suggest a semi-messianic appeal. The emphasis was placed firmly on the way in which he symbolised Welsh culture and traditions:

> Never in the annals of Welsh history has any single leader been known so to dominate Wales with the force of his personality or to set his impress so deeply on the national interests of the Principality as has 'David Lloyd George of Criccieth'. By common consent he is to-day the most representative figure of the Cymric race. In keenness of insight into the Cymric character, in force of eloquence in the articulation of Cymric ideals, and in the passion of devotion to Cymric interests, he stands supreme.
>
> (Edwards 1913: 263)

Yet by this time the nationalist politics being expressed in Wales were also starting to have an impact in Cornwall. Local opposition to Irish Home Rule in 1886 had undermined the supremacy of Cornish Liberalism. It was the breakaway Liberal Unionists who became the dominant political force in Cornwall and this prevented any meaningful discussion of regional issues in contrast to Wales. In 1906, however, the Liberals completely monopolised Cornwall's parliamentary representation. Their success meant that a Cornish agenda could now emerge based on a combination of constitutional, economic and religious concerns (Tregidga 1997: 140). Significantly, it was the Welsh model that was often deployed in political arguments. When George Hay Morgan, MP for the Cornish seat of Truro and a former member of Cymru Fydd, was criticised in 1910 by Charles Williams, his Unionist opponent, on the grounds that he was not Cornish he responded by pointing to his Celtic credentials. Morgan declared that he respected Mr Williams,

> because he was a Cornishman, a Celt, and he [Mr Morgan] was that. They all belonged to the same stock, of the same blood and line but the ancestors of one went to Mid Wales and of the other to West Wales. Cornwall was only the wall between Mid and West Wales. They were all Welshmen.
>
> (*Royal Cornwall Gazette*, 8 December 1910)

Such comments reinforce the point made by David Boyce (1988) that the Irish Home Rule debate in the late nineteenth century had acted as a catalyst to create a 'crude simplification' of politics based on Victorian ideas of racial differences, with the '"Celtic" lands ranged against the "Saxon"' (33). Even in Cornwall there were increasing references to the new tensions between 'Saxons' and 'Celts' for control of the British state (*Cornish Guardian*, 6 September 1912). There were further similarities with Wales in the way in which Lloyd George was often seen as a symbol of Celtic culture. When local Methodists proposed the disestablishment of the Anglican Church in Cornwall in 1912 it was argued that 'it could be said of Cornwall, as Mr Lloyd George had said of Wales, that the established religion was an imposition' (*Cornish Guardian*, 15 March 1912). Similarly, when a local newspaper editor attempted to explain the strength of religious nonconformity on Celtic grounds, it is noticeable that the Welsh politician was again co-opted into the explanation:

> The Celtic temperament. It produced Mr Lloyd George, and it is the vivifying spirit of Methodism. No doubt there are pure Saxons from the ethnic point of view, who are Methodists, but it probably remains true that the extent to which a man is distinctively Methodist is the extent to which he has in his composition an element which may be most nearly described by calling it Celtic.
>
> (*Cornish Guardian*, 20 February 1914)

Another revealing insight came when Lloyd George visited Cornwall during the general election campaign of January 1910. At a series of meetings in places like Penryn, Newquay and Perranwell he remarked upon the Celtic passion of Cornwall and stressed the theme of Celtic solidarity with references to the Cornish as 'a brave, fearless and independent race'. This culminated in a key election rally in Falmouth with the symbolic performance of Cornish and Welsh music, including *Forward Cornwall* and *Land of My Fathers*. Lloyd George then declared to the cheers of the crowd that he was addressing 'a gathering of his fellow countrymen' of Cymru. He 'did not care whether Cornwall was a part of Wales or Wales was only a part of Cornwall' (*West Briton*, 10 and 13 January 1910). The decline of the Liberals, partly as a result of the split between Lloyd George and Herbert Asquith in 1916, was to undermine the rationale for, what might be termed, this period of Cornu-Welsh politics. Yet in the short term it was to continue, with Lloyd George's supporters emerging as the leading Liberal group in Cornwall in 1918 and 1922 in the seats of North Cornwall, St Ives and Camborne. This included Sir Clifford Cory, MP for St Ives from 1906–22, who was a Welsh colliery owner (*The Times*, 4 February 1941). Paradoxically, the final example from this period relates to a successful Asquithian challenge to the Lloyd George coalition. In 1922, Isaac Foot, who was to emerge as the hero of Cornish Liberalism during the inter-war period, stood as an Independent Liberal in the Bodmin by-election and successfully defeated the coalition candidate. Significantly, press reports at the time interpreted this victory as a triumph of Celtic nonconformity:

The scenes on Saturday afternoon at the declaration of the poll beggared description. They were Cornish of the Cornish; the enthusiasm of nonconformist farmers, of earnest young preachers, of dark-eyed women and fiery Celtic youth had something religious about it. No such fervour could be seen elsewhere outside Wales.

(*Cornish Guardian*, 3 March 1922).

This depiction stands in stark contrast to Elliott-Binns's portrayal of Brittany that was mentioned earlier. Once again there is an emphasis on religious identity, with the newspaper correspondent subsequently referring to Foot's 'crusade' and the area's 'ancient faith in Liberalism'. But there is a sense of dynamism about this quote that is absent in the 'grim' and 'grave' imagery of a Brittany that still lived in the past. It suggests that the ongoing cause of Liberal Nonconformity remained a powerful force in inter-war Cornwall and North Wales. When fused with Celtic imagery, it created a powerful narrative that could be articulated in popular culture.

The past in Cornish history

What explains these rival attractions of Brittany and Cornwall? Robert Gildea (1994), through his pioneering study of France, provides a possible explanation since he highlighted the importance of cultural memory in relation to religious and political movements both at the centre and in the provinces. He concluded that 'there is no single French collective memory, but parallel and competing collective memories elaborated by communities which have experienced and handle the past in different ways' (10). From this perspective, rival communities could perceive the same historical event or personality in different ways. Those groups would then seek to 'win universal acceptance of their interpretation of the past and to suppress interpretations which were likely to deprive them of legitimacy' (11). This meant that events, such as the French Revolution or the Second World War, were subsequently co-opted in different ways into the political vocabulary of opposing groups from the left to the right. By studying the discourses of competing groups it is possible to gain a greater insight into the 'values and ideals that define, bind together and legitimate political communities'. Gildea added that the past is therefore 'constructed not objectively but as myth' in order to serve the interests of particular communities (10).

This idea of competing narratives can usefully be applied to the situation in Cornwall. Payton (1997b) interprets the Celtic Revival as a 'movement which … determined to look back over the "failure" of the industrial period to a time when Cornwall was unequivocally "Celtic"' (4). But there is a need to broaden existing constructions of the Revival to consider wider developments in popular culture. Whilst Jenner and his supporters articulated a pre-industrial and Catholic narrative with reference to Brittany, this was just one particular view, since by the early years of the twentieth century the concept of Celtic Cornwall had already been accepted by other groups in society. The evidence suggests that the Liberals in particular were co-opting elements of the Celtic Revival in order to justify their party's support for wider policies like Irish Home Rule and the ultimate goal of a federal Britain. Echoing Gildea's view that historical events could be interpreted in different ways, it is possible to apply this perspective to Cornwall. A good example is the way in which notions of Celtic history were applied to Anglican disestablishment. Thus, Cornish Anglicans claimed that their connections with their 'sister church' in Wales dated back to the old pre-Medieval Celtic Church and for this reason they should show solidarity when it was threatened by disestablishment (*Royal Cornwall Gazette*, 24 February 1910 and 29 February 1912). In contrast, Cornish Methodists could argue that it was Cornwall's ability to maintain 'its independence for so long' during the so-called Dark Ages that ensured 'the established religion was an imposition' and justified the need for ecclesiastical reform (*Cornish Guardian*, 15 March 1912). Similarly, the Western Prayer Book rebellion of 1549 reinforced the traditional Revivalist narrative since it linked Cornish culture with a defence of Roman Catholicism. But for Methodists the event's Catholic overtones meant that it needed to be forgotten in favour of other aspects of Cornish identity. A good example was the Rev. Samuel Drewe (Drewe and Hitchens 1824) who criticised the Cornish rebels of 1549 for defending Catholicism when their ancestors had once been loyal to the 'more simple worship' of the ancient Celtic Church (488). From this perspective the competing visions of Cornwall and Brittany reflected deeper divisions over how the past should be used to provide a new sense of legitimacy in the present.

Cultural memory also helps to explain the role of external personalities in Cornish nationalism. It was noted earlier that Gildea's work highlights the importance of individuals and events in sustaining the values and ideas of political movements. But what if a party or organisation lacks a politicised past? The official Revivalist movement that eventually developed under Jenner was ostensibly apolitical until the formation of Mebyon Kernow. Even then it was not until the 1960s that it started to make the transition into becoming a political party and it is only in recent years that it has become a serious force in local government; it still remains weak in parliamentary elections (*Guardian*, 26 January 2012). This chapter commenced with a consideration of why Gwynfor Evans should have been remembered so affectionately in Cornwall. It is no coincidence that *Cornish Nation* is the official magazine of Mebyon Kernow, which reinforces the political significance of this association. Evans's historic achievement in becoming the first Plaid Cymru MP at Westminster following a by-election victory in 1966 provided the inspiration for Mebyon Kernow's own initial 'Golden Age' in the latter part of the decade. One might add that his ultimately successful campaigns to establish a range of national institutions like the Welsh Assembly and SC4 (the Welsh Language television channel) created a legacy that Cornish nationalists could co-opt into their own political aspirations. Lacking similar memories and achievements, the life and times of Evans unconsciously provided Mebyon Kernow with both a substitute form of cultural memory and a practical model for the future. Similarly, Lloyd George became the hero of the embryonic cause of Cornish regionalism in the early 1900s. The absence of an existing tradition of political nationalism, combined with the concept of West Wales, meant that it was natural for Cornish Liberals to mention his name when discussing regional issues, since it made ideas like Anglican disestablishment for Cornwall appear more credible.

Conclusion

The early 1900s was an important period in the construction of 'Celtic Cornwall'. With the emergence of Cowethas Kelto Kernuak, a specific organisation now existed and Catholic Brittany provided a meaningful model for its supporters. But this particular direction was hardly likely to appeal to the nonconformist majority in Cornwall. It could be argued that this explains the relatively slow progress made by the movement in attracting support from a wider audience. Yet there is evidence to suggest that Celtic rhetoric and regional policies were being deployed in the public life of Cornwall before the First World War. The model of West Wales enabled progressive political opinion to make a meaningful connection between past and present. However, this popular side of the Celtic Revival was to be marginalised as a result of the national decline of the Liberal party and the removal of external factors following the creation of the Church in Wales in 1920 and the Irish Free State in 1922. As a result, the initiative passed back to the official Revivalists and opportunities to engage with the wider public had to wait until the movement, notably Mebyon Kernow, was transformed into a more effective pressure group in the 1960s.

Bibliography

Borlase, William. *Antiquities, Historical and Monumental of the County of Cornwall.* 1769 edition.

Boyce, D.G. *The Irish Question and British Politics, 1868–1986.* London: Macmillan, 1988.

Carew, Richard. *The Survey of Cornwall.* 1602.

Cornish Guardian, 15 March 1912.

—— 6 September 1912.

—— 20 February 1914.

—— 3 March 1922.

Cornish Nation. July 2005.

Deacon, Bernard. 'The Cornish Revival: An Analysis'. Unpublished paper. Cornwall Centre, 1985.

Drewe, Samuel and Hitchens, Fortescue. *The History of Cornwall.* Self-publication, 1824.

Elliott-Binns, Leonard. *Medieval Cornwall. London:* Methuen, 1955.

Gildea, Robert. *The Past in French History.* New Haven: Yale University Press, 1994.

Guardian, 26 January 2012.

Hale, Amy. 'Genesis of the Celto-Cornish Revival? L.C. Duncombe-Jewell and the Cowethas Kelto-Kernuak'. *Cornish Studies: Five.* ed. Philip Payton. Exeter: University of Exeter Press, 1997: 100–111.

Hugh Edwards, J. *The Life of David Lloyd George with a Short History of the Welsh People.* Volume one of two. London: Waverley Book Company, 1913.

Jaggard, Edwin. *Liberalism in West Cornwall: The 1868 Election Papers of A. Pendarves Vivian, MP.* Exeter: Devon and Cornwall Record Society, 1999.

Jenkins, Geraint. *A Concise History of Wales.* Cambridge University Press, 2007.

Jenner, Henry. *A Handbook of the Cornish Language,* London: David Nutt, 1904.

—— *Who are the Celts and What has Cornwall to Do with Them?* Self-publication, c.1929.

Lach-Szyrma, W. S. *A Church History of Cornwall and of the Diocese of Truro.* London: Elliot Stock, 1889.

Lake, Jeremy, Cox, Jo and Berry, Eric. *Diversity and Vitality: The Methodist and Nonconformist Chapels of Cornwall.* Place?: English Heritage/Methodist Church, 2001.

Morgan, Kenneth O. *Rebirth of a Nation: A History of Modern Wales.* Oxford: Oxford University Press, 1980.

Morrish, P. S. 'History, Celticism and Propaganda in the Formation of the Diocese of Truro'. *Southern History,* Vol 5, 1983: 238–66.

Pawley White Interview, 25 January 2000.

Payton, Philip. *The Making of Modern Cornwall: Historical Experience and the Persistence of 'Difference'.* Redruth: Dyllansow Truran, 1992.

—— *Cornwall.* Fowey: Alexander Associates, 1996.

—— 'Introduction'. *Cornish Studies: Five.* ed. Philip Payton. Exeter: University of Exeter Press, 1997a: 1–8.

—— 'Paralysis and Revival: the reconstruction of Celtic-Catholic Cornwall 1890-1945'. *Cornwall: The Cultural Construction of Place.* ad. Ella Westland. Penzance: The Patten Press, 1997b: 25–39.

Programme of the Gorseth at Carn Brea. Gorseth Kernow, 1929.

Royal Cornwall Gazette, 24 February 1910.

—— 8 December 1910.

—— 29 February 1912.

—— 20 August 1924.

Seward, Andy. 'Cornish Rugby and Cultural Identity: A Socio-Historical Perspective'. *Cornish Studies: Five.* Ed. Philip Payton. Exeter: University of Exeter Press, 1997: 164–179.

Taylor, Thomas. *The Celtic Christianity of Cornwall.* London: Longmans, Green and Co, 1916.

Taylor, Tom. *Ballads and Songs of Brittany.* London: Macmillan, 1865.

The Times, 5 February 1912.

—— 7 January 1913.

—— 4 February 1941.

Tregidga, Garry. 'The Politics of the Celto-Cornish Revival, 1886–1939'. *Cornish Studies: Five.* ed. Philip Payton. Exeter: University of Exeter Press, 1997: 125–150.

West Briton, 10 January 1910.

—— 13 January 1910.

14

FROM APOCALYPTIC PARANOIA TO THE MYTHIC NATION

Political extremity and myths of origin in the neo-fascist milieu

Andrew Fergus Wilson

Introduction

As the nation-state undergoes a continuous and complex unravelling by the forces of global politics, culture and capital, there is an increased tendency for communities to become mobilised around ideas of 'the nation' which are less reliant upon the structuring effect of 'the state'. The nation becomes increasingly, consciously, experienced in forms of cultural practice and tradition and it is these knots of solidarity that maintain the bonds that exist between the constituent members of national communities. Celtic nationalism can be considered in this way, the establishment of national assemblies in Wales, Northern Ireland and Scotland notwithstanding. From Yeats' aims in *The Celtic Twilight* to the resurgence of the Cornish and Breton languages, there has been a clear and conscious movement towards realising self-determining national identities which draw upon predominantly cultural resources to produce, in part, the particularities which circumscribe the resurgent national forms. Nonetheless, whilst such 'nations without states', to borrow Guibernau's conceptualisation (Guibernau 1999), may point to an increasingly common mode of transnational identity, they are also replete with the dangers of any form of nationalism. Indeed, to speak of any kind of European nationalism is to run the risk of calling to mind the belligerent strains of nationalism unleashed by the collapse of the Soviet Union and its satellite states or endemic in the emergence of neo-nationalist groups such as the English Defence League.

Whilst there are many examples of progressive uses of mystical or legendary 'pasts' within recent history, be it the cultural case for self determination within the former 'Celtic fringe' or the appropriation of 'witch' identities and practices by feminist women and men there are also a significant number of instances of the use of mythic national or communal pasts for less progressive political or ideological ends. This chapter will explore the presence of themes of mythical or legendary cultural and communal origins within contemporary nationalist discourse as they are used on internet websites dedicated to extremist nationalism. White nationalist discourse typically draws upon a range of cultural markers which incorporate Celtic identities and others into a syncretic 'Northern European' heritage. The aim is to demonstrate the manner in which these sites draw upon the polyvalency of mythic symbols and how the syncretic tendency within the contemporary cultic milieu uncritically absorbs paranoid nationalist rhetoric thus problematising commonly-held national myths and legends. The opportunities for networking amongst and between nationalist groups afforded by the internet mean that white nationalism is, paradoxically, increasingly transnational; it is in this context that Northern European cultural traditions have become key in the attempt by these groups to formulate a shared identity.

Racialist apocalyptic paranoia

> Today, in the year 2005, approximately two percent of earth's population is White female of child bearing age or younger. The White race is dead!!! Murdered by a coalition of Jews, Christian universalists, anti-nature dupes, opportunistic political whores, media moguls, over educated intellectuals, dogmatic nationalists, feminist fools, assorted misfits and cowards.
>
> The remaining whites are hopelessly integrated, terrorized, brain washed, miscegenated and are rapidly being overrun by six billion coloreds. As a viable entity with a means to survive, the white race is extinct. The few of us who resisted genocide are analogous to a few living cells within a corpse.
>
> (Lane 2005, §1–2)

The quotation above comes from David Lane, a figure whose status amongst white supremacists borders on that of a holy martyr. Lane died in jail whilst serving consecutive sentences totalling some 190 years for a variety of offences committed as part of the Brüder Schweigen (also known as The Order, or the Silent Brotherhood). In jail he produced a number of texts which have gone on to become highly influential within white supremacist and nationalist circles. The extract above comes from a text entitled, 'Open Letter to a Dead Race,' in which Lane calls upon white males to throw off their inhibitions and to partake of a racial revolution with the aim of creating a new white homeland. The possible outcomes, he suggests, are total: glory or a glorious death. The enemies that he describes are non-whites, led by a Jewish/Zionist conspiracy which has pacified and shaped the coalition described above: 'Zionist control of the media, as well as of all essential power points of industry, finance, law and politics in the once White nations is simply fact' (Lane 1999, 3). He sees his home country, the United States of America, at the heart of this conspiracy, describing its state symbols as coded manifestations of the conspiracy:

Over the eagle on the Great Seal are 13 pentagonal stars which form the Star of David, the clear symbolism being that the United States would finalize the World Zionist Empire. So we see that the Pentagon is the home of the police department for a World Zionist government of those who use the six-pointed star.

(Lane 1999, 330)

What becomes evident in this is the rejection of the USA as the vehicle by which Lane's fantasies of a racially-segregated white homeland might be reached. While, say, the Southern Poverty Law Center, a leading US civil rights organisation, described Lane as a 'White Nationalist' (SPLC 2010) there is little consideration of what constitutes the 'nation' for a nationalist who forswore the nation. What, then, is the white supremacist nation? It is varied and contested.

Lane's separatist outlook typifies a strand of American white supremacism which marked a turning away from the patriotism of traditional U.S. far right white nationalist discourse. The strong strand of separatism was exemplified by the establishment of the Aryan Nations communities during the mid-1990s. Even so, in these self-defined redoubts of Aryan folk there were sufficient grounds for ideological conflict between the predominantly Christian Identity organisers and white supremacists of other beliefs. Lane's own spiritual history was one notably marked by a trajectory which shifted from the Christian Identity movement to a racist paganism. Lane is described as an Odinist (Gardell 2003; Kaplan 1997), or follower of Asatru, but he is quite precise in delineating between Odinism and his variant, Wotanism. Wotanism allowed him to stress the religio-mythical basis of a shared 'Northern European' mindset:

So, I first chose the name Wotanism over Odinism. First because W.O.T.A.N. makes a perfect acronym for Will Of The Aryan Nation. Secondly because he was called Wotan on the European continent and only called Odin in Scandinavia.

(Lane n.d.a, §24–25)

Thus Lane demarcates the broad, international but ethnically discrete boundaries and beliefs of the 'nation, culture, and way of life,' that underlines his ideological outlook. The 'racial imaginary' Lane's religious formation draws upon becomes vital in providing an historical re-tension for the 'people' he sought to defend. The tradition that is alluded to must be established in order to make possible the validity of the racial–cultural complex. The Northern European sagas, myths and religious constructs that Lane draws upon provide a geographic, ethnic and historical origin story for him. Many of the elements that are drawn upon are well-established tropes of white supremacist and neo-Nazi discourse with Lane's pan-Aryan mysticism a synthesis of a pre-existing racist mythos. Nicholas Goodrick-Clarke's work on esoteric Nazism attests to a continuity at work within the fascist milieu (Goodrick-Clarke 2003, 2004).

Myths of nation

Myths of nation become crucial in this. National myths (as opposed to, say, legend or sacred history) are often overlooked in considerations of the 'lore' of a nation but it is argued by Misāne and Predīte that myths are 'authorized by traditions and by their specific relation to sacred time and space,' and thus are also active in the process by which 'the nation' is sacralised. In this way:

> Myths develop a sense of togetherness, they are the means by which human beings tie themselves to the world, feel at home there, and become the heirs of their ancestors.
>
> (Misāne and Predīte 1997, 160)

The collective conscience which this implies, however, in addition to organising itself around shared myths (and legends and a sacred history) also draws upon the religiosity of myth as a powerful, transcendent, legitimator of the nation and national community. Lane is clearly aware of the pressures involved in maintaining a unity amongst a dispersed and (perceptually) disenfranchised community:

> 24. No race of People can indefinitely continue their existence without territorial imperatives in which to propagate, protect, and promote their own kind.
>
> 25. A People without a culture exclusively their own will perish. [...]
>
> The folk, namely the members of the Race, are the Nation. Racial loyalties must always supersede geographical and national boundaries. If this is taught and understood, it will end fratricidal wars. Wars must not be fought for the benefit of another race.
>
> (Lane n.d.b)

Although 'the Nation' is to be territorially defined, the actual location is not of great consequence because the Nation, here, is founded entirely through 'the folk'. But, again, even here, what is the nation that Lane and other white 'nationalists' appeal to? Clearly there is a strong sense of a shared Aryan/Amanist destiny but the nation in which the race is realised is an imagined one, reliant upon a fantasy of blood purity and a 'race-soul'. Given the rootedness of Lane's 'nationalism' in images of Germanic heritage and spirituality and yet re-membered in a North American context and with the express purpose of becoming a 'Folk preserving religion,' (Lane 1999, 171) the nation is imagined at once as the awakening of a 'Folk' to their current and future racial destiny, but also legitimated through the appropriation of heathen forms as a means of providing a 'traditional' spiritualised ethnic identity to Lane's fellow racists. Simultaneously Northern European and Northern American, it provides a bridge to culturally disparate white nationalists.

Despite the emphasis that Lane places on blood and faith, his stark vision of an Aryan warrior race, 'fighting to save the future' is also one of a nation which seeks a territory, as the 24th precept, cited above, suggests. This search for a nation, couched in the fear-filled rhetoric of the paranoid spokesman, is one which is evident in much of the literature of the far right. English 'national anarchist' Troy Southgate evidences much the same paranoid nationalism as David Lane:

> The task we have set ourselves is a great one. The fight for race and nation – the renewal of the bond between blood and soil – is a cause that gives us a great sense of purpose and destiny. And yet, for those who are called to this fight in the immediate future, we can only offer a long and difficult road which is often characterised by disappointment and pain.
>
> (Southgate 2003b, §1)

The terms used by Southgate are strikingly similar to those employed by Lane: 'race', 'blood', 'purpose', 'destiny' and, indeed, the threat (or promise) of a potentially cataclysmic fight forever looming on the horizon of history. For all that Southgate espouses a broadly leftist 'anarchist' position, his politics are clearly racial and even in delineating his belief in the possibility of an anarchism that is informed by nationalism, the similarities with secessionist U.S. racial groups becomes increasingly evident:

> Q. Why 'national' anarchism? Surely nationalism is incompatible with anarchic principles?
>
> A. National-Anarchists do not support nationalism in the sense that we look to artificial nation-states or borders and boundaries [...] When we speak of nationhood we are referring to its tribal and organic implications. Therefore our concept of the word 'national' relates not to territory but to the racial identity which is a natural facet of all peoples.
>
> (Southgate 2006, §1)

The cultural tolerance which is implied in the recognition of the 'naturalness' of 'all peoples' is negated by the racial boundaries which are suggested to have supplanted the 'artificial boundaries' of the nation-state. Again, Southgate is writing in terms recognisable to participants in the white racist milieu because this image of racially-defined communal groupings living alongside but separate from each other is one that was common to racist ideologues and groups in the U.K. and U.S. during the latter half of the twentieth century. For Southgate, just as for Lane, the central purpose appears to be to sound a call to arms in defence of a threatened racially-defined but territorially diverse 'nation'.

The virtual pan-Aryan nation

Who constitutes this nation is not as simple as might first be thought. For sure, there are clear racial boundaries but the commitment invested in a racist identity will vary enormously between self-identifying 'citizens'. In *Online Belongings: Fantasy, Affect and Web Communities*, Debra Ferreday cites the play of the 'real' and the 'virtual' in online subjectivity and the role of fantasy for the cyber-subject (Ferreday 2009). This may well explain to some extent the 'play' of internet occult fascists who revel in the theatricality and transgression of the role whilst also being afforded the comfort of a supportive community in which to do so. Thus the 'not-real' status of virtuality provides an excuse for indulging in what would be 'rejected knowledge' (to borrow from Barkun, 2003) in any other form of mass communication. This gives a nebulous spectrality to the internationally dispersed but racially focussed white nationalist nations; around a hard core of 'permanent nationals' there flickers into and out of existence a tertiary nation of online-only self-identified members of the nation(s) who log on and log off from the nation. These 'virtual nationalists' are drawn to the discursively-constructed national 'space' which is constructed through the symbolically created and linked network of nationalist sites and signifiers. Speaking of web communities in general, Ferreday writes:

> By reading websites as texts, it is possible to track the precise means by which a 'sense of community' is constructed: through intonation, through explicit or implicit addresses to an 'ideal' reader, through intertextual references and hypertextual links, to name but a few.
>
> (Ferreday 2009, 54)

It is clear from both Lane and Southgate that the 'ideal reader' is white (and predominantly male) and the white Aryan nation is repeatedly explicitly addressed *en masse* and individually, whilst less overtly racist discourse relies upon the implicit intertextualities to which the myths of the Aryan nation are able to allude. Simi and Futrell describe the importance of internet communities to individual white supremacists for it is here that many geographically isolated racists coalesce into an indefinable social group (Simi and Futrell 2010). What is of key pertinence here is that they note that 'embracing the Aryan aesthetic and conveying the commitment to others online sustains members' identification with the collective "we" of the movement' (Simi and Futrell 2010, 89). Thus, the aesthetic realm becomes crucial in maintaining the idea of a shared (national/racial) collectivity. Of course, the cultural dimension is a key informant of national identity and one of the means by which the idea of any nation is mobilised and maintained. For the disparate 'nationalists without a nation', however, it may become the sole means by which they are able to construct an identity out of affiliation as opposed to (racial) difference. In a different context, Douglas Cowan describes the possibilities that the internet offers for exploring the cultic milieu and aspects of the spiritual self. Of particular relevance here is his observation that 'two other particular benefits [...] are the potential for community represented by the Internet and the stage for the experimental performance of identity that it provides' (Cowan 2005, 199). Thus, it is here that the appropriation of Northern European spirituality and myth become active in the construction of the tertiary virtual nationalist community. It is argued that the use of polyvalent myths of 'tradition' and 'spirit' are purposefully drawn upon by a primary core of Aryan nationalists to act as lures and fetishes for tertiary virtual nationalists and for potential converts. Before examining an example of how mythic archetypes of an Aryan nation are rehearsed within the paratext of white nationalist discourse, it is useful to explore further the intangible but always present 'spirit' of the nation.

The spirit of the nation

In *The Magic of the State*, Michael Taussig captures the irreducibility of the role of the 'spirit' of the nation in the popular imagination of a people (Taussig 1997). Based upon fieldwork in Venezuela, *The Magic of The State* is written from an intellectual space that sits between the academy and ethnography, documentary and fiction. The magic that the state draws upon to maintain the national 'whole' is conveyed well in the interplay between the nation's 'spirit queen', its other national archetypes, and its subjects. The spirit queen is appealed to by, and possesses, willing worshippers; she invests the landscape with meaning and power whilst revealing occult secrets of the nation, illuminating memory, 'the spirit queen, enigmatically smiling in her mountain with the spirits of the dead' (Taussig 1997, 147).

Taussig explores the use of the power of the dead by the nation-state and by its subjects in drawing upon the state's invocation of that power. He suggests that it is the reified mythos of the nation of the dead that underpins a nation state's claim to power. In an interview he makes evident this relationship:

> People today gain magical power not from the dead, but from the state's embellishment of them. And the state, authoritarian and spooky, is as much possessed by the dead as is any individual pilgrim.
>
> (Strauss and Taussig 2005, §7)

The Aryan nation-without-a-state does not have a dead-nation publicly preserved in war memorials, statues and the like; instead its shrines are frequently virtual, dispersed and largely hidden to all but the nation itself. Lane himself survives predominantly through repositories of his writing. Indeed, the sidebar menu of the main online resource for Lane's writings (David Lane's Pyramid Prophecy and Der Bruder Schweigen Archives) is headed by RIP notices for Lane and other key white supremacists, Bruce Carroll Pierce and Robert J. Matthews. The pages dedicated to them feature eulogies, personal memories and photographs of commemorative occasions (in some instances the term 'rituals' might be applied but in general would be too suggestive of a uniformity of event). In each instance the dead are described as heroes, martyrs; in Lane's writings similar epithets are used about earlier white supremacists and, of course, his appropriation of Wotanism borrows from long-dead (albeit recently revived) traditions. And so the Aryan nation to which Lane and others appealed and belonged becomes sedimented in these layers of death, of the dead Lane referring to yet more dead and, through them, the embellished dead provide the 'magical' centripetal forces that hold the virtual nation together. In these myths of dead heroes and Gods, the neo-fascist Aryan nationalists re-imagine a lost nation which is bequeathed a (borrowed, stolen) past that predates historical memory.

Taussig's work allows us to consider the ephemeral plane upon which the popular performance of the nation is sometimes staged. As such he is supplementing rationalist accounts of the nation with one that considers the mystic-spiritual dimension of 'belonging'. In a similar vein, so too does the work of Walker Connor, except he disassociates that sense of belonging from any consideration of the state and concentrates instead on the intangible bonds between the individual and the greater national community. So, rather than the bonds between a subject and the institutions and infrastructures that constitute the state, Connor's work places its emphasis upon the bonds between the people that constitute a nation. Connor's concept of 'ethnonationalism' is useful in that it foregrounds the 'deep emotional thrust' that unites a people in 'the irrational belief that, descending from common ancestors, we are all related and form part of the same "extended family"' (Conversi 2002, 2). Connor offers an account of nationalism as it is produced and maintained subjectively, that is to say that he demonstrates the emotional and imaginative work that is done to mobilise national identity. It is here that the role of myths of national belonging and destiny are at their most fecund. Further, by emphasising the centrality of ethnicity to nationalism, he underscores the familial metaphor through which nationalism is understood. This metaphor is part of the fabric of national identity and he points to its use in successive phases of American history (independence and union – the failure of the English to recognise their consanguinous ties and the ancestral blood shared by the 'people' of the union; Connor 1994, 200–1).

Whilst being an important, if unrecognised, element in established nations, the emphasis upon ties of kin loyalty is evidently more keenly felt in racialist discourses of nation and comes to the fore in the narratives in which the nation is invoked or theorised. Lane's renown within the racist underground was founded upon his actions as part of the Der Bruder Schweigen; the kin affinity that lay behind their nationalist identities made evident through their nomenclature. The far right, in diverse ways, are actively constructing a mythic past from which destiny has borne them. The process is not unique to the current generation of mystic racialists as Nicholas Goodrick-Clarke's work attests. Nonetheless, it is an endeavour that is currently augmented by the huge expansion of the individual subject's capacity to disseminate their views and materials pertaining to them on the internet.

It is here that we see the setting in which the subcultural drift of signifiers of the far-right milieu may occur. Increasingly, websites promoting the ideologies of the Aryan mystics are multi-faceted and incorporate elements that are bereft of overt ideological content. Although inactive since 'Walpurgis Night' 2009, Troy Southgate's 'SYNTHESIS: Journal du cercle de la rose noire' (http://www.rosenoire.org/) is emblematic of this trend.[1] The site is presented as an 'irregularly-published intellectual and cultural journal devoted to Anarchy [...] Occulture [...] and Metapolitics' (Southgate 2003a) and features a Romantic-Gothic design ethic that is maintained throughout the site's various sections. These are given over to reviews, articles, essays, interviews and two sections of hyperlinks, one dedicated to links to individual books on amazon.com and the other to a range of subject material. In all sections there is a diversity of content that would belie the site's nature were it not that the preponderance of texts are by figures associated with the mystical fascist milieu such as Miguel Serrano and Julius Evola. On the surface, the choices of text might appear to be the accidental cultural drifting of a blogger with European New Right tendencies were it not for Southgate's active espousal of 'national anarchism' and a stated strategy of entryism:

> This new way is entryism, working within society's institutions and organisations with committed revolutionaries. At this stage in our development, it is the only logical course of action. In the long-term, it is the only possible road to victory.
>
> (Southgate 2003c, §18)

Thus familiar cultural texts become lures by which active seekers become immersed in an intertext that is predominantly formed from neo-Nazi cultural obsessions and icons. As will be discussed below, a semiotic drift from the cultural underground to the neo-fascist underworld occurs and, on the grounds of Southgate's statement above, it would appear to be a purposeful misdirecting of the seekers' curiosity. Despite competing visions of a racially 'correct' religious belief, Betty Dobratz indicates the manner in which perceived ideological alignment between religious identity and racialism can be used as a bridging technique by racist groups (Dobratz 2001); Southgate's aims affirm her analysis.

Of course, it can be suggested that neo-fascism is subject to the same cultural tides and patterns as other formations within a culture; that its intertext is formed from a syncretic tendency within its national source. In a discussion of a suggested predilection for violence in American culture, Denis Dudos makes the case that festivals of the dead with a strong Nordic origin (such as Halloween, *Alfablot* and Yuletide) have embedded within the broader host culture an obsession with their themes and, ultimately, the deeply encoded remnants of Odinist warrior cultures. He states that:

> If the neo-Nazis and their 'intellectual' supporters have espoused a 'traditional' interpretation of these holidays, this should not hide the fact this secret obsession with death has arisen – to the point of permeating international culture – from the Gothic British novel and later from American syncretism and its fictional film versions. It was not by 'purist' Nordic-culture enthusiasts selling earthenware incense burners decorated with swastikas that this myth was introduced, but, more trivially, by the sale of Halloween gadgets and the international toy industry.
>
> (Dudos 1998, 150)

Leaving aside the ease with which Dudos equates 'neo-Nazis' with 'Nordic-culture enthusiasts', it should be noted that if Dudos is correct in this assertion then the semantic pathways which Southgate and his allies seek to exploit are already well-travelled and easily mapped. It will be suggested below that the heavy metal webzine *Mourning The Ancient* (http://www.mourningtheancient. com) exploits this shared semantic space to generate an association between neo-fascism, a David Lane-inspired Odinism, 'magick'[2] and heavy metal. To be sure, these associations are not unique, nor is *Mourning the Ancient* seminal, but what the webzine does attempt to do is to produce a visual manifestation of the neo-fascist national 'spirit queen': clearly, not intentionally, as such, but part of its operation is dedicated to heavily stylised erotic images of (white) women in a variety of mythically-inspired scenarios.

Imagining the mythic homeland

The 'extreme metal' website *Mourning the Ancient* is divided into three sections. The main section, certainly the one with the most content, is dedicated to an eponymous webzine which features interviews with bands, music reviews, poetry, articles and other related documents; the second is primarily a collection of images of women in what might best be described as 'white nationalist archetypal scenarios'; the third section is dedicated to a band named 'Primitive Supremacy' which initially provided backing music to CD-based slideshows of images that visited the same themes as those featured in the second section of the website before recording a music-only CD.

The index page of the site presents visitors with a choice between the three sections with each one represented by a banner logo.[3] These banners offer pictorial and linguistic devices which reflect the website's repeated concerns: the colour palette is simplistic, echoing the colours of the Nazi swastika flag design: red, black and white; a slogan proclaims, 'Tomorrow belongs to us!'. The webzine section is indicated by a blonde woman wearing an iconic German World War II *Stahlhelm* helmet emblazoned with the site's logo. The logo is repeated throughout the website and is described in suitable self-mythologising terms as being the product of a 'vision':

> As the vision unfolded the coming winter, the symbol of our doings, the 'Expansion Rune' (the five pointed star with four points reaching outward) was born. We designed this using two ancient runes. The 'pentagram' and the 'expansion points.' While both can be found in a number of ancient cultures, the five pointed star was known in some as a 'symbol of truth.' The two runes combined can be defined as 'the expansion of truth.'
>
> (*Mourning the Ancient* 2001, §2)

The banner for the photography section features two images of a blonde woman, one with blood dripping from her mouth whilst in the other she looks more serene, wearing a tiara of ivy topped with a crescent moon. These frame a subheading which reads 'Where Beauty and Barbarity Meet...' The third section, the band's area, has the slogan 'Melody and Madness' and is decorated with images of a mud-encrusted woman clutching a skull. These visual themes abound on the website and all of the images are taken from the photography section. Throughout the site there is an emphasis on loss, decline and a championing of a mythic past; this past is a syncretic amalgamation of Germanic, pagan, heathen, martial, magickal and Gothic visual tropes. This combination of themes provides a register of elements from which the aesthetic of a racially-defined, geographically-dispersed, neo-fascist nation is realised. That this register is composed mostly of polysemic signs which are not exclusive to the neo-fascist community points to the scope for the entryism that Southgate described. It must be said that this may well be one of the inherent dangers of a past unfixed from common knowledge; as possible readings of poorly understood beliefs proliferate and what is firmly known of them becomes overwhelmed by speculation, they then become increasingly available for appropriation and reductionist perversion by disparate groupings within the fascist milieu.

In the photography section of *Mourning the Ancient* a variety of images of nude and semi-nude female models are offered. It is within these images that the website produces an imagined iconography for their particular rendering of the mythical neo-fascist nation. With the over-riding theme of 'beauty' and 'barbarity', fifty galleries are filled with photographs of heavy breasted women in, for want of a better phrase, 'cultic tableaux'. The images are a curious meeting between 'glamour modelling' and atavistic primitivism with neo-fascist mystic overtones: gallery six ('Krieg') contains the original of the image used for the webzine banner, a topless model in *Stalhelm* and 'Expansion Rune' armband; gallery eleven ('Fallen') has the same model naked barring thickly encrusted mud, in this set she sports a set of wings, nipple rings and a sword and cavorts with skulls; unlike six and eleven, gallery sixteen ('Blut') is in colour and features a blonde, blue-eyed woman who is naked and smeared in what appears to be blood; gallery fourteen ('Magick') features, once more, a topless blonde model. In this set, wearing a long, flowing black skirt and with a pair of deer antlers on her head, the same model poses topless holding a sword in her right hand and a large, unidentifiable, antiquarian book in her left.

The images border on camp but the intent is clear: to invoke a mythical past which is marked by a primal simplicity in addition to tokens of the cultic and fascist milieux. The atavism is recognised by the authors of the website who state,

> Our photography, to us, represents many different thoughts and emotions, but primarily, anger and sorrow. It is those two emotions that have fueled us since day one. An anger and burning contempt for the lies paraded as truth in this tired world, and a bitter sorrow for the seemingly powerless position all of us stand. [...] 'Light' has always been seen as symbolic of truth, life and guidance. In this reckless age all three are reaching their points of extinction. [...] We long for the simple truths and freedoms of yesterday. Which is why our photography usually centers on more natural, antique themes.
>
> (*Mourning the Ancient* 2001, §5–6)

Their sense of loss carries the same melancholic apocalypticism that is found the writings of David Lane. *Mourning the Ancient* has clear sympathies with Lane's position and the repeated use of Aryan women in the website's imagery can be understood as representing the fertile vessels through which Lane's future, as demanded in 'the fourteen words', is to be secured. Additionally, the website includes an essay which recounts Lane's life and views and includes an interview with Lane (Mourning the Ancient 2003) and, although the website davidlane1488.org is the primary internet resource for Lane's writing, it is worth noting that the Wikipedia entry for David Lane's interpretation of Wotanism links to an article by Lane posted at *Mourning the Ancient* and not davidlane1488. org (Lane n.d.a). In addition to Lane's writing and links to websites sympathetic to him, *Mourning the Ancient* also features, amidst interviews with heavy metal groups of a variety of political leanings, interviews with the webmaster of racist Wotanist website, W.O.T.A.N. and with the current editor of the works of the Nazi mystic Savitri Devi. The romanticised ancient past that is being mourned is clearly a racially distinct one.

As stated, the images featured in the gallery pages of *Mourning the Ancient* are varied but thematically linked; visual tropes suggestive of mythic archetypes abound and, whilst neo-fascist belief is never overtly referred to in the images, the context of the website's political leanings frames the interpretative strategies open to the viewer. Typifying the tropic repetition is the ninety-seventh image from gallery forty-one ('Satori in Red'). In the centre of the image stands a blonde woman in a red micro bikini, a few strands of her fringe are dyed red, her face is made up in *kabuki* style, around her neck is an Iron Cross. Painted in red on a white backdrop, a series of runes frame the model. *Eihwaz* dominates the backdrop, five others encircle it and the model's crotch obscures the position that the spatial logic of the image suggests a sixth should occupy. The red of her thong mimics the red paint used for the runes and suggests a pseudo-connotative chain (Eco 1995) which sets sexual desire and spiritual iconography in relation to each other, but not dependent upon each other, for meaning. Thus the viewer can drift (ibid.) between sexual and spiritual readings of the image, all the time contextualised by the white supremicism that underlines the rationale of *Mourning the Ancient*. The central rune, *Eihwaz,* is also known as *Wolfsangel* and associated with Berserker werewolves and, pertinently, a number of Nazi divisions including the late and post-war Werwolf guerrilla groups (Biddiscombe 1998). Boyd Rice, of Death in June, the neofolk/industrial musical group, has made frequent use of the symbol and it is in this context that it is most well known in popular culture, although it is also an actively used sigil within the Church of Satan. These two currents converge in an online forum called '(The Satanic Network's) Undercroft'. In a thread dating from 2006, a Magister of the Church of Satan advertises the sale of a limited edition silver 'Wolfshook/Wolfangle' ring. On the fourth page of replies and responses, the original poster makes a further post which includes an attached jpeg graphic file showing Boyd Rice wearing the *Wolfsangel* ring (Magister Lang 2007).

Conclusion

It is in this fertile co-mingling of popular culture and the cultic milieu that *Mourning The Ancient* operates. At once drawing upon the national-spiritual resonances of appropriated Scando-Germanic heathenism, whilst resetting them within a sexualised subcultural context, *Mourning the Ancient* satisfies both post-pubescent fantasies of available and objectified women and the imagery of the subculture. Fecund and flirtatious, the spirit queen that Taussig identifies in a Venezuelan *barrio* is here transtemporal, emerging from a long lost (read: newly invented) past, shrouded in myth and magic and bearing an ancient knowledge. It is in this nexus of myth, longing and desire that the neo-fascist nation is imagined and it is heavily charged with a spirituality that becomes embodied in the warrior-woman imagery of *Mourning the Ancient*. The valkyries ride out to heavy metal in neo-fascist corners of the world wide web.

The imagery of *Mourning the Ancient* lends weight to the neo-fascist appropriation of Northern European heathenism. It recasts the runes, already much abused by Nazism past and present, in a self-mythologising setting of sexualised spirit queen and subcultural alterity. This is, however, more than a superficial toying with transgressive imagery as might sometimes be associated with subcultures. *Mourning the Ancient*'s sympathies with David Lane are evident and Lane is in no doubt of his 'destiny' in shaping a modern day racial heathenism:

> To that end I began teaching an updated form of our most common indigenous religion about 20 years ago. Its major deity is called Wotan, or Odin or Woden. Updated to be racial rather than tribal, and to remove any conflict with modern science. The Gods, Goddesses and myths of Wotanism represent the forces of Nature. [...] History shows that a religion must have a founder, often called a "prophet." Since no one else assumed that role, I have done so.
>
> (Lane c.2002, §4)

Through an association with Lane's messianic atavistic racism, *Mourning the Ancient* becomes a virtual safehouse for racist ideas as well as a cultural resource for dreaming the Wotanist nation into being. The webzine section co-mingles relatively well known heavy metal bands, such as Deicide and Carcass, with more obscure ones, many of the latter, such as Pagan Hellfire and Capricornus/ Thor's Hammer, being identified with far-right politics. The bleak outlook shared by many heavy metal artists, intensified in the lyrics and imagery of what Keith Kahn Harris describes as 'extreme metal', is here used to provide an apparent coincidence of perspective between the better known acts and the obscure nationalist groups. Whilst a band such as Deicide, described by Kahn-Harris as typifying extreme metal's 'discursive transgression' (Kahn-Harris 2007, 34–43) are certainly bleak, if not apocalyptic, in their lyrics they could not be characterised as subscribing to the kind of racial apocalypse that David Lane espoused. Nonetheless, bassist and vocalist Glen Benton's 1998 interview with *Mourning the Ancient* touches upon his wish to limit immigration to the U.S., on excessive taxation, surveillance and the kind of anti-federalist conservatism that would now be associated with the Tea Party (Benton 1998). His political views are conservative, certainly, however it is only in the context of interviews with avowed fascists such as Sturmfuhrer that the reader's interpretation becomes framed within a neo-fascist register.

Although there is no concrete connection between Southgate and *Mourning the Ancient*, this interweaving of subcultural texts and spiritual belief with racial nationalism on the *Mourning the Ancient* website intertextually insinuates neo-fascist values into broader cultural consumption. This then is the cultural tactic proposed by Southgate and described by George Macklin as an attempt to 'forge the 'political space' necessary for political and racial hegemony' (Macklin 2005, 319) and also described elsewhere by Cristoph Fringeli as an attempt by 'elements of the organized far right who are trying to use a "metapolitical" strategy of intervention to fight their fascist kulturkampf'(Fringeli 2011). The recent motion picture *Thor* (2011), itself an adaption of the popular Marvel Comics strip, further sedimented a germinal idea of the Norse pantheon in the popular imagination but the neo-fascist right has been active in digging over the ground within which these seeds can grow. Here, at the heart of the neo-fascist project, is an attempt to colonise the past and to reinvent the religion and myths of a people long dead. David Lane reinvented and recontextualised those beliefs within a violent racism whilst projects such as *Mourning the Ancient* have promulgated Lane's modern myths of 'Wotan'. In doing so, the waters of what constitutes Northern European paganism become increasingly muddied by the neo-fascist jackboot. For instance, the well-established Danish neo-pagan community Forn Siðr has been forced to make a statement distancing itself from neo-fascist use of its symbols.[4] The building of a deterritorialized neo-fascist nation is a project that draws upon and colonises existing cultural constructs, forcing them to be re-read within the terms set by the virtual nationalists. It is thus that a set of beliefs which are recognisable, but poorly understood, slowly become eclipsed by the black sun and neo-fascist groupuscules are able to build myths of their own. It is clear here, then, that myth is always an ongoing project, it is re-visited, reworked, and revised and, crucially, must be contested and re-won when attempts are made to appropriate it in ways that would crush its polysemous pleasures into a solitary, bleak, vision.

This, then, is the dilemma faced by a resurgent Celtic nationalism. On the one hand there is the call to redeem marginalised and silenced cultures and yet, on the other, is the dangers of tarrying with an embittered rhetoric which intersects with the exclusionary outlook of extremist nationalism. The stakes are clear: for those national communities, be they existing nation-states or 'nations without a state', whose past is being pilfered by extremist nationalist projects, there is a need to consolidate their cultural history in terms which reduce the polyvalency of the symbols drawn upon extremists. For nations supported by the institutions of a state have at their disposal the means to shore up the parameters of their cultural vision through galleries, museums and educational curricula which narrate the national concerns but for nations-without-a-state, there are diminished opportunities to do so. In some cases, they must negotiate with institutions that reflect colonial cultural and linguistic dominance. Thus the importance of works such as the present one become much clearer: in revisiting and revitalising the spirit of the Celtic nation in ways which illuminate its richly diverse and, at times, contradictory heritage, the dynamism of these cultural visions prevent the ossification of cultural tropes which might otherwise provide nationalist extremists with the basis from which to fashion *their* myths of nation.

Notes

1 *Synthesis* has been taken offline and Southgate's efforts appear to now be focussed upon 'National Anarchism'.
2 I have placed magick in inverted commas here to denote that whilst the website uses iconography associated with magickal systems, it does not do so within a framework which could be identified as belonging to any one magickal system and, as such, can be seen as a generalised 'populist magick'.
3 Since this chapter was written the website has modified a number of its images but the symbolic paradigm is maintained.
4 The English language homepage of Forn Siðr states explicitly, 'We wish to make it clear that Nazi activity, or misuse of pagan symbols for Nazi purposes IS NOT compatible with membership of Forn Siðr'. Available from HTTP: <http://www.fornsidr.dk/dk/17> (accessed 5 July 2011).

Bibliography

Barkun, M. (2003) *A Culture of Conspiracy: Apocalyptic Visions in Contemporary America*, Berkeley: University of California Press

Benton, G. (1998) Interview with *Mourning the Ancient*. Online. Available HTTP: <http://www.mourningtheancient.com/deicide.htm> (accessed 12 July 2010)

Biddiscombe, P. (1998) *Werwolf!: The History of the National Socialist Guerrilla Movement, 1944–1946*, Toronto: University of Toronto Press

Connor, W. (1994) *Ethnonationalism: The Quest for Understanding*, Princeton: Princeton University Press

Conversi, D. (2002) 'Conceptualizing Nationalism: An Introduction to Walker Connor's Work' in D. Conversi (ed.) *Ethnonationalism in the Contemporary World: Walker Connor and the Study of Rationalism*, London: Routledge, 1–23

Cowan, D. (2005) *Cyberhenge: Modern Pagans on the Internet*, London: Routledge

Dobratz, B. (2001) 'The Role of Religion in the Collective Identity of the White Racialist Movement', *Journal for the Scientific Study of Religion*, 40 (2): 287–301

Dudos, D. (1998) *The Werewolf Complex: America's Fascination with Violence*, trans. A. Pingree, Oxford: OUP

Eco, U. (1995) 'Unlimited Semeiosis and Drift: Pragmaticism vs. "Pragmatism"' in K. L. Ketner (ed.) *Pierce and Contemporary Thought: Philosophical Inquiries*, New York: Fordham University Press, pp. 205-220

Ferreday, D. (2009) *Online Belongings: Fantasy, Affect and Web Communities*, Oxford: Peter Lang

Fringeli, C. (2011) 'From Subculture to Hegemony: Transversal Strategies of the New Right in Neofolk and Martial Industrial', *Who Makes The Nazis?* Online. Available from HTTP: <http://www.whomakesthenazis.com/2011/07/datacide-from-subculture-to-hegemony.html> (accessed 15 July 2011)

Gardell, M. (2003) *Gods of the Blood: The Pagan Revival and White Separatism*, Durham, NC: Duke University Press

Goodrick-Clarke, N. (2003) *Black Sun: Aryan Cults, Esoteric Nazism, and the Politics of Identity*, New York: New York University Press

—— (2004) *The Occult Roots of Nazism: Secret Aryan Cults and Their Influence on Nazi Ideology*, London: I. B. Tauris

Guibernau, M. (1999) *Nations without States: Political Communities in a Global Age*, Cambridge: Polity Press

Kahn-Harris, K. (2007) *Extreme Metal: Music and Culture on the Edge*, Oxford: Berg

Kaplan, J. (1997) *Radical Religion in America: Millenarian Movements from the Far Right to the Children of Noah*, Syracuse, NY: Syracuse University Press

Lane, D. (2002) 'Why Wotanism and Pyramid Prophecy'. Online. Available HTTP: <http://www.freetheorder.org/DavidLane/whywotan.html> (accessed 3 July 2010)

—— (2005) 'Open Letter to a Dead Race'. Online. Available HTTP: <http://www.freetheorder.org/DavidLane/openletter.html> (accessed 7 July 2010)

—— (n.d.a) 'Wotanism (Odinism)'. Online. Available HTTP: <http://www.mourningtheancient.com/dl-2.htm> (accessed 9 July 2010)

—— (n.d.b) '88 Precepts'. Online. Available HTTP: <http://www.freetheorder.org/DavidLane/88.html> (accessed 7 July 2010)

Lane, K. (ed.) (1999) *Deceived, Damned and Defiant: The Revolutionary Writings of David Lane*, St. Maries: 14 Word Press

Macklin, G. (2005) 'Co-opting the Counter Culture: Troy Southgate and the National Revolutionary Faction', *Patterns of Prejudice* 39 (3): 301–326

Magister Lang (2007) 'Now Available'. Online. Available HTTP: <http://www.satannet.com/forum/ubbthreads.php?ubb=showflat&Number=152301> (Accessed 14th January 2011)

Misāne, A. and Predīte, A. (1997) 'National Mythology in the History of Ideas in Latvia: A View from Religious Studies,' in G. Hosking and G. Schöpflin (eds) *Myths and Nationhood*, Hurst and Co.: London, 158–69

Mourning the Ancient (2001) 'History'. Online. Available HTTP: <http://www.mourningtheancient.com/history.htm> (accessed 15 June 2010)

—— (2003) 'David Lane and the Brüder Schweigen: The Men Against Time'. Online. Available HTTP: < http://www.mourningtheancient.com/dl.htm> (accessed 23 June 2010)

Simi, P. and Futrell, R. (2010) *American Swastika: Inside the White Power Movement's Hidden Spaces of Hate*, Plymouth: Rowman and Littlefield

Southern Poverty Law Center (2010) 'David Lane'. Online. Available HTTP: <http://www.splcenter.org/get-informed/intelligence-files/profiles/david-lane> (accessed 12 July 2010)

Southgate, T. (2003a) *Synthesis: Journal du Cercle de la Rose Noire*. Online. Available HTTP: <http://www.rosenoire.org> (accessed 4 July 2010)

—— (2003b) 'From Sacrifice Comes Victory'. Online. Available HTTP: <http://www.rosenoire.org/essays/sacrifice.php> (accessed 5 July 2010)

—— (2003c) 'The Case for National-Anarchist Entryism'. Available HTTP: <http://www.rosenoire.org/articles/entryism.php> (accessed 7 July 2010)

—— (2006) 'What Is National-Anarchism?' Online. Available HTTP: <http://www.folkandfaith.com/articles/anarchy.shtml> (accessed 5 July 2010)

Taussig, M. (1997) *The Magic of the State,* London: Routledge

Taussig, M. and Strauss, D. L. (2005) 'The Magic of the State: An interview with Michael Taussig', *Cabinet* no. 18, 2005. Online. Available HTTP: <http://www.cabinetmagazine.org/issues/18/strauss.php> (accessed 23 June 2010)

15

ALBION'S SPECTRE

Building the new Jerusalem

Jason Whittaker

> What do I see? The Briton Saxon Roman Norman amalgamating
> In my Furnaces into One Nation the English: & taking refuge
> In the Loins of Albion. The Canaanite united with the fugitive
> Hebrew, whom she divided into Twelve, & sold into Egypt
> Then scatterd the Egyptian & Hebrew to the four Winds!
> This sinful Nation Created in our Furnaces & Looms is Albion.
>
> (*Jerusalem* 92.1–6 E252)[1]

Blake has, of course, been adopted regularly as a significant English national poet in the near two centuries after his death. Julia M. Wright, in *Blake, Nationalism and the Politics of Alienation* draws attention to that old truism that the national space in which Blake lived and worked is constituted by "overlapping and competing categories of 'British' and 'English'",[2] but with a few rare exceptions his reception outside academia as a national poet – as opposed to an exemplar of Romanticism, revolutionary politics or an artist of imagination – demonstrates almost no overlap and no competition. He is nearly always *English* Blake (as Bernard Blackstone described him in 1949). Yet while this is the case in the popular imagination, Blake, in his conception of Albion in later works such as *Milton, A Poem* and *Jerusalem or the Emanation of the Giant Albion* had a great deal to say with regard to the Celtic prehistory of this island.

Though the term Celtic had begun to be used as a technical term during the eighteenth century to describe the pre-Roman inhabitants of the British Isles, as in Edward Lhuyd's *Archaeological Britannica* (1707) and Rowland Jones's *The Origin of Languages and Nations* (1764), Blake generally preferred the terms "Briton" and "British". Indeed, as can be seen from the quotation with which this chapter begins, Blake's use of the term "English" is very different from the usual way in which it is considered with regard to ethnic or pseudo-racial terms.

Speculation was rife from the Renaissance onwards with regard to the origins of the various groups of Britain, with widespread attempts to reconcile the Celts in particular with the semitic peoples of the Bible. William Camden in his *Britannia* was one of the first to presume that the migrants from the continent, as noted by Caesar, were perhaps the descendants of Gomer, son of Japhet, whose inheritance of the islands of the Gentiles in Genesis 10.5 was a prophecy that those descendants would inherit the world. The link between the Cimbri or the Cimmerii of Germany and Gaul and the ancient Hebrews via Gomer became a commonplace of seventeenth- and eighteenth-century antiquarianism. Some, such as Aylett Sammes in his *Britannia Antiqua Illustrata*, even went further, positing a more direct link between the ancient Britons and the Phoenicians who, he argued, had come to Britain to trade for tin. Having populated the coast, they gave to the island the name "Barat-anac", that is "a field of tin".[3] Blake was familiar with all these historically peculiar arguments (as well as some of the more esoteric ones, such as Edward Davies' assertion that Noah's ark had even landed on Penmaenmawr, thus giving rise to the ancient religion of the Druids), and they fed into the British-Israelitism of *Jerusalem* and *Milton*. For Blake, if the nation aspired to greatness it was because the English combined within them these mythic origins of their Celtic forebears who had been blessed with more direct access to the divine than Hengist and Horsa.

The evidence of Blake's writings, then, does not entirely connect to his popular status as a poet with what is often viewed as a specifically *English* perspective. Considering the fact that as a writer he ranks alongside Shakespeare, Milton and Wordsworth in terms of his status as a national poet, Blake's various comments on the nation hold a few surprises, not least of which is the rarity with which he specifically refers to England and the English. Indeed, as we shall see – and despite some very determined efforts to recuperate him to a specific nationalist cause – Blake in his poetry much more clearly sees himself as bard of a much wider poetic community, one that must embrace the Celtic (as well as Scandinavian and even Latin) heritage of these isles. In his illuminated books, the adjective is only mentioned eleven times – nine of those in *Jerusalem*, twice more in reference to the "English boy" who will stand before the throne of God alongside the little black boy in *Songs of Innocence*. His use of the term "England" is a little more extensive, occurring twenty times in *Jerusalem* alone and being mentioned once in *Europe a Prophecy*, as well as twice in *America a Prophecy* and four times in *Milton*. Actually, Britain does little better (appearing only in *Jerusalem* in the illuminated works, and again four times as "Brittannia" [*sic*]), Blake's preferred name for this island of course being Albion; and while Blake cannot take credit for the invention of the phrase "perfidious Albion", his references to this country often share a great deal with the spirit of the Marquis of Ximenez and the medieval Europeans who often viewed the island with suspicion. In the speech of Los that begins this chapter, the English are a sinful nation, but it is worth emphasising immediately that there is no suggestion in Blake's writings of English being used to suggest an ethnic or racial identity (his preferred term is "Saxon" in such contexts). Englishness is, rather, a linguistic, political and cultural identity, as when in Chapter 3 of *Jerusalem* he refers to Los using English as a "rough basement" with which to build the "stubborn structure of language".[4] Inevitably, perhaps, we find ourselves in the territory of Benedict Anderson's imagined communities, and Blake would have had no difficulty whatsoever with the conception of the nation state as a product of imagination.

At the conclusion of *Jerusalem*, Blake offers a particularly idiosyncratic view of what he means by England when he refers to "England who is Brittannia" awakening on Albion's bosom, the same phrase having previously been used in Chapter 2 when describing how "England who is Britannia" divides into Jerusalem and Vala.[5] England, then, appears to have been taking shape in Blake's later works as the emanation of Albion, but that idea was never as clearly distinguished as the figure of Jerusalem herself who, from the title onwards, is more consistently described as Albion's emanation. Nonetheless, "England who is Brittannia" remains a trace within this myth, sometimes more explicitly so as in the following lines from plate 24:

> They walked before Albion
> In the Exchanges of London every Nation walkd
> And London walkd in every Nation mutual in love & harmony
> Albion coverd the whole Earth, England encompassd the Nations,
> Mutual each within others bosom in Visions of Regeneration;
> Jerusalem coverd the Atlantic Mountains & the Erythrean,
> From bright Japan & China to Hesperia France & England.[6]

If England is Albion's emanation, then Albion in Blake's mythology would be more commonly recognised by most readers (should they venture further than the famous lines beginning "And did those feet in ancient times…" that preface the epic poem *Milton*) as resolutely *British*. As we have already seen, Blake's conception of English as a pure term is a palimpsest that covers all ethnic aspects of the island's history, Celtic as well as Anglo-Saxon. As Robert N. Essick has argued with reference to Blake's invocation of Erin as a figure in his later poetry, Blake was fascinated by the "Celtic revival" that took place throughout the British Isles in the late eighteenth century, whether the fashion for the Ossianic forgeries of James Macpherson or the invocations of bardic poetry that came into vogue following the success of Thomas Gray's poetry.[7]

Blake was certainly capable of nationalistic jingoism as Steve Clark, Susan Matthews and Julia Wright have observed,[8] but in general Blake's vision of England – or Britain – is an anti-imperialist one. Furthermore, drawing on a line of indigenous jeremiads stretching back to Gildas's *De excideo et conquestu Britanniae* and transmitted to him via Milton's *The History of Britain, that part especially now called England*, Blake is more concerned with the sinfulness of the nation and the warmongering of the Sons and Daughters of Albion than with any false notion of their glories. For all that Blake may be seen as a poet of English nationalism, his conception of Albion draws much more on the Celtic prehistory that was being uncovered (and frequently constructed) by antiquarians during the eighteenth and early nineteenth centuries. England as part of Albion is more than a synthesis of Saxon and Briton: it is also the synthesis of both with the entire world.

This makes his recent adoption by the far right all the more surprising, perhaps. This is Blake's spectre, as it is Albion's spectre. There are a few easy blows that can be landed in defence of Blake concerning his adoption by the British National Party and other right wing groups – not least that most of those misappropriations are based on ignorance of what Blake wrote. I emphasise "most" – not all. Just as Blake, perhaps the most prominent of philo-Semitic writers from the Romantic period, could not resist the occasional anti-Semitic sneer, and as the most prominent of philo-British (by which I mean Celtic) of the Romantics could occasionally appear to neglect the earlier inhabitants of the British Isles, so there is dangerous activity in his critique of nationalism from his chosen perspective of a prophet of and to the nation. If Blake is so often considered a great *English* (rather than British) poet, a great national – even, in some quarters, a nationalist – poet, it is because of one single use that outweighs all other references throughout the body of his work.

> And did those feet in ancient time,
> Walk upon England's mountains green:
> And was the holy Lamb of God,
> On England's pleasant pastures seen![9]

Of course, in the context of the Preface to *Milton a Poem*, these lines and the other three stanzas that precede Blake's epic are part of a denunciation of the corruption and warmongering of perfidious Albion, yet as transformed by Hubert Parry – and, more significantly, as arranged by Edward Elgar – it is of course this single poem that has done more than anything else to enable the identification of Blake with the political right. For nearly a century these four quatrains have been invoked as a touchstone of English mysticism, sometimes imbuing their singers with a sense of dangerous prophetic vision regarding the magical bonds between English men and women and their green and pleasant land. Nor is this perilous prophetic sense a recent phenomenon. Shirley Dent points out that in 1917, a year after Parry's hymn was composed, the homeopath John H. Clarke used Blake's words in *The Call of the Sword* to call for a new crusade against the Jews of Europe. As we shall see, anti-Semitism has generally been replaced by Islamophobia but, as Dent also observes, the present-day desire by many on the left to recuperate "Jerusalem" as a socialist anthem for England is frequently motivated by "identity envy", whereby "it is in the very attempt to forge a new and progressive myth of nationhood that the left comes within touching distance of the right".[10] There is always something disturbing about an alliance of nationalism and socialism, no matter how honourable its motives.

The association between "Jerusalem" and the BNP is surprisingly recent. After its emergence as a breakaway group from the National Front, established in 1982 by John Tyndall, the BNP was mired in a few typical scandals around anti-Semitism and Holocaust denial during the 1990s.[11] Two features are key to the transformation of the party, however, in the opening decade of the twenty-first century: the first of these was the "modernisation" of the BNP following Nick Griffin's assumption of the leadership in 1999, and related to this was the shift, following the attacks of 9/11, away from its traditional anti-Semitism to Islamophobia. Following a pro-Zionist article by Lee Barnes in 2006, "Nationalism and Israel", a party editorial announced that the BNP had cast off "the leg-irons of conspiracy theories and the thinly-veiled anti-Semitism which has held this party back for two decades". The new threat was "the endless wave of Islamics who are flocking to our shores to bring our island nations into the embrace of their barbaric desert religion".[12]

It is the rejection of anti-Zionism, combined with a shift towards a more overtly Christian stance, that has made certain members of the BNP so willing to take on Blake's "Jerusalem" in particular. While there are certainly recidivist neo-Nazi pagans and Thule Society mystics who remain engaged with the party, they were increasingly marginalised in the years following 2000 as Griffin sought to make the BNP more mainstream. Until this point, "Jerusalem" tended to be redolent either of a patrician watered-down Conservatism or a kind of British-Israelitism that undermined any claims to racial purity: Blake, despite the occasional anti-Semitic remark, was simply too friendly to the Jews. From 2000 onwards, however, a change began to take place beginning with the period just before the election of George W. Bush to the White House, when Griffin joined a group of 70 American sympathisers led by Mark Cotterill of the American Friends of the BNP (AF-BNP), in Arlington, Virginia. It was at this event that Griffin spoke alongside the former leader of the Ku Klux Klan, David Duke, and led the group in singing "Jerusalem", "God Save the Queen", and "The Star-Spangled Banner". In 2001, the reporter Christopher Goodwin (2001) believed that Cotterill's troubles with the authorities over his involvement with white supremacist groups could have spelt the end of the BNP. Just seven days after his story, the attacks on the World Trade Centre gave the BNP a new enemy, one far more effective than anti-Semitism and one that would increasingly legitimise it with wider sections of the British public.

Islamophobia was one driver for the adoption of "Jerusalem", but other social transformations also conspired to metamorphise the Blake-Parry hymn into a suitable vehicle for the aspirations of Griffin and the BNP, particularly uncertainties around the status of English nationalism and the increasing popularity of "Jerusalem" as a sporting anthem. In 2005, Griffin, along with John Tyndall and Mark Collett, was charged with race hate offences brought as a result of a 2004 BBC documentary, *The Secret Agent*, during which Griffin referred to Islam as a "wicked, vicious faith". Answering bail at Halifax Police Station on April 6, Griffin warned supporters outside against rioting, saying "We will leave that to the Far Left and the Muslims".[13] After this, as most newspapers reported on the day of his appearance before magistrates in Leeds, he led those supporters in "rousing" renditions of "Jerusalem" and the Lord's Prayer. Although Griffin had received a suspended sentence for inciting racial hatred in 1998, Tyndall and Collett were acquitted at both the original trial that took place in February 2006 and a retrial that occurred in November that year, and by the end of the decade the hymn had become an important fixture in BNP meetings and rallies, becoming a theme tune for example at the Red White Blue Festival held near Codnor, Derbyshire, between 2007 and 2009. Likewise, as part of the modernising agenda, Rev. Robert West (who stood in the 2009 European Elections as a BNP candidate), launched the Christian Council of Britain in April 2006 as part of an attempt by the party, in the words of the anti-fascist magazine *Searchlight*, to "erect a veneer of respectability for its anti-Muslim campaign".[14]

Any links between "Jerusalem" and the far right should not be surprising, of course. Regardless of Blake's meanings, the hymn has often served jingoistic patriotism, but it is only in the past half decade that BNP members have unashamedly come to adopt it as suitable, so much so that in the past few years it has come to serve as a token for a particular "modernising" attitude within the organisation as with Richard Barnbrook, member of the London Assembly for Dagenham and Barking, who, as several commentators took sly pleasure in observing during the 2008 elections, had "Jerusalem" as his mobile ringtone. Similarly, BNP Councillor Martyn Findley, representative on Nuneaton and Bedworth Borough Council, Warwickshire, included a post on his blog with various renditions of "Jerusalem" accompanied by the heading "Jerusalem – pure magic: If this does not stir you then you are dead already".[15] Such associations are not inevitable and, interestingly, it is as much in the right-of-centre press that a backlash is taking place, with other conservatives attempting to prevent Blake's hymn becoming synonymous with the far right and even, as in a letter to the *Daily Telegraph*, observing that as the metre of "Jerusalem" corresponds to that of the Anushtubh metre of the Hindu Vedas, and its imagery of burning bow and arrows of desire is also drawn from Hindu mythology, it "should be sung lustily not only at the Proms, Twickenham and at marriages, but also in every Hindu temple".[16]

"Jerusalem", however, although extremely important as a shaping influence in English nationalism, is not the only factor in the far right's adoption of Blake. The now defunct website Landandpeople.bnp.org.uk used Blake as one of several English writers to provide a short-lived green connection between Albion and the rights of his indigenous population. Similarly, Lee Barnes has adopted Blake's painting of the Angel of St John as his emblem and regularly invokes Blake in tirades on contemporary politics, in such delightful posts as

"Why our country is going down the shitter" and more disturbingly thoughtful ones as "William Blake and slaves of Urizen".[17] I say disturbing because it is quite clear that Barnes has read Blake in some detail. A common assumption on the part of those opposed to the BNP is that the party is somehow intrinsically ignorant. Whatever the case with regard to the organisation as a whole, it is false security to presume that individual members are themselves ignorant. Blake's Jeremiads against warmongering Albion can be depicted in one, extremely restricted, sense as a parallel to the sense of injustice against the military opportunism in Iraq and Afghanistan of the Labour government during the first decade of the twenty-first century. The important distinction is that the far right wants to continue combat on its own terms and, as is immensely clear from the use of "Jerusalem" by other organisations such as the English Defence League (EDL), it is a hymn that for them celebrates the corporeal warfare of "our boys in the field" just as it condemns the donkeys that lead these lions – ignoring that for Blake those lions are as much a part of the sinful nation as their leaders.

To conclude this section with just one final example, Blake's "Ecchoing Green" was cited in December 2009 on the right-wing forum, The Green Arrow, to illustrate an example of what was being lost by "Nu-Labour's" land grab, or "great garden theft", the appropriation of land from town gardens and village greens to build accommodation for a horde of immigrants.[18] The argument itself is depressingly familiar, but here fashionably greened in terms of its rhetoric and Blake invoked as part of a *faux* lineage of English conservative radicalism. Blake, of course, is not the only figure or motif to be so invoked: Shakespeare and Arthurian legends have long been more popular with the far right, to say nothing of spitfires and, libel-suits permitting, Marmite. The concern here, however, has been to examine a little of what the far right takes from Blake: a notion of Albion as the centre of all things, a nostalgia for the past, and also a sense of the self as outsider in its own land – itself an idea as old as that of the prophet without honour in his own country. What is new in the re-appropriation of Blake by the right, and something not offered by Shakespeare or King Arthur, is the way in which the cumulative energy that has amassed in the past century in particular around Blake as a popular radical outsider is harnessed by the BNP.

What, then, of the Britain that Blake himself invokes? Although, as I have indicated, specific mentions of England are relatively unusual in Blake's works, it would be foolish to neglect the fact that references to the locales and habitations of the British Isles abound in Blake's works, particularly *Jerusalem*. Sometimes those references build up to a solid mass in their own right, as in plate 16 of *Jerusalem* in which the counties of England, Wales and Scotland are listed as an impenetrable density, reminiscent of those biblical lists and genealogies that so influenced Blake's British-Israelitism. Such masses, built from the rough basement of English, form not England so much as *Albion*, a combination of British, Saxon, Roman, Norman and Hebrew cultures. It is clear, from descriptions of Albion extending from "Caithness in the north, to Lizard-point and Dover in the south"[19] that Albion is not simply England but Britain and, as has long been recognised, Blake's ideas were informed by the activities of British and European antiquaries working between the sixteenth and nineteenth centuries who managed to fashion a plausible falsehood that the British (if not, exactly, the English) nation had descended from the same tribes that were to become the nation of Israel. William Camden, Aylett Sammes, Jacob Bryant, William Stukeley, William Borlase, Rowland Jones and countless other antiquaries (including the pornographer John Cleland) all contributed to the invention of this tradition, a tradition so cluttered by the end of the eighteenth century that it was impossible to move through etymological and archaeological fields without stumbling on fragments of evidence that "proved" the connections between Britain and the Holy Land. It is this "evidence" that Blake alludes to in plate 27 of *Jerusalem* when he writes:

> Jerusalem the Emanation of the Giant Albion! Can it be? Is it a Truth that the Learned have explored? Was Britain the Primitive Seat of the Patriarchal Religion? If it is true: my title-page is also True, that Jerusalem was & is the Emanation of the Giant Albion. It is True, and cannot be controverted. Ye are united O ye Inhabitants of Earth in One Religion. The Religion of Jesus: the most Ancient, the Eternal: & the Everlasting Gospel – The Wicked will turn it to Wickedness, the Righteous to Righteousness. Amen! Huzza! Selah! "All things Begin & End in Albions Ancient Druid Rocky Shore".[20]

Blake's conception of the origins of the "Everlasting Gospel" in "Albions Ancient Druid Rocky Shore", so obviously behind his use of the legend of Joseph of Arimathea visiting Britain in the lines that comprise "Jerusalem", can be distorted to the pernicious nationalism of groups such as the BNP. In full prophetic mode, Blake makes those – frequently infuriating – statements that operate completely outside any positivistic or empirical framework: "It is True, and cannot be controverted". Omitting any argument here with Blake's epistemology, it is worth recognising that Blake appears to understand entirely that his statements regarding mythic nationalism may be turned to nefarious purpose: "The Wicked will turn it to Wickedness, the Righteous to Righteousness". It is also worth noting more precisely what Blake is claiming here: that Albion is a source of the Everlasting Gospel because *all* nations are the source of the Everlasting Gospel: "Ye are united O ye Inhabitants of Earth in One Religion. The Religion of Jesus: the most Ancient, the Eternal". Steve Clark has interpreted lines such as these as indicative of a more sinister aspect to Blake's use of national myths, the imperative to convert that was a prerogative of imperial, Christian Britain.[21] Such ambiguities are, unfortunately, attendant on much of Blake's rhetoric concerning the nation state and the point where his mythology descends into the very mysticism he detested. But the tenets expressed in his earliest illuminated tract, *All Religions are One*, had in fact expressed something very different – that all people, of all nations, possessed divine inspiration in the poetic imagination, and that this – the very basis of their imagined communities – meant that no single country, whether Britain or Israel, had privileged access to God.

Anderson's (1991) notion of imagined communities has, of course, become a staple – even a cliché – of discussions around nationalism. While there are some flaws to Anderson's notion of the invention of these sovereign, limited communities during the nineteenth century with regard to Britain (dominated by England), which had demonstrated the more advanced features of nationalism at least a century before, the idea remains a useful one, particularly in contrast to essentialist and racialist notions of the nation state. However, when dealing with Blake's nationalism in contrast to the reactionary, ethnic version espoused by organisations such as the BNP, I wish to consider it in relation to more recent work by Anderson with regard to *internationalism* and imagined communities in his book, *Under Three Flags: Anarchism and the anti-colonial imagination* (2007). In relation to this, an important point is made by Hardt and Negri in *Empire* regarding limitations of postmodernist and postcolonialist critiques of imperialism, particularly insofar as they feed into a new localism that is "false and damaging" as it presupposes that "the global entails homogenization and undifferentiated identity whereas the local preserves heterogeneity and difference".[22] Roger Whitson has shown the useful ways in which Hardt and Negri's re-reading of Spinoza and, more provocatively, St Francis of Assissi, can also be applied to Blake in order to give a new relevance to the New Historicist project of the 1990s, and my own approach shares some features with his. By exploring Blake's ideas within the globalist struggles of the twenty-first century, Whitson suggests, "his insistence [on] the building of Jerusalem in the present… can totally change every aspect of the hard material reality that many historicists are too quick to preserve" (2008: 98).[23] A not dissimilar approach has been taken by Sarah Haggarty and Jon Mee in *Blake and Conflict*, in which they employ Nancy's "inoperative community" as a means of exploring how Blake's conception of a political community may neither be reduced to an aggregate of individuals nor hypostasised as totalitarian communal substance.[24]

Because the nation was so evidently important to Blake's anti-colonial imagination, I would like to conclude this chapter with a few brief pointers how Anderson's *inter*national imagined community can provide a useful means of engaging with Blake's conception of Albion. By invoking anarchism as an alternative to the totalising, recidivist tendencies of the BNP, it could appear at first glance that I am courting precisely the potential irrelevance of postmodern politics that Hardt and Negri find in the works of Deleuze and Guattari or Agamben when those philosophers place liminality at the core of radical politics. I am also concerned that the easy dichotomy of fascism and anarchism is misleading, and although Hardt and Negri come perhaps closest among post-Marxist political philosophers to embracing anarchism as their preferred term, in the follow up to *Empire*, is *multitudes*. Anderson's *Under Three Flags* does not appear immediately helpful to my re-evaluation of Blake's nationalism in that it deals not with the 1790s, nor the twenty-first century, but the transition from the nineteenth to twentieth century. Furthermore, his careful reading of anarchist politics in Spain and the Philippines does not seem instantly applicable to Blake's Englishness, nor his vision of Albion. However, in his examination of the careers of figures such as the novelist José Rizal (*Noli Me Tangere*) and folklorist Isabelo de los Reyes (*El folk-lore Filipino*), Anderson quickly follows them through Europe and the Americas, reminding us that in the 1890s it was anarchism – not Marxism – that was *the* movement of internationalism, the black flag being more frequently raised alongside the banners of Spain and the Philippines than the red one. Significantly, with regard to de los Reyes in particular, the contribution of what Anderson calls "the riches of local knowledge"[25] have an important part to play in this internationalism: de los Reyes's work on the folklore of the Philippines contained an "unknowness" that contributed to its "future-oriented character". For such local knowledge – what Blake might have called the "minute particulars" of the history of the Philippines – to gain credence, it had to avoid the common assumptions of nineteenth century colonialism. If Filipino traditions were assigned significance only insofar as they were translated into Spanish, then they would be relegated to minority status. To insist on the hegemony of local nationalism, however, risked rendering this hard-earned knowledge irrelevant outside the borders of his country. As such, de los Reyes imagined instead "a sort of global folklore which included the regional portion of the Philippine Islands".[26]

It is something akin to this "global folklore", I would argue, with which Blake wishes to engage in when writing about Albion in his prophetic books. When all the nations walk "before Albion / In the Exchanges of Albion" and "London walkd in every Nation mutual in love & harmony" the past tense is important as a reminder that the present glory of imperial Britain is a false idol, the fall from Albion's original status as but one of the Eternals. When Blake locates the patriarchal religion of Noah and Abraham among the British Bards and Druids, this is not an act of colonial appropriation but of an epistemological imagination in which all nations are but a portion of the infinite which man, were the doors of that imagination sufficiently cleansed, would perceive: "The Religions of all Nations are derived from each Nations different reception of the Poetic Genius which is every where call'd the Spirit of Prophecy".[27]

The nation, then, is an important foundation for Blake, but, geography, culture and identity, like language, are no more than "rough basements". The spirit of prophecy, like folklore, is international and global. In plate 11 of *The Marriage of Heaven and Hell* he provides his account of the fall of this spirit of prophecy into what would more commonly be considered nationalism:

> The ancient Poets animated all sensible objects with Gods or Geniuses calling them by the names and adorning them with the properties of woods, rivers, mountains, lakes, cities, nations, and whatever their enlarged & numerous senses could percieve.
>
> And particularly they studied the genius of each city & country. placing it under its mental deity.
>
> Till a system was formed, which some took advantage of & enslav'd the vulgar by attempting to realize or abstract the mental deities from their objects: thus began Priesthood.[28]

Here we see the sin of nationalism defined most clearly: nations are a product of *poiesis*, the abundance of language, imagination and energy, a creative act of mythologising in which the poet speaks a particular condition in a particular location – but when systematised via religion, the father- or motherland degenerates into a mysticism that cannot be questioned, only loyally obeyed.

Blake is resolutely *English* and the nation never disappears from his work, quite the contrary: the gods and geniuses he names are adorned with the properties of England's green and pleasant land, but these are an act of poetics, not the systematic theology that he identifies with mysticism. These local gods are to be created continually within the human form divine rather than reified into objects that demand our loyalty. The experiences of José Rizal and Isabelo de los Reyes are instructive: these Filipinos were inducted into a Hispanicised, Catholicised colonial system through their equivalent rough basement of Spanish, but rather than react against this induction by a retreat into Tagalog, Ilocano, Maranoa or one of the many other indigenous ethno-linguistic localities of the Philippine islands, they expanded into a multicentred and global perspective in which their national – even regional – differences were on a par with the colonial empires of Spain, Britain and the United States: for both of them, all things begin and end in Filipino rocky shores, and Manila walkd in every Nation mutual in love and harmony. Similarly, *The Four Zoas* and *Jerusalem* end with Albion's resurrection not to ensure the domination of his empire, which is merely the addition of territories to an *imperium* itself formed by the negation that is his fall (and is in turn sustained by corporeal war), but in the building Jerusalem which unites the English, the Celts who existed before them, and even the Jews in Blake's own form of British Israelitism. In contrast to the exclusion desired by narrow nationalist groups such as the BNP, Blake desires rather a mental fight in which all participants recognise that the sin of their nationhood is itself a precursor to forgiveness of sin, the proper state of Eden.

Notes

1 All quotations are from David V. Erdman, 1998. *The Complete Poetry and Prose of William Blake*. Revised edition. New York, London, Toronto, Sydney and Auckland:

Doubleday. Citations are indicated by the letter E followed by the page number in Erdman's edition.

2 Wright, Julia M. 2004. *Blake, Nationalism and the Politics of Alienation*. Athens, OH: Ohio University Press. xviii.

3 Aylett Sammes. 1679. *Britannia Antiqua Illustrata*. London. 16.

4 *Jerusalem* 36.58–9, E183.

5 *Jerusalem* 94.2-, E254; 32.28, E178.

6 *Jerusalem* 24.41–7, E170.

7 Essick, Robert N. 2006. "Erin, Ireland, and the Emanation in Blake's *Jerusalem*" In Steve Clark and David Worrall, eds *Blake, Nation and Empire*. Houndmills: Palgrave. 204–5.

8 See: Clark, Steve. 2006. "*Jerusalem* as Imperialist Prophecy". In Steve Clark and David Worrall, eds *Blake, Nation and Empire*. Houndmills: Palgrave. 167–85; Matthews, Susan. 1992. "Jerusalem and Nationalism". In Stephen Copley and John Whale, eds *Beyond Romanticism: New Approaches to Texts and Contexts 1780–1832*. London: Routledge. 79–100; Wright, Julia. 2004. *Blake, Nationalism, and the Politics of Alienation*. Athens, OH: Ohio University Press.

9 *Milton*, plate 1, E95.

10 Dent, Shirley. 2012. "'Thou readst white where I readst black': William Blake, the Hymn 'Jerusalem' and the Far Right". In Mark Crosby, Troy Patenaude, and Angus Whitehead eds *Re-Envisioning Blake*. Houndmills: Palgrave. 48–9.

11 Andrew, Anthony. "Flying the Flag". 2002. *The Observer* 1 September. www.guardian.co.uk/theobserver/2002/sep/01/features.magazine37 (accessed June 14, 2010).

12 Barnes, Lee. 2006. "Nationalism and Israel", web.archive.org/web/20071014195726/http://www.bnp.org.uk/news_detail.php?newsId=1057 (accessed June 3, 2010).

13 Duff, Oliver. 2005. "BNP leader faces jail after being charged with inciting hatred". *The Independent*, 7 April. www.independent.co.uk/news/uk/politics/bnp-leader-faces-jail-after-being-charged-with-inciting-hatred-481297.html (accessed May 26, 2010). See also, Martin Wainwright. "BNP leader faces racial hatred charge". 2005. *The Guardian*. 7 April. Paul Byrne. 2005. "'Race Hate' Griffin". *The Daily Mirror*. 7 April.

14 Williams, David. 2006 "The BNP and Christianity". *Searchlight*, www.searchlightmagazine.com/index.php?link=template&story=170 (accessed June 5, 2010).

15 Findley, Martyn. 2009. "Jerusalem – Pure Magic", http://martynfindley.blogspot.com/2009/03/jerusalem-pure-magic.html (accessed June 7, 2010).

16 Hill, Stephen. 2010. "The Hindu imagery in William Blake's 'Jerusalem': How the hymn 'Jerusalem' is suited to multicultural Britain", *Daily Telegraph*, 22 July. www.telegraph.co.uk/comment/letters/7903076/The-Hindu-imagery-in-William-Blakes-Jerusalem.html (accessed July 23, 2010).

17 Barnes, Lee. 2007. "William Blake and the Slaves of Urizen". *21st Century British Nationalism*, 28 November, leejohnbarnes.blogspot.com/2007/11/william-blake-and-slaves-of-urizen.html (accessed May 30, 2010).

18 Yorkshire, Dave. 2009 "Nu-Labour's Great Garden Theft". *The Green Arrow*, 21 December. www.thegreenarrow.co.uk/index.php/writers/others/965-nu-labours-great-garden-theft (accessed May 15, 2010).

19 *Milton* 6.7, E99.

20 *Jerusalem* plate 27, E171.

21 Clark, Steve. 2006. "Jerusalem as Imperial Revelation". In Steve Clark and David Worrall eds *Blake, Nation and Empire*. Houndmills: Palgrave. 201–15.

22 Negri, Antonio and Hardt, Michael. 2000. *Empire*. Cambridge, Mass.: Harvard University Press. 44.

23 Whitson, Roger. 2008. "Applied Blake: Milton's Response to Empire." *Interdisciplinary Literary Studies*. 9.2.98.

24 Haggarty, Sarah, and Mee, Jon. 2008. *Blake and Conflict*. Houndmills: Palgrave.18.

25 Anderson, Benedict. 2007. *Under Three Flags: Anarchism and the Anti-Colonial Imagination*, London and New York: Verso.14.
26 Ibid. 16.
27 *All Religions are One*, E1.
28 *The Marriage of Heaven and Hell*, plate 11, E38.

Bibliography

Anderson, Benedict. 1991. *Imagined Communities: Reflections on the Origin and Spread of Nationalism* (2nd ed.). London and New York: Verso.
——. 2007. *Under Three Flags: Anarchism and the Anti-Colonial Imagination*, London and New York: Verso.
Andrew, Anthony. 2002. "Flying the Flag". *The Observer*, 1 September. www.guardian. co.uk/theobserver/2002/sep/01/features.magazine37 (accessed June 14, 2010).
Barnes, Lee. 2006. "Nationalism and Israel", web.archive.org/web/20071014195726/ http://www.bnp.org.uk/news_detail.php?newsId=1057 (accessed June 3, 2010).
——. 2007. "William Blake and the Slaves of Urizen". *21st Century British Nationalism*, 28 November. leejohnbarnes.blogspot.com/2007/11/william-blake-and-slaves-of-urizen.html (accessed May 30, 2010).
Clark, Steve. 2006. "Jerusalem as Imperial Revelation". In Steve Clark and David Worrall eds *Blake, Nation and Empire*. Houndmills: Palgrave, pp. 201–15.
Dent, Shirley. 2012. "'Thou readst white where I readst black': William Blake, the hymn Jerusalem and the far-right". In Mark Crosby, Troy Patenaude and Angus Whitehead, eds *Re-Envisioning Blake*. Houndmills: Palgrave, pp. 48–62.
Duff, Oliver. 2005. "BNP leader faces jail after being charged with inciting hatred". *The Independent*, 7 April. www.independent.co.uk/news/uk/politics/bnp-leader-faces-jail-after-being-charged-with-inciting-hatred-481297.html (accessed May 26, 2010).
Erdman, David. 1988. *The Complete Poetry and Prose of William Blake* (2nd ed.). New York, London, Toronto, Sydney and Auckland: Doubleday.
Findley, Martyn. 2009. "Jerusalem – Pure Magic", martynfindley.blogspot.com/2009/03/ jerusalem-pure-magic.html (accessed June 7, 2010).
Fletcher, Martin. 2008. "By all means name us, but you won't shame us, says the 'ordinary' face of the far Right". *The Times*, 22 November. timesonline.co.uk/tol/news/politics/ article5209802.ece (accessed May 26, 2010).
Gilligan, Andrew and Ralph, Alex. 2009. "BNP threat at the polls is looking hollow". *Evening Standard*, 18 May. http://www.standard.co.uk/news/bnp-threat-at-the-polls-is-looking-hollow-6797677.html (accessed June 2, 2010).
Goodwin, Christopher. 2001. "How American Racists Could Finish the BNP". *Evening Standard*, 4 September.
Haggarty, Sarah, and Mee, Jon, eds 2008. *Blake and Conflict*. Houndmills: Palgrave.
Hill, Stephen. 2010, "The Hindu imagery in William Blake's 'Jerusalem': How the hymn 'Jerusalem' is suited to multicultural Britain", *The Daily Telegraph*, 22 July. www. telegraph.co.uk/comment/letters/7903076/The-Hindu-imagery-in-William-Blakes-Jerusalem.html (accessed July 23, 2010).
Matthews, Susan. 1992. "Jerusalem and Nationalism". In Stephen Copley and John Whale, eds *Beyond Romanticism: New Approaches to Texts and Contexts 1780–1832*. London: Routledge 1992, pp. 79–100.
Morton, Cole. 2008. "The art-school liberal who now won't allow blacks in his party." *Independent on Sunday*. 1 June. www.independent.co.uk/news/people/profiles/richard-

barnbrook-the-artschool-liberal-who-now-wont-allow-blacks-in-his-party-837840. html (accessed May 19, 2010).

Negri, Antonio and Hardt, Michael. 2000. *Empire*. Cambridge, MA: Harvard University Press.

Whitson, Roger. 2008. "Applied Blake: Milton's Response to Empire." *Interdisciplinary Literary Studies*. 9.2, pp. 87–101.

Williams, David. 2006. "The BNP and Christianity." *Searchlight*. www.searchlightmagazine. com/index.php?link=template&story=170 (accessed June 5, 2010).

Wright, Julia. 2004. *Blake, Nationalism, and the Politics of Alienation*. Athens, OH: Ohio University Press.

Yorkshire, Dave. 2009. "Nu-Labour's Great Garden Theft". *The Green Arrow*, December 21, 2009. www.thegreenarrow.co.uk/index.php/writers/others/965-nu-labours-great-garden-theft (accessed May 15, 2010).

INDEX

Printed in Great Britain
by Amazon

59231149R00143